MANUAL
OF GRAPHOLOGY

Scriptor Books

Acknowledgements

I wish to express my gratitude to Joanna Tzoura-Panagiotopoulos, who first suggested that I translate this major textbook, and to my husband, Ian, who read every chapter with care and patience and made some very useful suggestions regarding the finer points of English, his native language.

MONIQUE STIRLING
Translator

Jacqueline PEUGEOT
Arlette LOMBARD
Madeleine de NOBLENS

MANUAL
of Graphology

Translated by
MONIQUE STIRLING

Edited by
Lorraine Herbert

Scriptor Books

an imprint of
The British Academy of Graphology
London

"Manuel de Graphologie"
Copyright © 1994 Masson, Editeur, Paris

English Edition first published in 1997
by SCRIPTOR BOOKS,
an imprint of
The British Academy of Graphology (Limited by Guarantee)
in association with The London College of Graphology Ltd.,
75 Quinta Drive, Barnet, Herts. EN5 3DA

Editorial Office: 123 Bickenhall Mansions, London W1H 3LB

A CIP catalogue record for this book is
available from the British Library.

ISBN 1-899653-13-9

Typesetting and layout by

EuroBuro '92 | Brigitte Froud
London, Tel 0181-788 3289

Printed and bound in Great Britain

CONTENTS

Introduction 1

Foreword : Scribbles 5

PART 1
The basics: handwriting as graphic material for the study of the personality

1. The Stroke (pressure according to Crépieux-Jamin) 13

Signs concerning weight (pressure)... 16
  strong (16), light (19), in relief - flat (22), deviated (24), spasmodic (27),
  sharp-pointed - clubbed (28), spindle-shaped (30), furrowed (31).

Signs concerning the quality of the stroke 33
  precise (33), pasty - porous (36), well-nourished - velvety (39), congested -
  smeary (muddy) (40), fine (42), thin - dry (33), blurred - washed-out (45),
  moirée (variegated) (46).

Tension, synthesis of pressure and movement in the handling of the stroke 48
  supple (49), firm (50), weak (52), taut (53), irregular pressure, quality and
  handling of the stroke (55).

The penhold and the choice of the graphic instrument 56
  The penhold (56).
  The choice of the writing instrument (61).
  Note on Hegar (66).

2. Form 71

Forms remaining close to copybook, personalised forms 75
  copybook (75), personalised (78), simplified (79), complicated - ornate -
  bizarre (81), acquired - artificial (84), conventional - typographic - stylised
  (87).

The major basic scriptural forms 91
  arcade (91), garland (94), rounded - inflated (101), angular (104), filiform
  (thready) (108), simple (111), clear - confused (113).

Emphasis on closedness or openness of forms 117
  Closed forms (117) : double-joined - lassos (118)
  Open forms : open - progressive (120)

The notion of homogeneity of form 122

3. DIMENSION 125

The middle zone 127
    The vertical axis : large (127), small (130), enlarging (134), diminishing (137).
    The horizontal axis : wide (139), narrow (144).

Proportions between the zones 146
    sober (148), prolonged up and down (149), prolonged up - prolonged
    down (151), low (154), superelevated (158), extensive movements -
    expanded (159), regularity - unevenness - irregularity (162).

4. MOVEMENT 165

    still (169), controlled - resolute (173), inhibited - restrained - constrained (177),
    floating - slack writing (180), flowing movement - effortless writing (comfortable)
    (182), dynamic movement - dynamogenic writing (185), propulsive movement -
    carried away writing - thrown writing (flying strokes) (188), vibrant - effervescent
    movement - animated writing (192), obstructed - reared movement (195).

5. CONTINUITY 199

Degrees of connection.. 201
    connected (201), disconnected (juxtaposed) (204), grouped (208),
    overconnected (210), secondary connections (212), combined (213), irregular
    continuity - nuanced - hopping (216).

Difficulties and peculiarities of connection 217
    fragmented - dissociated letters (217), false connections (219), jerky -
    telescoped (218), suspended - unfinished - lapses of continuity (223),
    amended - covering strokes - supported - shark's tooth (226).

6. FREE SIGNS... 229

Accents and punctuation.. 229

T - bars (Chart 1) 235

Initial strokes. Finals (Charts 2 and 3) 238

7. DIRECTION 245

The slant of letters 247
    vertical (247), left-slanted - straightened-up (249), right-slanted - very right-
    slanted (252), irregularity of direction - pulled-about (vacillating) - variably-
    slanted (255).

General direction of the stroke.. 259
    right-tending (259), left-tending (261), soaring (263), reverse - twisted
    (Chart 4) (264).

8. SPEED 271

    slow - slowed down (275), poised (280), accelerated - rapid - precipitated (281).

9. SPACE 287

Spacing between words 290
    compact - very compact (292), spaced-out - very spaced-out - with inter-
    word gaps (294), aerated (298), irregular spacing (300).

The layout 302
    trajectory of lines (302), spacing between lines (308), margins (309), new
    paragraphs (312), overall arrangement (314).

10. T HE SIGNATURE 317

Position on the page and in relation to the text 319

The formal elements of language 320

Signature similar to the text 320

Signature very different from the text 324

A few men's signatures 326

Remarks 333

A few women's signatures 334

PART 2
Guiding syntheses, methodology, writing of left-handers

11. EVOLUTION OF HANDWRITING AND ORGANISATION 341

Age as a factor of evolution. Children's handwriting and intelligence 345

Relationship of handwriting to educational and socio-cultural levels 349

Intelligence and handwriting 366

Disorganisation of the handwriting through old age 369

Dysgraphia 372

12. HARMONY, FORMLEVEL, RELATIONSHIP BETWEEN FORM
    AND MOVEMENT 379
Harmony 379
Form Level 383

viii

Relationship between Form and Movement 386

13. METHODOLOGY AND PRACTICAL APPLICATION 393

14. HANDWRITING OF LEFT-HANDERS USING THE LEFT HAND 409

Left-handed writing and cursive movement (continuity) 411

Left-handed writing and the fine motor skill of the hand 413

Is there a left-handed writing identifiable as such? 414

Can a left-hander's writing be as reliably analysed as that of a right-handers? 415

Appendix 1: The symbolism of the graphic space 427

Appendix 2: Reflections based on the observation of the signatures of a
homogeneous group 429

BIBLIOGRAPHY 435

INDEX 441

Introduction

Handwriting, which is an activity specific to human beings, a personal tool and a social act, performs several functions: it is needed for for acquiring and transmitting knowledge; it often allows deeper elaboration of thought than would speech alone; and finally, its role is to provide communication in the general sense of the term.

It is a synthesis of a language based on thought, and a graphic gesture which is a very fine psychomotor activity, directed by the brain, for the reproduction of a whole complex of coded signs which translate that language.

In to-day's evolved civilisations, with compulsory education, it tends to have become for everyone, as Marcel Cohen [1] wrote : "a kind of individual function, like speech, of which it is the visible replica" and therefore just as expressive as one's voice or one's gait ... and probably more profoundly so, in view of all that is involved [1].

Graphology is founded on the expressive factors of handwriting, a coded trail which has the advantage that it can be studied away from the writer.

Because handwriting becomes automatic only after many years of training and practical use, it was thought for a long time that graphological analysis could be applied only to handwritings which had got past the stage of graphomotor difficulties. That view has had to be changed, as some recent studies both in France and abroad have proved that even from childhood, a graphological approach is possible, although to a lesser degree, and furthermore, that it has the merit of helping to understand the handwriting of adults. For the latter reason the reader will often find in this book that we revert to the origins and development of the act of writing.

---

1   It should be noted that according to neurologists and with reference to pathology, handwriting may be related to several functions of brain activity: through the temporal lobe, it is supposed to be linked to speech, and through the parietal convolutions, to symbolic gestures [2].

Graphology can also be used in other spheres : historical, owing to the fact that there are styles of writing which correspond to certain periods; national, because handwritings are liable to show the marks of collective characteristics to some extent, Latin countries, especially France, being the least affected .

Cultural, historical and national aspects of handwriting will not be dealt with in this manual.

Graphology is both a human science and a science of man.

As a science belonging to the humanities, it differs from the exact sciences, which does not mean that it is not "true", nor that it is founded only on intuition in the derogatory sense of the word; real intuition, in its higher sense, is a factor in all sciences.

Graphology is indeed an original science, the methods of which rest on a rigorous technique of observation and the interpretation of which is based on analogical reasoning, founded on the direct expression of graphic gestures and on the archetypal symbolism of form and space, which are to be found in all civilisations [2].

Graphology is also a science of man. It requires a thorough knowledge of human beings, and, on the part of the graphologist, a maturity which enables him both to understand others and to be capable of objective judgments.

The reader will not, in this book, find characterological, ethical or philosophical theories of the sort that he can find in the works of the pioneers in particular. We have in fact made ourselves familiar with the data of psychological findings of the last few decades, especially with regard to depth psychology, while at the same time avoiding the use of psychological terms, which the graphologist does not need in his written analyses.

What we have aimed at is to stay constantly close to handwriting as a graphic gesture intimately bound up with personality by the laws of psychomotricity, and we have used no particular typologies, as each writing reveals its own syntheses.

We have not tackled the very specialised area of diagnosed mental illnesses

---

2 In Appendix 1, the reader will find, together with commentaries, a chart of the Symbolism of Space which, although sketchy, indicates the essentials.

here.

The book is divided into two parts : in the first part, which sets out the bases of graphological study, we have kept the French signs, rich and nuanced, classifying them in categories close to Crépieux-Jamin's, but with variations, as a sign often belongs to several categories, and our choice being sometimes different to that of Crépieux-Jamin.

In the second part, we have considered the syntheses of orientation and the methodology, ending with a chapter on left-handers' left-handed writing, putting forward an attempt at an overall view of this subject that has, so far, been incompletely examined.

Finally in Appendix 2, we have quoted a statistical study of signatures, done by the authors, thus indicating a possible line of study to students.

A science of expression, graphology is not founded on statistical observations, but research is necessary in order to validate and confirm classical interpretations, or sometimes alter them, modify them, or treat them cautiously, eliminate preconceived ideas, establish landmarks and also to launch new hypotheses: this is what research is for, and that is why it is necessary to the progress of all science.

Jacqueline PEUGEOT
President of the Société
Française de Graphologie

4

NOTE

There exist at the moment graphometric scales based on numerically-graded assessments, or on very precise measurements of graphic characteristics, set out in relation to standardised and statistically validated reference groups.

This type of approach can be developed in a positive way in the future, but only on condition that its results attest to the seriousness and competence of their authors.

Graphologists will then be helped in the same way as doctors are with medical tests in a laboratory.

But the use of these scales is not without danger. To be effective, a thorough knowledge of graphology is required, which is essentially the aim of this manual.

Foreword
Scribbles

In this preface, we have thought it of interest to discuss the scribbling of very young children, a socially - approved activity, but nevertheless almost instinctive.

Very early indeed, towards the age of one, the hand, a subtly evolved organ, makes holding a pencil possible. At about eighteen months, the temptation to draw signs on a piece of paper is liable to be unleashed in the child, if the conditions are suitable; that is to say, if pencils are to hand, if an adult asks him to do so, or if he has a brother or a sister whom he wants to imitate [1].

Straight away an observer will understand that this is no ordinary game. The child's enthusiastic acceptance, his hesitation or his refusal, make one think that he himself senses that this act is not without significance. As Marthe Bernson [5] has noted, it is as if the child were fascinated both by the limited space of the paper and by own his movements, which, by leaving a trail, give him tangible proof of himself. He experiences a feeling of both wonder and disappointment, for he never gets what he thought he could. And the gap between what he is and what he thought he was marks the beginning of his desire for progress.

For the first time perhaps, his movements leave a visible trace and, depending on the result he gets, he feels either joy or annoyance. He displays his scribble for adults to admire, or else crosses it out violently, or throws it away. What is most important here, and what he expresses in this scribble, is himself.

The observation of scribbles is of major interest to graphologists[2]

---

1 L. Lurcat has studied very objectively and without interpreting them, the stages of scribbling of young children from the age of 18 months up to the school age [3, 4].
2 In order to ascertain their relationship with writing movements, A. Lombard has studied some 400 scribbles of children aged between 18 and 24 months, who were regularly observed from January to July 1968, at the staff crèche of the Beaujon Hospital in Paris [6].

because it enables them to see the genesis of the writing movement : a dot which, more often than not is thrown, then a pattern, whose qualities, heavy or light, connected or disconnected, wide or narrow, curved or straight, its position within the graphic space and, lastly, its general appearance, contain the seed of all that makes for expressiveness in handwriting.

Graphologists will also appreciate how valuable this gesture is in terms of communication, through the particular response it evokes from the entourage. The attitude of adults is not the same as it would be if they were faced with another kind of activity. From the start, a split occurs between those who consider the scribbles of children as "nothing" (in which case, why would the child continue?) and those who stimulate the child and appreciate the value of a product in which his intelligence and his motor skills are put to use.

Scribbles should be studied most carefully, for children are extremely mobile, and one should watch them making the scribbles, as it would be difficult afterwards to retrace the way they went about it. One can then notice that a certain type of pattern ends up being repeated and thereby becomes representative of a specific child. This can be verified if a whole series of numbered scribbles is available.

Although they are meaningful only if taken as part of a series, rather than in isolation, we shall show a few samples coming from children who do not yet talk, and which, it seems to us, represent their authors sufficiently.[3, 4]

---

3 We are deliberately restricting ourselves to the very first scribbles, as we are not attempting here to treat this subject extensively. The reader interested in the later development of scribbles, in the pre-school age period, can refer to L. Lurcat's book already quoted [3].

4 The arrows appearing on the right of the scribbles indicate the downward direction.

a

a) Girl, 20 months.

A non-centred scribble, with no real density but expanding over and beyond the page, a usual thing with that child. On the other hand, the pattern is skilful; pressure is uneven and occurs mainly on the movement of extension, that is, contrary to the norm, and thus is related to deviated pressure (see Chapter 1) with the significance of deviated energy - sometimes with attitudes of opposition - which it introduces.

Abandoned by her mother at birth and in the process of being adopted, this small girl was very coddled in her adoptive family; she showed, however, in her behaviour, both seduction and opposition, aiming at monopolising adults' attention.

b

c

b) and c) Boy, 19 and 24 months.
Scribbles comprising many different phases. The first pattern was the broken line which goes upwards, a gesture of communication and effort, reflecting inhibition, the difficulty of coming out of himself. Then comes the production of two concentric, lighter patterns placed on either side of the first pattern without covering it and which respect the limits of the paper. The concentric movements were drawn in a single stroke involving few dents, but light and porous. This preparation work enables the child to make linear strokes back and forth, which have strong pressure, are thrown and rapid, and are fairly expanded, something he would not have allowed himself or been able to make at first.

A shy boy, serious-minded, attentive, obedient, with a deep need for affection. He had a brother six years older.

Five months later, we can see maturity of gesture, mastery of space, enough self-confidence to allow freedom of movement with enough tonicity for it to remain firm and directed. A continuous movement, with no penlift, therefore sufficiently supple and assured so that it has no interruptions or dents. Colour is used which, for a long time that child had refused.

This is one of his last scribbles. Since then, his first attempts at drawing figures have totally separated him from that stage.

d

d) Boy, 21 months.
Violent and dense scribble, in the middle of the page, with numerous thrown dots. The pattern, concentric and quite light to start with, was soon covered with black, precise, rapid and very heavy strokes, complex and lively in their back and forth movements. An angry pattern which certainly expresses the impact of this aggressive young bossy boots.

Indeed, as soon as language appears, the child wants to make an act of representation: the scribble is called house, dog, plane, mum, or all these, one after the other. Along with the development and practice of graphic movements, the child's intelligence, his need to differentiate, like his need to communicate by means of oral or written language, soon leads him to go beyond the stage of the first scribbles and to start making approximations of handwriting.

(d) Boy, 24 months.

He has drawn scribbles, in the middle of the page, with numerous through-ups. The strokes are varied and quite light to start with, and soon reveal bold blacks, vivid and rapid emphases accentuated locally in their back-and-forth movements, after rather indecisive attempts the imprint of this systematic young scrib-bler.

Indeed, as soon as language appears, the child wants to make use of representation; the second is called house, dog, plane, man, or all these, one after the other. Along with the development and practice of graphic movements, the child's intelligence, his need to differentiate, like his need to communicate by means of oral or written language, soon leads him to go beyond the stage of the first scribbles and to start making approxima-tions of handwriting.

PART 1

The basics :

handwriting as graphic material
for the study of the personality

The STROKE

Pressure according to Crépieux-Jamin

Both the term pressure and the more recent one, stroke, which graphologists have been using more readily since Hegar [7], have their ambiguity. Pressure evokes the weight exerted on the paper by the writing instrument (writing is possible only if there is sufficient tonicity), but with this word, Crépieux-Jamin indicated both the various degrees of pressure, that is to say the weight, and also the quality of the line left on the paper[1].

The term stroke, on the other hand, evokes more the intrinsic qualities of the ink flow : pasty, precise, etc.

To the array of the characteristics defined by those two terms, are also added general notions of tension, connected to the graphic progression as a whole.

We think it desirable, for the sake of a unified terminology in France and abroad, to use the word stroke, less specific than that of pressure and capable of encompassing all the characteristics deriving from the results of the graphic act, when it is produced with an inked instrument, and to keep that of pressure, if so desired, as a synonym for weight.

In the study of the stroke[2], explained in detail a little further on, we shall therefore consider:

1) *The signs concerned with weight* (pressure in the strict and narrow sense).

2) *the signs concerned with the quality of the stroke.* (When examining the stroke, one can distinguish between the inside and the edges if the writing instrument makes this possible).

---

1 We were thinking of starting this manual with Form, the aim of handwriting, but in the end, we opted for the Stroke which is more primitive, more personal, and a constitutive element of handwriting.

2 **Stroke** : line made with a pen. Handwriting. (Littré)*.

3) *the signs and components concerned with the tension of the stroke*, the resulting synthesis of both movement and pressure in the handling of the stroke.

4) In the fourth part (at the end of the chapter), we shall talk about *the penhold and the choice of the writing instrument.*

Former copybook models, in the days of quill pens, prescribed a distinction between up and down strokes which is hardly ever taught today (but perhaps will again be in the future[3] and is reduced by modern instruments, especially felt pens. That differentiation, which creates a rhythm, corresponds to the fact that it is easier, and therefore more the norm, to press during flexion (downward movement, adduction, downstroke) than during extension (upward movement, abduction, upstroke). Having said this, observation of the development of children's handwritings shows to what extent this pressure, in the broad sense of the term, becomes at, a very early stage, eminently personal, freed from the motor difficulties of learning which have been statistically recorded[4] [8], and closely bound up with children's individual development. In certain cases, a child's pressure can change very significantly at brief intervals, indicating changes in his tonicity and in his behaviour[5].

The same thing applies to the adult, whose stroke is so closely linked with the writer that Hegar had the idea of identifying it with a reflex; the stroke is a basic material where an element of stability, the image of the writer's profound identity, links up with changes which express, in a very direct, temporal way, the writer's history, his periods of dynamism, of physical and psychological health, as well as the difficulties, either emotional or organic, which he may encounter. The stroke does not allow the making of an exact medical diagnosis, but it is what one chooses to study in the observation of handwritings done in collaboration with doctors. The stroke, to quote only this example, alters in the case of depression [10].

---

3   Project of 'L'Education Nationale': finding a writing instrument for a renewal of the teaching of handwriting, 1986.
4   This refers to the items of the Children's Scale.
5   Graphomotor activity is directly linked to tonic muscular activity and we know to what extent tonicity is related to character.

Lastly, the stroke leaves on the paper - the graphic space symbolising the outside world in a wide sense - a very revealing print of the writer's attitude towards both others and reality, of his personal way of acting, reacting and communicating.

Besides weight and all the particular features relating to the course of the writing gestures, the stroke is also an element of :
- the paper on which the writing has just been set down,
- the writing instrument used and the way it is held.

There is not much to say on the nature of the paper, the quality of which is good enough nowadays not to have an important influence on the quality of the stroke. Nevertheless, the possibility of notes taken, by chance, on porous paper, giving a 'blurred' stroke should not be overlooked. This is one of the limits of the validity of graphology; it requires prudence on the part of the graphologist, and also shows the need for several documents, or one which is suitable. The very choice of a writing paper can be indicative if it is very marked; it is an immediate clue offered to the graphologist : paper with a very smooth, almost glazed surface, expresses the desire for a gliding movement, unlike rough paper which offers resistance.

The colour of the ink in itself can be informative when it is the result of a systematic choice. The most used colours are blue and black; black, supposedly more virile is, when overdone, sadder than blue, which is warm. Green is frequently and temporarily used by adolescents; later it is the sign of a rather doubtful attempt at originality and youthfulness. Red, colour of passion and excitement, is rarely used on a regular basis, just like purple, which conforms to traditions of old, (it was, in the past, the ink colour prescribed for schoolchildren), but is not often used nowadays, except with felt pens.

Much more important is the choice of the writing instrument used; unless used by chance, it is revealing, as is the way it is held. The appearance on the market of new instruments as widely used as the fountain pen, poses problems of observation and assessment for the graphologist. In this chapter, we have thought it preferable to deal first with all the signs pertaining to the stroke, before discussing that point, thus making it less abstract and more explicit.

We draw the reader's attention to the fact that observing the stroke requires the original document and, in most cases, a magnifying glass. A photocopy, as compared with the original, especially if it is reduced, may wildly exaggerate the differentiation of pressure.

The interpretations put forward at the beginning of this book necessarily involve signs dealt with in the later chapters, owing to the didactic necessity of respecting an analytical plan. Right from the second chapter, the reader can begin to gain a better understanding of how the various associations of signs are formed and their combined significance. We advise students, once they have finished studying this manual, to reread the first chapters attentively.

1. Signs concerning weight (Pressure in the strict sense)

STRONG PRESSURE

A writing has strong pressure when the writer accentuates the pressure on the gesture of adduction, that is, a downward gesture pointing to self-assertion. Its stroke leaves a discernible imprint on the back of the paper, especially with a biro, thereby showing that the graphic movement inscribes itself forcefully in the third dimension of handwriting, which is depth. With a pen-nib, specially if it is soft, under the effect of strong pressure, the stroke tends to widen and the points to separate if the nib is split. It is sometimes difficult to distinguish this type of stroke from the wide stroke with medium or weak pressure produced by a wide nib (false pressure) rather similar to the effect given by a thick felt.

Whatever its source, quality and use, strong pressure is the expression of a force signifying that the writer feels called upon to stand fast in his relationship with others and reality. The origins of this attitude can be multifarious : vital energy, demanding affectivity, strong convictions, search for power, or inner tension.

If the handwriting is sufficiently elastic, it comes from an active person who involves himself in his actions especially since it is there that he finds part of his justification. The position he adopts is the result of a choice, of a decision with a definite plan of action. The obstacle is accepted as part of a job. It follows that the involvement is considerable, sometimes making it difficult for him to assume a distance in his relationship with himself and with others.

If the elasticity of the stroke diminishes, the writing becomes less supple, making it less lively; strong pressure slows down the progression at the same time as elements of inhibition or stiffness appear. In the first place, the force of assertion is less well controlled, hence a risk of being authoritarian, foolhardy or stubborn, especially if there are also double-joins.

If the movement is static, betraying inhibition, the energy finds no outlet. The writer tenses up, becomes bogged down and he does not use his potential.

Comme les vacances durent je pense y aller après Noe enfants - Vous pourriez di seule avec vos enfants jus

Woman, 30 years

1

Writing with strong pressure, precise, connected, double-joined, with arcades, garlands, angles, slight left slant, aerated. Self-assertion, decision, pugnacity, stability in the pursuit of goals. Clear, lucid and efficient intelligence. The movement is controlled, the intensity reserved for the pressure. The writer's strong convictions do not prevent her from being prudent and clever.

Like many components of writing, the adjustment of pressure is a progressive phenomenon. It often happens that children press too much. They do this as part of their efforts to reproduce the required form and, although it results in hindrances, heavy pressure seems preferable to too much lightness, which generates an uncertain execution of the stroke.

Among adolescents, it is rare to find writings with strong pressure in a supple context; it is stiffening and resistance which cause this pressure, rather than any real conviction. Assertiveness is applied in opposition to the outside world rather than in compliance with it .

---

l intervient en concrétisant les potentic
nternes que toute personne a en elle m
ne sait pas utiliser. Et je suis persuade
pue des cellules mutées, ne répondant plu
u corps, sont normalement éliminées ,

Man, 25 years.

2   *Writing with strong pressure, precise, very connected, clear but straightened up; rather angular, arcaded, more or less narrow, constrained movement. The elasticity is insufficient, hence lack of suppleness in the behaviour of this young man who is serious, conscientious and organised, but whose communication is affected by the defensive and slightly stiff aspect of the writing.*

Man, 40 years

3   *Writing with strong pressure, precise, inharmonious, with extensive movements, wide, not very clear, damaged forms, bad rhythm of the distribution of space. The progression is chopped up and very uneven. A strong personality, desire for power, but little inner cohesion. Strong pressure combined with lack of homogeneity may bring out the contradictions of this person in a dangerous manner.*

LIGHT

In LIGHT writing, the pressure on the paper is weak; most of the time there is a slight differentiation between up and downstrokes. But, in extreme cases, the upstrokes can even disappear, so much so, that the pressure on the downstroke itself is abnormally reduced. The graphic movement does not penetrate very deeply, thereby showing a fundamentally different attitude to life from the one brought about by heavy writing. In a supple writing context, lightness increases speed.

The energy potential is sometimes less considerable, but it is mainly the desire for self-assertion which is different. The writer uses his strength in another manner, trying to smooth down antagonism, preferring to work around events rather than try to act directly upon them. He does not feel he has to intervene, because he prefers to keep various options open, or because he feels less confident. Consequently, he is prepared to revise his opinions if the person he is dealing with demonstrates the validity of his own views. Action is less important for him than it is for the writer with strong pressure; yet his interventions can be more rapid and just as effective, although the effectiveness may be of a different kind.

The writer here does not so much take charge as make himself adaptable to unexpected events; he uses less force and more finesse.

Light writing reveals receptivity, delicacy, hypersensitivity, modesty or relative self-assertion. It lends itself to intellectual and psychic mobility. It is related to intuition, to questioning and also to an activity which promptly adjusts itself to what is required.

But, in order to indicate such qualities, lightness must occur in a context of suppleness; for light pressure also expresses the danger of lack of self-confidence, of uncertainty, of difficulty in involving oneself and often, with pursuing a goal. It shows the tendency to lack powers of resistance and to show oneself vulnerable and impressionable.

With regard to lightness, the quality of the stroke is paramount [6]. This is what will determine the self-confidence and the efficiency of the person, and his sense of reality. The lightness of the stroke can be compensated for by its precision, or increased by its porousness.

Delicacy then becomes a weakness; erratic attitudes or excitability dominate. There can be emotional lability and relationships with others can be superficial.

The less supple the stroke is, causing either a slack or stiff writing, and the more the forms dissolve or become spoilt, the greater the risk of lightness bringing with it signs of weakness and discouragement.

In adolescents, light writing is frequent [11] and corresponds to the period of expectancy and transformation they go through.

In an elderly person, it shows wear and lassitude.

---

6   This may be why very light writings are found among high-level sportsmen whose
     reserve of vitality cannot be doubted, but whose speed of judgement and estimation
     is essential.

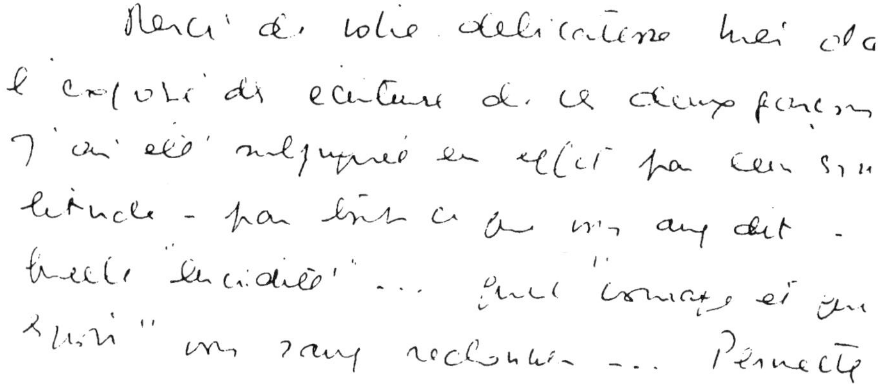

[handwritten text in French cursive]

Woman, 42 years.

4

Small, light writing, hopping, in relief, supple, rapid, rhythmic, personal and progressive. The writing movement, full of subtleties, serves a receptive intelligence, enriched by intuition and sensitivity; the lively mind, which also has finesse and agility, is ready to respond quickly to a new idea. Self-assertion is achieved through the intellect, but the precise stroke suggests efficiency and a certain distancing for self-protection.

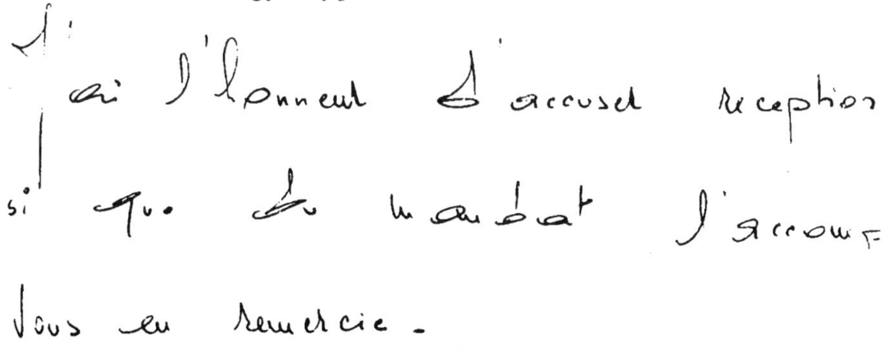

[handwritten text in French cursive]

Man, 45 years.

5

Light writing, with lessened pressure mainly on the downstrokes, disconnected, with a few gaps in the continuity, both narrow and wide, very fragile and monotonous. Contradictions, between the superelevations and the suspensions, the simplifications and the complications. Difficulty in asserting himself can be suspected, in spite of the writer's ambition.

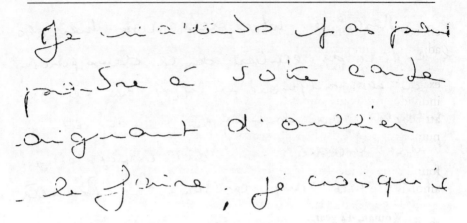

Woman, 40 years.

Light writing, both filiform and inflated, wide with left tendencies, imprecise, slack, with a weak, poor quality stroke. The progression of the writing gives the impression of slithering, which suggests an elusive personality. A lot of irrationality, subjectivity, and behaviour lacking in independence in this impressionable person.

6

IN RELIEF
FLAT

In writing IN RELIEF, the difference of pressure between up and down strokes is no longer slight, but pronounced; it is the result of a firm movement with very personalised pressure. The stroke is particularly differentiated, thus increasing the impression of relief and therefore of the volume of the writing; this happens no matter how thick the writing is, but becomes especially noticeable in a sufficiently well-nourished writing.

Since we are dealing with a differentiation of pressure which, through contrast, produces relief between flexion and extension movements, writing in relief therefore indicates that the relationships of the writer, both with himself and with others, are experienced in a personal and intense manner; his way of expressing them stimulates exchanges with the environment. Strong individuality emanates from this tonic writing.

A writing in relief which is also harmonious, probably makes the most effective use of pressure, because it involves at the same time strength, adjustment and personalisation and generates a rhythm in itself.

However, too strong a relief carries with it the shortcomings of all exaggeration, especially if the writing is jerky and not very clear. Because the individualism is too imperious, the originality may generate a very closed attitude and interfere with communication, restricting it to a limited number of people. By becoming too different, one can appear strange [10].

In order to be able to master this stroke in relief, the writer must have found his own identity; it is therefore not surprising to find it only rarely amongst adolescents.

Hegar made a special study of the dimension of the relief in relation to the connection in space, consisting of the arc in space in which strong and light pressure alternate in a continuous movement. The arc can be concave, denoting harmony between sensory perception and achievement, or convex, denoting by its reduced pressure that reality is felt too strongly [7].

In FLAT writing, there is no difference between up and downstrokes, whatever the thickness of the stroke may be. However it is more often associated with light writing.

This lack of contrast leads to the production of a uniform stroke, which is the opposite of the stroke of exchange contained in writing in relief.

A graphologist will deduce either passivity, or a defensive attitude on the part of a writer, who denies his emotions so that they do not affect him.

Man, 25 years. (sample on previous page)
Writing in relief, firm, rhythmic, personal, simplified and rapid. The writing
7 *is very expressive; originality can be seen both in the way the writer lives and*
in his intelligence. His level of intelligence enabled him to get into a renowned
science college, but one can guess that the personality is too strong to be satisfied
with a classic business career.

---

i and strengthened by the cord

has been placed in us.

Margaret Thatcher

Woman, 55 years.
Arc in space and stroke in relief in this personal and rhythmic, somewhat
8 *spaced-out writing. Authority without sectarianism and cleverness of this*
British Prime Minister. Intuition, imagination, freedom and awareness of
what she represents.

DEVIATED

Pressure is called DEVIATED when the weight is not exerted as it ought
to be, on the vertical axis, the normal axis of affirmation. Instead, it appears
elsewhere, particularly on the upstrokes or, even on horizontal strokes. Now,
to strengthen the upstroke which is a gesture of extension, directed out-
wards and normally lighter in pressure, creates a resistance with regard to

the environment; to increase pressure horizontally on the baseline makes it heavier and slows down graphic progression to a surprising extent.

Wherever the area of pressure is, that area is in itself significant - there is a phenomenon of deviated energy which is uneconomical for the writer since it is easier to press on descending than on ascending or horizontal movements and, here, he does the opposite. One can assume that the life flow is wrongly channelled and used in a forced, unnatural way.

The graphic movement is predominantly constrained; both action and communication are carried out only in certain conditions, or are channelled in a restrictive manner. The fact that one does not let oneself go and that one refuses to admit any weakness, shows a strength and considerable personal involvement on the part of the writer in what he does, but also an inner tension, the origins of which have to be investigated.

This tension will be indicated in other signs apart from deviated pressure : signs of stiffness such as lines that are too straight, for instance.

Woman, 45 years.
Strongly deviated pressure on the horizontal, causing straight-lined writing and secondary width. The deviation is related to the inner intensity which the writer tries hard to keep under control by making herself fit into a rather conventional social pattern. A lot of presence, a desire for concrete achievements, stubborn pursuit of personal objectives. There is energy and courage in these tense movements. The underlying ethical sense is strong.

9

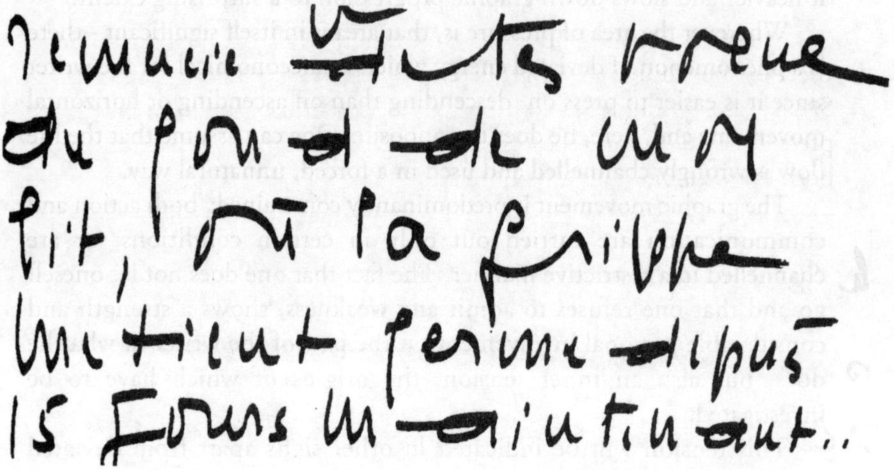

[handwritten sample in French]

Woman, 35 years.

10 *Inharmonious writing, yet with relief; contradictory in its association of both narrow and wide letters, with emphasised secondary width, suspended, enlarging and clubbed finals, superelevations, double-joins and discordances. The deviated pressure increases the risk of impulsiveness, of lack of prudence, of authoritarianism.*

One can assume that the unnatural effort resulting from deviated pressure is the consequence of an inner obstacle which the writer tries to overcome; it is a sort of active compensation which is not devoid of courage. The writer with deviated pressure is not indifferent; the mere fact of his insistence calls for consideration to be given to the efforts made in the name of a demanding moral or social conscience.

But precisely when this moral conscience is insufficient, the force embodied in deviated pressure can show up in an anarchic or aggressive manner.

SPASMODIC

This concerns contrasts in pressure, reminiscent of spasms. Here, there is no supple alternation between pressure and its reduction. SPASMODIC writing generates a tense, irregular stroke, where not only is the pressure stronger, but also arbitrarily placed; the discharges seem to aim at both the writer and his environment

Man, 50 years

11 *Spasmodic writing, inharmonious, heterogeneous (narrow and wide, diminishing and enlarging). Arbitrary personality, disconcerting, tense and possessive, authoritarian (connected to overconnected). Unpredictable behaviour, if one takes into account the ill-controlled strength which emanates from this personality.*

In this difficulty of controlling pressure, one can sense a strong underlying impulsiveness. Emotivity or even aggressiveness may irrupt; one can assume irritability and impatience which make fitting in with a working team precarious.

The graphologist should look for elements in the writing which are liable to correct the slightly explosive appearance of the stroke : order, for instance, can show possibilities of self-control.

SHARP-POINTED
CLUBBED

SHARP-POINTED writing is shown by a discharge forming a sharp point at the end of the final stroke. Sharp points can also be found in some free signs; t-bars, for instance. They occur mostly on rightward strokes with horizontal pressure which is much stronger than in the case of a mere jerk. But sharp points can be found in any direction, particularly leftwards and downwards. The direction of the sharp point informs us against whom or what it is aimed.

Whether in a final letter or elsewhere, it is a sign of the release of an impulse or of tension in the form of impatience, nervous violence if not of aggressiveness. We know that the final stroke, in finishing a word, prepares the connection with the following word; the discharge placed on it does not make for a sympathetic rapport with others; there is a tendency to contradict, or others are not trusted.

Woman, 70 years

12

Sharp-pointed writing, but in relief, thrown and personalised. Surprising combativeness in this intelligent, original, woman who is still out to conquer the world with her propulsive movement, which is nourished by her convictions and her radiance. Relationships with others are not tender; they may be provocative, but she also carries others along with her.

Man, 60 years

13

Clubbed writing, thrown, large, personalised, angular, connected, with little clarity and propulsive movement. This pugnacious and imperious writing makes a strong impact. The originality, the need for power, the uncompromising convictions must have been difficult to keep under control for this writer, a former president of the Assemblée Nationale. The clubs can be seen in the finals, the accents and the t-bars.

The meanings of sharp-pointed writing vary, particularly in relation to speed and pressure. If the thrust involved in a rapid movement can be put down to impulsiveness, it is more alarming in a slow context where one can suspect calculated nastiness or some resentment. On the other hand, the critical sense belonging to a sharp-pointed writing can be made to serve an incisive intelligence - as do fine sharp points in a light and rapid movement, for example - but the stronger the sharp-pointed movement is and the more pressure it has, the greater the risk of unexpected, touchy reactions and of a vindictive or distrustful attitude.

The sharp-points at the end of words which can be found in the rather slow writings of some children point to the awkwardness of a clumsily stopped movement and are not necessarily synonymous with aggressiveness; they are part of the difficulty in controlling the movement, which Crépieux-Jamin used to call the final stroke of released tension.

CLUBBED writing is based on a thickening of the stroke, especially in finals. Unlike sharp-pointed writing, it derives from a constrained and braking gesture. It comes from tension arising from an impulse or ardour which has been repressed. The movement gets crushed on the spot, producing a club-like shape which makes the word heavier and does not allow easy connection with the following word.

The frequency and intensity of clubs, just as the layout and the rhythm of distribution do, enable us to appreciate the extent to which the writer manages to control himself.

Clubbed writing represents the impetuosity, the combative spirit of a fiery, intense personality holding strong convictions, who means to impose his point of view.

Like all excessive gestures, clubs tend to give some discordance to a writing. Anything that compensates for this discordance, such as rhythm, spacing (as was the case in the last writing) or anything which increases it, such as monotony, stiffness, compactness, confusion, etc., must be attentively looked for.

SPINDLE-SHAPED

SPINDLE-SHAPED writing arises from differentiated pressure, strong pressure in the middle of the downstrokes, in upper and lower extensions in particular, shaped like spindles. It used to exist mainly with the pen-nibs used at the time when the copybook model prescribed light upstrokes and heavier downstrokes. It constitutes an anomaly of pressure, connected, it would seem, with the presence of emotional, or sensuous discharges.

sont comme les femmes

accessoires essentiels

srg gainsbourg

Man, 50 years

14

Dazzling writing, full of sudden discharges. Inharmonious, angular, connected, prolonged up and down. A showy writing with emphasised spindles. The personality of the writer tends to assert itself with a contempt for any convention, excessively so, but not without a certain flourish.

FURROWED

FURROWED writing is produced by a stroke which digs into the paper, that is to say with very strong and particularly constant pressure on both up and downstrokes. Thus there is excessive pressure with no differentiation. Consequently, rhythmic alternation is not possible and the expenditure of energy is exaggerated.

It can be deduced that the writer expresses a force without being able to relax or to stand back; both self-assertion and expansion are unilaterally pursued, with inevitable excesses as a result.

The furrowed stroke is the opposite of the nuanced stroke, which is one of exchange; the writer is apt to be vulnerable due to that permanent tension [12].

Woman, 35 years

15 *Furrowed writing; the inner tension brought to light by this dug-in stroke , is also found in the double-joins, the looping, the free strokes and the finals.*

2. Signs concerning
the quality of the stroke

PRECISE

PRECISE writing consists of a precise[7], homogeneous stroke, with well-defined edges requiring firmness of movement.

The precise stroke is that of the introverted [8] writer who, having mastered his emotions, adopts a resolute and determined attitude; like this he expresses a distance between himself and his environment and retains his independence.

He gains in autonomy what he loses in receptivity. That is why a sharp-edged stroke is considered to symbolise a form of protection for the writer. Incidentally, the edges of a precise stroke are sometimes called defended edges. The writer, less affective and more active than one with pasty writing, is better equipped to resist influences; so one can predict greater objectivity, lucidity, courage of one's convictions, and greater discipline.

The inner attitude which gives rise to precise writing, favours the intellect, concentration and cerebral sensitivity, hence fewer variations in mood and more constancy, but also less readiness to listen and less warmth.

Preciseness is all the more interesting in that the writer has responsibilities forcing him to maintain a critical mind and self-discipline.

But we should be aware that the precise stroke retains all its positive interpretations only if it is also supple, for the snag with this type of stroke, is possible stiffening; combined with signs of closedness which tend to isolate the writer, a precise stroke generates intransigence and coldness.

---

7   We are using Crépieux-Jamin's definition, more general than Hegar's which arises from a short penhold as indicated at the end of this chapter, when we comment on the way the instrument is held and where the precise stroke is contrasted with the pasty stroke, as they originate from a fundamentally different psychomotor attitude.

8   The term introversion is used from the point of view of the innermost attitude in the Jungian sense, rather than in the sense of what appears on the surface. This association is owed to C. Boureille's research [13].

dans votre lettre au sujet de de votre courrier, j'ai le reg taire part que j'ai un peu à vous lire. Je pense aussi q- dû parce que je n'ai pas l

Woman, 40 years

16 *Precise writing, supple and firm, comfortable, aerated, in garlands, although close to the copybook model. Simplicity, seriousness, uprightness, ability to organise and stability in this writer who did not have a higher education. Preciseness here indicates a good balance between lucidity and emotions.*

Precise writing, owing to the choice of attitude it involves, is not very frequent in adolescence, so its presence will be more positively interpreted when found in a sufficiently supple graphic context.

me demande si je dois l'employer et

l'embaucher pour un poste très élevé.

Est-il stable ? Créateur ? A-t-il les

qualités de chef ?

Man, 60 years (see sample opposite page)

Precise writing, small, with strong pressure, sober, personalised, connected, angular, with held back movement, a slight left slant and wide spaces between the lines. The precise stroke indicates the intellectuality of this intelligent and hard-working writer for whom any weakness would mean a surrender. Here, the precise stroke does not have perfect elasticity; in combination with angles and the left slant, it betrays the inner tension of this director of one of the leading international advertising agencies. The very considerable spaces between the lines is a measure the writer imposes between himself and between events. What is more, the irregularities show the interiorised sensitivity of this very selective person.

17

Man, 25 years

Precise writing with rather strong pressure, connected, small, taut, spaced out and irregular. The precise stroke indicates the desire not to let a shaky self-confidence and strong sensitivity dominate. In spite of the clumsiness of the jerky graphic progression, a courageous, stubborn and clear-headed personality can be discerned.

18

PASTY
POROUS

PASTY writing[9] has an evenly wide stroke, over half a millimetre wide, with slightly imprecise edges; the pressure is more or less strong. It often is a writing with few contrasts, because neither the penhold nor the inner attitude, which is less determined and from which the penhold arises, favours contrasts.

Pastiness of the stroke is related to a sensory and affective approach to life and also to a spontaneous and direct one.

The writer is an extravert[10] instinctively ready to be receptive to the environment with which he wishes to become one and not to be distanced from. The whole attitude to life is different from that of the writer with a precise stroke; the writer with a pasty stroke is, up to a point, not bothered if he is dependent on his environment, since this is the source of his inspiration.

The result is a more physical presence, a permeability, a harmony which facilitates adaptation and enriches communication. Self-assertion is marked with an emotional tone and the intensity and bias which derive from it. What the writer gains in warmth and contact with others, he can partially lose in objectivity and autonomy.

Pastiness, through what it symbolises, brings an interesting quality to writers whose professions give importance to human relationships, or are founded on a world of sensory images such as all the professions involving communication or the arts, for instance.

For a pasty stroke to have radiance, it must be combined with good pressure and a firm handling of the stroke, and the writing must be lively; in this case, activity is maintained.

Otherwise, the passive element of this stroke takes over, betraying the

---

9   We are using Crépieux-Jamin's classical definition and not Hegar's; the latter is very specific and will be found in Part 4 of this chapter.

10 The term extraversion, like that of introversion, is used from the point of view of the innermost attitude in the Jungian sense, according to C. Boureille's researches [13].

writer's dependence as far as his environment, his own emotions or sensations are concerned. The pasty stroke then is that of a writer who offers no opposition, is apprehensive of obstacles and who may, in the end, look for the easy way out in order to give himself pleasure, for reasons of material self-interest, or of weakness.

When the permeability of the pasty stroke is exaggerated, it results in POROUS writing, the edges of which communicate too much with the paper, indicating a person's lack of resistance as far as the outside world is concerned.

Man, 35 years

19 *Writing produced with a fountain-pen, having a good blue pasty stroke with strong pressure and some relief. Connected writing, wide, individualised, rhythmic, largely right-tending. Here, pastiness reflects a developed sensuousness used on an artistic level.*

Pou nous aider à Tracea les de la prochaine" année sce d'autout qu'un grand chan, una grande éclosion occanhe

Man, 50 years

20

Pasty writing, permanent choice of felt pen; the writing weighs heavily on the line, is double-joined, left-slanted, with angular arcades. The progression is hindered by left-tending movements. The predominantly sensory approach is not easily channelled; the hermetically closed writing reveals a certain anxiety. The pastiness, owing to the permeability to the environment which it involves, indicates that the writer is dependent on his emotions and his surroundings. Notice the superelevations and the very shortened lower-extensions.

d'occasion d'aller à Paris et, voir tous les amis je ne dois dan occasion.

i à Paris le mercredi 16 juin

Man, 50 years

21

Pasty writing, clumsy, precipitated and progressing unevenly. Yet, some successful connections show the pragmatic intelligence of this engineer destined to work on site. The pastiness brings emotional warmth, but also a lack of impartiality and difficulty in self-control.

WELL-NOURISHED
VELVETY

WELL-NOURISHED writing has a well-inked stroke, sufficient pressure and well-defined edges; it strikes a happy medium between fine and thick writing. It has a good quality stroke, solid and most often supple.

It shows a good potential, personal equilibrium and autonomy. It is a sign of self-confidence, of the capacity to use one's abilities; it is also a sign of healthy relationships with others, neither too close nor too distant.

It is the stroke of an adult, because its pressure, homogeneity and handling presuppose choices and the decision to bring them into effect.

A well-nourished stroke always has a positive meaning.

nécessité, pendant quinze jours,

un traitement à forte dose de

cortisone et d' antibiotique et

qu' elle risque de supporter plus

Woman, 45 years

22 *Well-nourished writing, with good proportions, supple, simple and clear, in garlands, orderly, controlled and rhythmic. Receptivity and autonomy, balance and sense of duty, ability to make choices, reflective and level-headed, ability to form relationships easily.*

VELVETY writing consists of a light but full stroke which glides on the paper. It tends to be slightly pasty. It does not have the firmness of well-nourished writing which is more resolute and offers greater resistance.

Velvety writing attests to naturalness, receptive emotions and seduction; it is imbued with sensitivity and indicates the writer's desire for smooth human relationships.

Man, 50 years

23 *Velvety writing, slightly pasty, supple, in garlands, clear, with an almost flowing movement, aerated. Simple, natural, warm and discreet attitudes in this perceptive writer who is readily liked by those working with him. A clear mind, open to discussion.*

CONGESTED
SMEARY (MUDDY)

According to Crépieux-Jamin, CONGESTED writing consists of ovals (a, o, e, d) filled with ink. This is more likely with a pasty or thick stroke, but it can also be associated with a finer stroke when congestions should attract the graphologist's attention, because of their contradiction with the stroke itself.

The fact that congestion applies to round letters is important because these letters are called "affective"[11] letters, due to their special sensitivity to

---

11 They are symbolically so for two reasons : their curved shape and their position in the middle zone.

the writer's sentimental reactions. The black inside the letters can, nevertheless also be found in upper and lower zone extensions.

If the obliteration of round letters with ink is not caused by a faulty instrument and is consistently repeated, it shows some anxiety, a difficulty in expressing oneself on an affective level and subsequent uneasiness. This can also be caused by fatigue.

In SMEARY (MUDDY) writing, the stroke is exaggeratedly pasty and stagnant; the edges are very blurred, which causes extensive congestion; there is a sort of clogging of the whole trail which appears as a heavy and muddy flow progressing with difficulty.

If this kind of stroke is usual, it reveals a subjective mind, lacking in clarity, frequently emotional anxiety and difficulty in getting down to action. Communication and adaptation are therefore considerably affected.

The hypothesis of a physical handicap, or of the writer suffering from the effects of medication is not out of the question.

Woman, 45 years

24

Severely congested writing, where connectedness and compactness increase the obliteration. The predominance of the middle zone, the static aspect, the straightness of the lines, tell how much the writer is a prisoner of strong inner tension. Communication is not at all easy and those around her find her a burden.

Cher Mademoiselle

Auriez-vous l'amabilité de m'envoyer la feuille de maladie avec les séances de Thomas depuis l'hiver 61.

Woman, 30 years

25   *Smeary writing, produced with a fountain-pen, congestions, slowed down progression, although the pressure is rather light. Neither the form nor the movement can escape from the clogging of the stroke; probable anxiety.*

FINE

FINE writing consists of a light and slender stroke the thinness of which is not necessarily detrimental to the elasticity [14] or the rhythm.

By its lightness, it shows that the writer asserts himself with discretion; by its dual qualities of thinness and liveliness - provided the stroke is supple - it indicates a receptive attitude, although one marked by prudence.

Fine writing attests to a slightly intellectual sensitivity, to finesse, to delicacy and, frequently, to intuition. A possibly precise stroke compensates for its slender quality; otherwise, there is not much resistance to obstacles. The writer runs the risk of being anxious and easily disturbed.

If, moreover, the writing seems inhibited, a fine stroke then becomes one of the signs to do with withdrawal, self-effacement and lack of self-assurance.

Man, 45 years

26 *Fine writing, precise, accurate, narrow, superelevated, simple, and spaced out. Sensitivity, delicacy and reserve are combined with a precise, thoughtful and rigorous mind; activity is carefully organised.*

THIN
DRY

When a precise stroke has neither weight nor width, it is called THIN.

A lack of sensuousness and affectivity increases along with difficulty in self-assertion. A lack of self-confidence, a feeling of loneliness, some difficulty in expressing oneself are frequent.

The thin stroke is one of the elements of a writing which has deteriorated with age, a kind of devitalisation arising from graphomotor difficulties caused by lack of tonicity; in this case, the writing is in the process of disorganisation.

This type of stroke can appear temporarily with certain diseases.

*avir samedi et tout est entendre
avec elle pour se rendre chez
vous - passer un moment - .
C'est avec beaucoup de
peine que j'écris ces quelques
mots excusez-moi de le faire*

Woman, 90 years

27
Thin writing, fragile and angular, but still connected and slightly rising. The stroke is both stiff and weak, but never slack in this old lady who is fighting old age with tenaciousness and lucidity.

*rès sensibles à votre délicate attention,
ous adressent leurs remerciements les
lus chaleureux pour la très jolie
mpe qui s'harmonisera à ravir avec*

Woman, 26 years

28
Thin, light writing, fragile in the quality of the stroke, precarious in the monotonous and disconnected progression, with many twisted strokes of self-assertion, concave and descending lines; capitals in the middle of words. Yet some control over the letters has been acquired in spite of considerable anxiety, but the difficulties of fitting in with a teacher's post are not surprising.

A thin stroke is mostly associated with jerkiness, tenseness, angles, not from choice, but from an inability to make curves.

This stroke reveals some suffering, some impoverishment, or helplessness in mastering reality.

The devitalisation found in a dry stroke is more alarming in a young person.

The DRY stroke is both thin and trenchant. It lends itself to stiffening. The writer often takes an abrupt and categorical standpoint, thereby betraying his affective discomfort. He is very touchy.

As in all cases of rather negative interpretations, we should look very carefully for elements of the writing which could compensate the dryness of the, stroke such as dynamism, balanced proportions, intelligent combinations, good space distribution or, on the contrary, those which accentuate it, such as angles, narrowness, sharp points and lack of cohesion.

BLURRED
WASHED-OUT

BLURRED writing lacks precision in its contours and density of texture, which implies indecisive pressure and inadequate tension of the stroke.

Consequently, the writing consists of a porous stroke (see PASTY writing). The subject is easily influenced, suggestible, and finds it difficult to channel his considerable emotivity; this can even make him indecisive. He tends to procrastinate and to show a lack of consistency in the pursuit of his aims.

The blurred stroke is on a par with a personality lacking in certainty and feeling insecure as a result.

Somatic or psychological problems and the wear and tear of old age can cause a blurred stroke.

The meanings which we are giving, will prove correct only if the blurred stroke is habitual. We must check that it is not due to a bad quality instrument or paper.

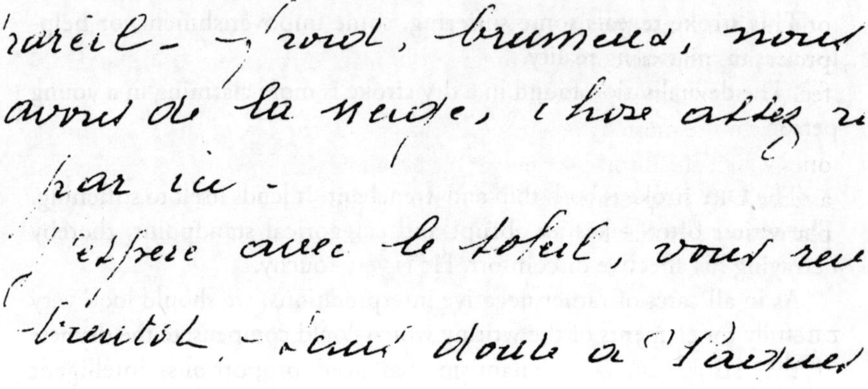

[handwritten French text:]
rareil - jroid, brumeux, nous
avons de la neige, chose assez n
par ici -
J'espère avec le soleil, vous rev
bientôt, - sans doute à l'avenir

Woman, 68 years

29 *This blurred stroke is irregular in pressure and quality; the writing, however, remains structured. The angles and some enlarging forms show the efforts the writer makes to adapt.*

WASHED-OUT writing has a rather faded stroke; both pressure and consistency are clearly insufficient. If it is habitual, the graphologist should take note, for it shows decreasing psychic energy, defencelessness, a feeling of surrender and sadness. There can be various causes for this and they are not conditioned by age.

MOIRÉE (VARIEGATED)

A writing is called MOIRÉE (or VARIEGATED) when an irregularity in the ink flow can be seen, causing a more or less marked irregularity in the colour of the stroke.

It is yet another manifestation of openness to the environment and of impressionability. Here the writer finds if difficult to assess himself or others and, consequently, does not cope very well with frustrations and is prone to subjective and unpredictable reactions arising from an inner feeling of anxiety and touchiness.

The more moirée the writing is, the greater the risk of gut reactions, or ones which are disproportionate. It can follow that the relationship within a team may be precarious. The writer with moirée writing needs to be placed in a familiar framework that can give him a sense of security.

Woman, 35 years

30 *Moirée writing, double-joined, with fairly square looped garlands, low and conventional. A lot of inner churning, uncertainty and anxiety in this writing dominated by emotions, but a courageous steadfastness in the achievement of projects.*

3. Tension, synthesis of pressure and movement in the handling of the stroke

In the components and signs which are to follow, we shall approach the handling of the stroke from the point of view of the application of tension, a notion which we have already mentioned.

The tension of the stroke is the result of the phenomena of contraction and relaxation inherent in the graphic gesture itself.

The different sorts of stroke handling follow from the different ways in which the movements of flexion and extension are related and indicate a general attitude to life which will, of course, be completely understood after the study of the other signs[12, 13].

---

12 The German graphologist, Rudolph Pophal, constructed a whole graphological system based on the observation of the degrees of tension of the stroke, which he related to specific areas of the brain.

Even if these specific areas are controversial, the very study of stroke tension in five degrees remains a definite contribution. Pophal observed stroke tension starting from slackness (hypotonic, degree I) up to excessive tension (hypertonic, degree V). These two extremes are connected with "archaic" cerebral centres (pallidum). The medium degree combines conscious, voluntary firmness with the suppleness of gestures and movements which go back and forth, and are connected with the most evolved part of the brain, the cortex (degrees III and IVa). Degree II, related to the suppleness of a writing, is connected with the subcortical area and degree IVb, stiffness, is connected with the striatum [15]. The reader interested in the above, can refer to C. de Bose's article on Pophal [6].

13 Roda Wieser also founded a graphological system on the twofold study of the elasticity of the stroke, which she calls basic rhythm. Her point of view, based on a large number of observations, is different from Pophal's. Her books, at present, have not been translated into French. We are quoting one of the most important books [17]. C. de Bose has written several articles on Roda Wieser's basic rhythm [18].

SUPPLE (a component of Gobineau)

A SUPPLE stroke is an elastic stroke which achieves co-ordination of flexion-extension[14] movements with an easy and natural flow. The effort of flexion, a movement requiring pressure, blends happily with the relaxation of extension, a gesture of release; there is a natural rebound from one gesture to the other as well as overall homogeneity.

A supple stroke involves a certain firmness of the graphic movement, since a confident movement is essential for a good distribution of pressure. The main thing about a supple writing is that its essence lies in relaxation rather than in control and this is what makes it different from firm writing; it thereby implies medium tension.

Because of its successful co-ordination, the supple stroke is economical in energy; because of its well-balanced alternation between pressure and release, it creates a rhythm; because of the freedom which pervades it, it is symptomatic of a self-confident person, who easily relates to reality and at the same time knows how to be detached from it; his energy is easily channelled without sudden changes or without emotional twitches.

Although the stroke is of medium tension, the penhold and the certainty of movement ensure consistent contours of forms and continuity of connections.

There is an affinity between supple strokes and curves, garlands in particular.

A supple stroke indicates naturalness, genuineness, ability to adapt, a conciliatory attitude, the ability to give, and self-confidence.

If the stroke is not quite firm enough, the suppleness is that of a relaxed person who is moderately combative.

A really supple stroke is rarely seen in adolescents, as self-confidence is not a strong point at that time.

---

14 H. de Gobineau and R. Perron [19] have listed the items of suppleness and stiffness, including them among the components of personality, called P.

te de cette lettre pour vous
+ de ma nouvelle adresse.
n haitant de bonnes vacan.
vous prie de croire à toute
mitié.

florence

Woman, 30 years

31

Rhythmic writing, round, supple and firm, simple, personal, pasty, slightly wide and with good distribution of the spaces. The suppleness of the strokes shows the open nature of the intelligence; the naturalness, the adaptability and the firmness give it autonomy and determination.

FIRM (one of Crépieux-Jamin's signs)

The graphic movement which dominates the FIRM stroke has tonicity, is well-controlled and resolute. The tension of the stroke is balanced; sufficiently strong to generate a sustained cursive movement, and sufficiently regular to make control the dominating factor of the writing.

The balance between form and movement in the writing shows a dynamic writer in full possession of his faculties; firm writing expresses a good degree of maturity. It is the sign of an autonomous, resolute, responsible and disciplined character who gets things done. It points to a decisive mind, to the ability to resist where necessary and to a purposefulness which channels the writer's energies.

There is more affinity between firm and precise than between firm and pasty, but this is not a hard and fast rule. If a precise writing can hardly be other than firm, a slightly pasty one can be firm also.

On the other hand, if firmness of stroke tends to produce slightly angular forms, curves which are both precise and firm do also exist and are

---

Woman, 26 years

Small and firm writing, a little held back, but rhythmic, sober, simple, simplified, angular, aerated, grouped to connected. The slight constraint which can be noticed still in this young woman who has just entered professional life, makes it possible to foresee real firmness of character, aptitude for taking decisions, stability of aim, sense of responsibility and independence of mind.

32

all the more positive as they soften what could amount to an excess of determination in the firmness.

The qualities of character giving rise to firm writing also give rise to a lively writing; firmness of stroke therefore goes together with a certain rhythmic quality, even if it is a little taut.

In adolescence, a firm stroke is particularly interesting, in that it shows the emergence of self-confidence, of a sense of responsibility and the capacity to assume definite standpoints; the sooner it appears, the sooner it indicates that the adolescent has made some choices.

WEAK (as opposed to firm)

The main factor of a WEAK stroke is the slackening; it lacks tonicity, tensile strength and elasticity, which is not naturally conducive to rhythm in the writing.

Neither flexion nor extension has sufficient tone for successful coordination; the pressure is generally light and therefore, the weak stroke is not conducive to the creation of good forms; connections often disintegrate and imprecision is frequent.

The writer gives the impression of being unaware of the efforts to be made, or that he does not have the energy to make them. Adaptation is haphazard; the subject shows himself to be changeable, easily influenced and dependent. There is a risk here of emotional instability, a tendency to escape responsibilities and to become discouraged.

The more weak and arhythmic the stroke, the more the writer shows himself indecisive in the utilisation of his potential.

If however, the weak stroke is incorporated in a regular movement with correct use of space, the passive element is then partly modified by an acceptance of discipline. People with this type of stroke will tend to adjust to certain routine tasks, which more reactive people would not put up with.

Man, 30 years

Weak stroke, light pressure, unsteady writing not conducive to a steady line.
33 *The stroke is precise in spite of its fragility and this modifies the slack aspect of the writing. Yet, the writer is an intelligent man, but with a weak character.*

TAUT (a component of Gobineau)

The TAUT stroke is dominated by constraint; it implies a movement that is constantly tense with little or no elasticity.

The stiffening disturbs the coordination of flexion and extension, and can go as far as interrupting it by an increasing number of penlifts. One can see elements of tautness appear in angular forms, narrow letters, poverty of movement and rigid organisation. The dominant factor of the writing is linear (based on straight lines). If the writing is curvilinear, then the curve is stiff and therefore lacks the quality of suppleness which is the essence of a curve.

Whether the writing is straight or curved, there is no easy transition from one form to another; nor is pressure well-managed.

However, there are numerous aspects of tautness and, in particular, numerous degrees of the elements of stiffness capable of influencing a writing without necessarily dominating it.

Medium stiffness is quite compatible with successful social conduct and the utilisation of one's potential. It is found, for instance, in obstructed movement, which, although to be treated with reserve, is also of a certain interest.

Acquired writing also, owing to the self-surveillance it needs, is often tinged with stiffness without this necessarily being a hindrance as long as the writing remains lively.

The steadfast character of a person with a medium degree of tautness in his writing, can find its place in professions where great vigilance is necessary and where one has to act with authority; in this case, the forms should be structured and the layout clear.

Baccalauréat Philosophie 156
Licence en droit mention 93 191
Diplomé du Centre d'Etudes Interna
de la Propriété Industrielle de

Man, 33 years

34   *Angular, connected writing, with strong pressure. Dynamism and strong convictions in this obstructed movement, but also inner opposition. The tension contained in the stiffness finds an outlet in combativeness and argumentation. Despite the qualities of intelligence, working within a group is difficult.*

But if a taut stroke appears in a monotonous or discordant context, it then reveals an anxious state of alarm, a feeling of insecurity, hyperemotivity, uncalled-for reactions and inhibitions.

The greater the stiffness, the weaker the resistance to frustrations becomes and the more the subject becomes wrapped up in himself through what we shall call an egocentricity of tension.

A taut stroke is fairly frequent in adolescence; it reveals dissatisfaction, multiple desires, fear of failure, and the unloading of anxiety on to others, but this could merely be a temporary phase

In this case, its significance should therefore be adjusted.

Whereas an adolescent's thin stroke can be followed with a firm stroke once examinations are over, or a suitable profession has been found, in an adult, on the other hand, it appears more constitutional.

The tension contained in moderate tautness is a potential force, which becomes a weakness only if it is excessive; one does not find that much stiffness in young people.

Excessive stiffness is found also in pathological writings amongst those writers whose communication and adaptability are really problematic.

We shall end these three first lines of approach with the global notion of irregularity which we will find afresh in each chapter.

IRREGULAR PRESSURE, QUALITY AND HANDLING OF THE STROKE

There can be great irregularities of pressure and we generally talk of irregularly light or irregularly strong pressure.

This is particularly noticeable in adolescence when self-assertion comes and goes or is ill-controlled. Irregular pressure in adults retains these characteristics of emotivity and reactivity.

The quality and colour of the stroke can also be irregular and this was discussed in the case of both moirée and washed-out writings. To a lesser extent, also in adolescence, one finds irregularly pasty and sometimes irregularly precise strokes, thus revealing general uncertainty; the same meaning is applicable to adults, but it is of course less justified.

More disturbing is the greater or lesser irregularity in the handling of the stroke, and consequently, of its tension. This is the case with a stroke which is simultaneously weak and stiff, and this combination is more frequent than one might expect. Here the stroke is anarchic and causes the writing to skid with excessive and badly-controlled movements; it prevents the creation of a continuous, homogeneous and clear writing, as the forms and connections disintegrate. Speed is consequently reduced, and bad rhythm becomes the rule.

Considerable alternation of stiffness and slackness in a stroke, reveals considerable inner conflicts, as the writer has trouble in managing his relationships with other people and with reality.

A stroke that has very irregular tension touches on pathology and remains the exception.

4. The penhold and the choice of the graphic instrument

1. The penhold. - The aim of this book is not to describe the motricity of the graphic act, nor the positions of the hand, the forearm or the posture. But we feel we should talk about the way the instrument is held, in view of the connection this has with the character of the writer and of the effect on the stroke.

The most common penhold, the one best adapted to the use of the graphic instrument and formerly taught in schools, is that where the pen is placed between the thumb and the index finger on the one hand and, on the other, the left side[15] of the middle finger, and is leaning on the hand at the point where the first phalanx of the index and the metacarpal[16]

---

15 For the penhold with the right hand.
16 When children are learning to write, one can point out to them that they have two fingers on top and three underneath.

articulate. Thus the fingers are half bent and half extended, placed at a distance of about 4 cm from the paper.

Fig. A

The hand, placed below the writing line, rests on the table on its side (particularly on the little finger and the ring finger joined together) as well as on the forearm; the angle formed by the pen with the paper is about 45 degrees [20].

This penhold always corresponds to the correct one, but nowadays, primary school teachers pay scant attention to it and children, when starting to learn to write, use penholds which in one way or another are faulty and this does not help in the acquisition of an efficient writing movement. But we need not deal with this subject here.

Indeed, we are studying adult or adolescent writers who have acquired a normal mastery of graphomotricity and whose penhold, even if not always conforming to the norm, is, however, adapted to a cursive movement presenting no major difficulties.

This penhold happens to be relatively stable and personal. The different forms it can assume have a direct relationship with the stroke and we have thought it interesting to describe the two main ones.

a) *The short, vertical penhold*. When a writer has too short a hold, i.e. places his fingers lower down than average, nearer the nib and the paper, he also straightens up his pen towards verticality, in order to keep skilful control of his graphic movement. The angle formed by the pen and the paper is definitely greater than the 45 degree of the average hold and causes a direct contact between the paper and the nib point, which gives, in the case of a fountain pen a *precise stroke*, the edges of which stand out clearly on the paper.

The pressure is generally fairly strong, but can be very differentiated, particularly between up and downstrokes.

When pressure becomes excessive, with too short a hold, too much flexion, tenseness and the index finger bent inwards, the gesture makes cursive progression difficult.

The graphologist, Hegar, pointed out that there is an affinity between a writing with a short, vertical penhold, giving rise to the precise stroke, and the straight stroke.

b) *The long, oblique penhold.* As opposed to the previous penhold, the fingers are placed on the writing instrument at a greater distance from the nib than average, and the angle formed with the paper becomes less than 45 degrees. Thus the nib comes into contact with the paper obliquely, and one can notice in certain cases, with a fountain pen, a pasty stroke as described by Hegar, that is to say with a precise outer edge and a pasty inner edge (corresponding to the underneath part of the nib), ending in fringes. In fact, more often than not, what the graphologist will observe is a pasty stroke in the classical sense, both edges of which communicate with the paper.

The more or less long penhold facilitates light pressure; if the fingers are placed very far up during extension, the penhold will tend to be weak and will give rise to a stroke lacking in firmness.

Hegar pointed out that a long penhold and a pasty stroke have affinities with the curved stroke.

We reproduce two figures, B and C, summing up the precise stroke and the pasty stroke according to Hegar, and their formation [21].

It is obvious that the notions quoted above are valid only in general terms, and that in the extreme diversity of penhold, one can find short holds with light pressure, or long ones with strong pressure, but these combinations are rarer.

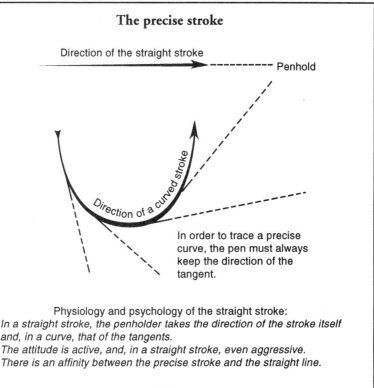

Fig.B

As a general rule, long penholds are more relaxed than short ones.

It is no less obvious that entirely precise or entirely pasty strokes are rarely found. The direction of the strokes and the differentiation of pressure all come into play.

A precise stroke requires the pen to be continually pointed in the direction of the movement. It also seems easier to execute a precise stroke on the down than on the upstroke (in flexion more than in extension). In relation to the symbolism of space, precise observation of the spots where pastiness or preciseness are found in a writing can give very nuanced information, but it must be admitted that present-day instruments do not allow such subtle descriptions, and that in most cases, a graphologist will have to be content with a more global approach.

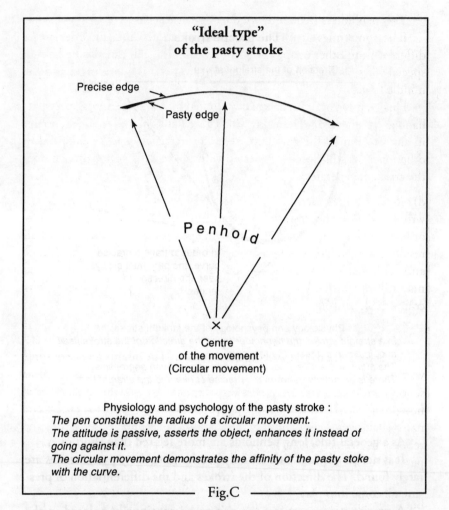

"Ideal type"
of the pasty stroke

Precise edge

Pasty edge

P e n h o l d

×
Centre
of the movement
(Circular movement)

Physiology and psychology of the pasty stroke :
The pen constitutes the radius of a circular movement.
The attitude is passive, asserts the object, enhances it instead of
going against it.
The circular movement demonstrates the affinity of the pasty stoke
with the curve.

Fig.C

c) *Remark on the lateral penhold.* All we have just said applies to the most common penhold, that is when the writing instrument is pointing in the same direction as the forearm and extends it.

Another grip, the "lateral", also exists in which the writing instrument is perpendicular to the forearm and parallel with the written line.

This penhold is frequently used by left-handers.

It is sometimes artificially adopted by adolescents in order to be different from other people, and in that case, the pen can also be held in special ways, as for instance in the joint between the forefinger and the middle finger.

Finally, it is a position habitually adopted by a small percentage of right-handers. Its effects on the stroke, which have not been well recorded, do not in any way hinder the graphologist's interpretation, as this penhold, like other ones, is still closely connected with the writer's personality, as does the stroke it generates.

d) *Remark on the pressure applied to the instrument.* - In some cases, the writer puts more neuromuscular effort into holding the instrument more or less tensely, than he does into applying pen pressure on the paper. This results in a light, ill-controlled stroke which is mainly noticeable in children and adolescents who have graphomotor difficulties, but some adults also may still retain that graphomotor deviation which, does not make for a comfortable writing.

2. The choice of the writing instrument. -The disappearance of some writing instruments such as pen-nibs dipped into ink (still in use in some schools, however), the decreasing use of fountain-pens, the appearance of new instruments with only one inked point, such as biros, broad and narrow felt pens, have obliged graphologists to make new observations and reflections, in fact to adapt, in order not to cut themselves off from that personal element of capital importance, the stroke.

The usual writing instrument, deliberately chosen, is in itself significant, but a graphologist must be certain that he is not looking at a text written by chance with a borrowed pen. These are the limits to validity with which a prudent graphologist is always confronted (to have several documents, not all written on the same day, is advisable).

a) *The biro* : it facilitates a rapid and spontaneous progression of the writing movement for a writer with a small script, who often has a short, vertical penhold, and who first and foremost considers his writing as a means for the transcription of language.

Graphologists have adapted well to studying writings executed with a biro; irregularity and the amount of pressure can be perceived with a degree of precision by running one's hand over the back of the paper.

b) *The broad felt pen* [17]: it suits a writer who writes large and likes to leave plenty of ink on the paper. It goes with a long, oblique penhold, almost that of people who are drawing : the paper is caressed, there is little differentiation and rhythm in the pressure; there is sensuousness, a need for warm, easy and smooth contacts, as opposed to the short penhold with strong pressure which expresses an attitude that imposes itself on the outside world in an incisive way.

But a broad felt pen can also go with a straight and rapid stroke, although more rarely so, in a large writing which takes up space : such writers know how to impose their will upon others, while maintaining good contacts (see, further on, writing no. 36 and, in the chapter on signatures, writing no. 208).

Broad felt pens are often used by writers with acquired[18], artificial or fabricated writing. In this case, the writing is considered as an aim in itself because its forms are chosen both for the communication itself and the impression it will make on others, even if the writer who has produced it is unaware of that aim. A felt pen can also be used to give an appearance of stronger pressure than is natural to the writer.

The broad felt pen is fairly often used by writers whose writing is spontaneous, but who have an unconscious need to make the black dominate the white, to leave a sometimes dirty-looking mark on the paper, corresponding to character traits of writers attached to certain objects, to money, who are difficult characters[19] or, who, conversely, need to

---

17 We use this term for the type of pen with a fibrous point.

18 See acquired writings in the Chapter on Form, p. 84.

19 In characterologies based on the Freudian stages, this is close to the anal stage.

neutralise, by means of the felt, the inadequate aspects of their stroke and the meanings related to it.

The stroke produced by a thick felt is close to that produced by a broad nib, but the graphologist makes a distinction, because the felt pen stroke is not differentiated. Writing executed with a biro has an affinity with a precise stroke, and writing executed with a broad felt pen, with a pasty stroke, sometimes with a smeary stroke if it is excessive.

There is, in actual fact, a contradiction between the biro and the thick felt pen, when it comes to a choice: the biro writer, with a small writing, cannot write with a broad felt pen (or else he is mistaken in his inner choices, see writing no.37), just as the writer with the broad felt pen writing suffers if obliged to write with a biro. Generally, biro writing is one in which Movement dominates and felt pen writing, one in which Form dominates.

c) *The fine felt pen*: basically, it can be used by a large number of writers. In fact as it slides without any elastic response to the pressure of the writer, like chalk on a blackboard, it is suitable for light pressure, and many fountain-pen or biro writers,who like to feel a response when they press, do not like using it on a regular basis. On the other hand, because it allows very fine, small and light writing, it can sometimes be used for amendments or additions.

Handwriting with a fine felt pen can be spontaneous, artificial, small, large, etc., but it nearly always expresses a desire for human relationships without friction.

d) *The fountain-pen* : although it is the most ancient of "modern" instruments, it does not seem necessary for us to write about it at length, as all the observations of classical graphology, and the signs described above apply perfectly in this case.

Let us recall that the nib has two prongs, that it allows thin upstrokes and thick downstrokes, that is to say a big differentiation of the stroke. Strong pressure makes it possible in principle (and with a magnifying glass) to distinguish both furrows of the pen, whereas light pressure does not.

There exist supple or hard nibs, fine or broad, whose multiple combinations produce great varieties of strokes described among the signs in this chapter.

The fine nib an has an affinity with the precise stroke, the broad nib, with the pasty stroke and the thick felt pen, but there can be cases where this does not apply.

Graphologists must beware of poor-quality inks, old cartridges for example, used out of necessity or by chance, which can temporarily cause a poor quality or a washed-out stroke, and which can mislead a graphologist (limits of validity). On the other hand, the very definite progress achieved with cheap biros, has almost completely eliminated the inconveniences of the early days, such as thickenings of the stroke, dots within the stroke, or blotches left on the paper; but a ballpoint in the process of drying up always needs extra pressure, and felt pens which are too old produce a stroke which crumbles away.

Neither the penhold nor the instrument can be seen by a graphologist, if he not looking at someone in the act of writing. Identifying these is the result of a hypothesis, of second-degree reasoning, which the graphologist must get used to doing, in order not to deprive himself, in his analyses, of the very important data given by the stroke and the choice of the graphic instrument, which is revealing if it is habitual.

Notre dossier est déjà parti.

Ne faudrait-il pas le compléter

avec les 2 annexes ci-jointes ?

Rozenn.

Woman, 25 years (see sample opposite page)

35 *Rapid, small, precise, written with a biro. The writer cannot write with a felt pen; lively mind, rapidity of decisions.*

J'aime écrire avec un feutre épais.

Woman, 55 years

36 *Large, pasty, connected, broad felt pen. The writer hates writing with a biro and does not manage to write small. Efficient in practical matters, taste for human relationships, need to play a part.*

*mon divin et ma tm 13
27 Avenue du maréchal
75016 PARIS*

Woman, 42 years

37 *The writer, who has a small writing, has made an unsuitable choice in using a thick felt pen; the writing becomes confused; an unconscious choice corresponding also to some difficulties in human relationships.*

3.   Note on Hegar. - The graphologist, Walter Hegar, in his book *"Graphologie par le trait"* [7], studies handwriting from four aspects : pressure (light, heavy), the quality of the stroke (pasty, precise), the curvilinear or linear tendency of the stroke (straight, curved) and its speed (slow, rapid).

THE 24 BINARY COMBINATIONS
TABLE A

		HEAVY		LIGHT
Straight	1.	Energy allied to decision. Energy applied to the pursuit of goals.	7.	Easy decision-making. Awareness of the decisions taken.
Curved	2.	Energy guided by imagination allied to the need to realise images and to give concrete expression to ideas.	8.	Imagination allied to sensitiveness. Imagination and perceptions influence and stimulate one another. Search for perceptions corresponding to their images. The larger the curve the more imagination prevails over perceptions which can be unconsciously distorted by it. Fantasy. Mythomania.
Rapid	3.	Energy increased by activity and vice-versa.	9.	Activity easily triggered off (compare no. 7).
Slow	4.	Intense inner activity; possible serious inhibition.	10.	Assimilation and observation to the point of hesitation, shyness, exhaustion, illness.
Pasty	5.	Energy taking reality, feelings and the life of the senses into account. Energy hindered by instinctive assertion of what is felt as existing. Conflicts between energy and pleasure. (Possible brutal pleasures).	11.	Impressionability of the senses. Ranges from a sense of colour to toal need to gratify senses. Thirst for impressions. Delicacy of feelings.
Precise	6.	Energy guided by rigorous personal moral laws or by some or other principles. Incorruptible or pitiless energy. Energy detached from the life of the senses, from physical states (from tiredness) or else surmounting them.	12.	Intellectual or cerebral sensitivity. Coldness of heart.

TABLE B

	STRAIGHT	CURVED
Rapid	13. Great decisiveness (lack of imagination).	17. Imagination closely bound up with a complex of ideas, stereotyped ideas, activity stimulated by a complex of ideas.
Slow	14. Decision-making together with prudence or hesitation. Resolute person, in spite of the fears provoked by a feeling of obstacles. Lack of self-confidence.	18. Imagination influenced by a feeling of obstacles. Sense of proprieties and ceremony. Feeling of obstacles increased by imagination. Anxiety, worry, distress.
Pasty	15. Decisions at the service of the senses or the heart (or vice-versa). Tendency to merge with decisions and needs. (Sadness arising from resignation). Corruptible decision-making.	19. Imagination nourished by the senses or by the feelings. Feelings and life of the senses sublimated by means of imagination. Appreciation of sensorially perceived forms (aesthetic sense). Imagination carried along by the senses (sensuous images).
Precise	16. Incorruptible decision-making based on personal or other principles. Cold and insensitive decisions unaffected by imponderables, feelings or life of the senses.	20. Imagination influenced by moral, social or religious ideas or by principles. Mystical imagination. Utopian illusions. Fanciful ideas.

Straightness and curviness of stroke play a decisive role only when there is a very clear dominance of one over the other - when sticks are curved, for instance - but observation, in most cases, gives a neutral result, writing being a combination of curved and straight strokes. Besides, the speed of the stroke, in itself, is very difficult to assess (see chapter 8 on Speed).

The last two aspects of the stroke quoted above are therefore less used by graphologists, whatever their interest may be.

It has nevertheless seemed to us useful to reproduce Hegar's tables concerning these four elements, in their combinations of two, for, in spite of a few exaggerations, they make a definite contribution in the case of writings where the elements are very clearly represented, and especially for associations which are not very frequent, such as curved and precise, for instance, or pasty and straight.

TABLE C

	RAPID	SLOW
Pasty	21. Activity at the service of the senses or the feelings or vice-versa (see no. 15). (Corruptible activity).	23. Awareness of obstacles and assertion through feelings, of what is felt as existing, stimulate each other. Passiveness allied to a need of contact with reality. Lack of activity or laziness accompanied by physical unease. Low-spiritedness. Fatigue. Exhaustion.
Precise	22. Activity inspired by ideas linked to personal morals or by rigorous principles. Cold and insensitive activity unaffected by imponderables, feelings and life of the senses.	24. Inner obstacles opposing the subject's freedom regarding the circumstances of life. (Repression of feelings and of needs of the senses).

38 **Man, 50 years**
Precise and curved, a less frequent combination than precise and straight, indicate, according to Hegar, imagination and creativity which can lose their

link with reality and feed on moral, religious and sometimes utopian ideas, in spite of the high level of the writing.

Woman, 50 years

39 *Pasty combined with straight is also less usual than pasty combined with curved; a decisive mind and some rigour coexist with a considerable affective and sensory potential in this writer.*

2

FORM

When one first learns to write, form is the first rule imposed by a calligraphy which is "the art of good letter formation" (*Littré*).

It is therefore quite logical that one should study this after studying the stroke.

It is necessary to know the basic copybook model and particularly the mopvements involved in it, in order to understand how handwriting, having first been based on a model, later deviates from it.

It is also desirable to be familiar with the copybook model of foreigners whose handwritings we wish to analyse.

However, it is quite obvious that to study how writing deviates from the original model, is not the only approach for a graphologist. There exist basic forms common to all styles of writing[1], and an evolved writing is a living entity with a stroke and a pattern which is inscribed on the space provided by the paper[2].

Calligraphy is a totality consisting of curves and straight strokes which create different sorts of letters having different dimensions and proportions.

In our cursive connected writing, one distinguishes between middle-zone letters and upper or lower extensions, whether looped or not .

---

1   Michon, for instance, made a brilliant attempt at studying and interpreting a writing in Chinese characters, which were unknown to him [22].

2   The German graphologist Klages thought, rather paradoxically, that with his law of expression, he could analyse any writing of a foreigner, without knowing from what copybook model the writer had learnt to write.

In the present day French copybook model (known as "English"), there are no angles in the shape of the letters; this has not always been the case in the past (Gothic, Sacré-Coeur, etc).

As far as connections between letters are concerned, these are also usually rounded, with slight variations depending on the different models, as well as on the teachers' handwritings. Indeed, some teachers, by nature, may have writings with slightly stiff connections.

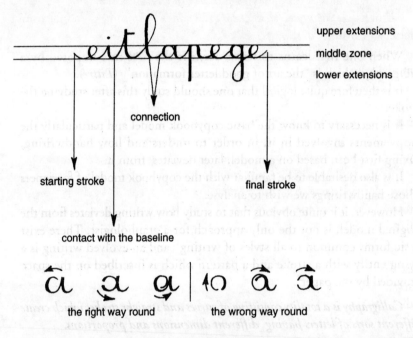

Fig. D. - Direction and starting point.

We would like the reader to be aware that the term 'form of connection', used by many graphologists[3] to describe garlands, arcades, etc., might, we think, lead to confusion.

---

3   "The forms of connection are the forms by which the downstrokes of a writing are
     joined to one another" [24].

For this reason, we prefer to keep the general term 'form' for the above aspects of writing, and, with reference to the genetic aspect, reserve the term 'connection' for the joining stroke between two individual letters[4].

The curve (or its angular transformation by some writers) takes different shapes in handwriting. These are mainly :
- the arcade : *n, m, p* (French model), *h,*
- the garland : *u* especially, *v* and *w* (French model), *y,*
- the circle, or what closely resembles it, concerning the inner round letters, or ovals *o, a, d, g, q,* part of *c,*
- the loops : *e,* looped upper and lower extensions *l, b, g, f* (French model), etc.

Through their movement, all the other letters come close to either the shape of arcades or garlands, or to straight sticks which should be drawn from top to bottom.

The copybook model also prescribes a direction for the writing of letters which follows the logic of a cursive movement going from left to right.

Consequently, round letters are formed anticlockwise (*a, d, g, q, o*) as are the looped extensions which start from the baseline and go upwards towards the top of the page (*l, b, h, f*), whereas lower extensions, which start from the baseline and go downwards are formed clockwise (*g, j, y, z*).

In our writing, which favours right-tending movements, there are exceptions to this : *s* and the first part of *x* (French model) whose final stroke is turned leftwards[5], as well as the downstroke of *f* whose leftward direction is opposite to that of other lower extensions.

When the direction of letters is not followed by the writer, it gives rise to "reverse" writing, the different aspects and significance of which will be described in the chapter on direction, although this sign also has a lot to do with form.

The school model is more hesitant on the matter of how to start *a,d, g, q* : from the right, which is more desirable, but often from the left, which

---

4   Moretti's graphology in Italy has the same viewpoint.
5   Some writers who like to connect, children in particular, finish these letters with a small lasso which joins with the next letter.

facilitates scrolling (which we shall look at in the sign called 'double-joined'), or the separations (which we shall look at under Continuity) .

On the other hand, it is never recommended that the starting point of these letters should be at the bottom, and we shall be able to see the significance of this when studying Direction.

We do not think it necessary to attempt to give an abstract philosophical meaning to the concept of form. The codes which have enabled language to be transcribed have varied with time and place. Extremes which come to mind are the writings where pictograms or ideograms are the main forms - and the ancient cuneiform writing, where form was reduced to its simplest expression.

On the other hand, what is significant is the importance which the writer may give to form, either consciously or unconsciously, and to its dominance over the movement which produces his writing, or vice-versa.

It is in the chapter on the relationship between Form and Movement that we shall be able to discuss Form as a significant graphological entity.

In the first part, we shall deal with the forms that have remained close to the copybook model, and the forms which have become personalised.

In the second part, we shall deal more precisely with the signs corresponding to basic scriptural forms, the constituent elements of handwriting.

In the third part, we shall look at the signs connected with the degree of openness and closedness of the forms.

Finally, in the fourth part, we shall end with the concept of homogeneity of form.

1. Forms remaining close to copybook personalised forms

COPYBOOK

One learns to write in order to master the copybook model; this is generally achieved towards the age of ten. The model may be adhered to in adulthood, yet without being reproduced exactly : this is COPYBOOK writing, that which keeps more faithfully than any other to the school forms, in its contours, proportions, controlled progression and layout.

Through this reproduction, respect for the forms learnt and the security this brings, self-discipline and the desire to be understood are expressed. Copybook writing reveals a serious-minded, conscientious person who has common sense and accepts reality as it is.

This writing which is often retained by writers who have not had a higher education[6], is nevertheless significant, since many such people are incapable of producing it, or have more or less drifted away from it.

Copybook writing is more commonly found in certain professions; teachers, accountants, whose professions oblige them from the start to watch the way they write, and who, after all, keep to a style that suits them.

Copybook writing is apt to be used also by those who write daily, but remain faithful to the model, thereby showing their attachment to a certain formalism. If, in this way, they demonstrate little originality, they nevertheless show their sense of regular effort, their discipline, and their correctness in social relationships.

Copybook writing, owing to its precise forms, tends to favour form at the expense of movement. The writer's relationship to his writing appears

---

6   In which case, there has been no graphomotor necessity to transfer the basic forms in order to increase the writing speed (see Chapter 1, part 2).

to be fixed. It is this that has sometimes led to the association of copybook writing with lack of imagination or with difficulty in evolving.

Nevertheless, it would be a mistake to think that forms which have remained close to copybook style are necessarily fixed; they can be transformed imperceptibly by personal proportions, by the quality of the stroke, or be enriched with a rhythm which entirely modifies the appearance of the script and gives it life.

The three following samples show how writings can differ, although they each share the same sign as a dominant, and this justifies the importance given to graphic syndromes throughout this book.

A writing is not defined by one sign only, but always by the overall context in which it occurs. Just as there is no such thing as two identical people, there are no two identical graphic milieus.

Je vous remercie très sincèrement, chère Madame, de votre délicate attention à mon égard.

Je vous souhaite - ainsi

Woman, 40 years

40 *Copybook, clear, controlled, orderly, connected, pasty, all factors indicating this primary schoolteacher's seriousness, her desire to be exemplary and her slightly conventional, but warm sociability.*

royant posseder les qualifications requ
joins à cette lettre mon curriculum v:
, étant entendu que je me tiens à

Woman, 28 years

Copybook writing, despite a few personal movements and proportions; very little movement in this conscientious, attentive, tenacious young female engineer. The almost scrupulous retention of the school model, particularly if one considers her high educational level, makes one assume her need for a stable and safe set of rules. Her good distribution of space lightens up this straight-lined writing.

41

'e plus fort curieux de co
sage de l'homme invisi
lequel il a travaillé,
Je vous prie de croire, (
mieur, à ma très vive co

Man, 65 years

Forms close to copybook, but drawn with freedom - proportions, sinuous baseline - despite a kind of clumsiness; more than discipline or the desire for security, it is simplicity, authenticity and freshness which dominate in the writing of this well-known advertising man whose source of inspiration is precisely a sort of almost childish mischievousness.

42

PERSONALISED

Handwriting generally becomes personalised very quickly, and one might even say, any modification, however small, is personalisation (see the personalisation of writing no. 42, although close to the copybook model). However, a writing is called PERSONALISED with regard to form, when it is definitely differentiated from the copybook model. It is this type of personalisation which we are talking about here, bearing in mind that handwriting, in fact, can be personalised in all its aspects.

Just keeping to the shape of letters, one finds a whole range of more or less accentuated, or more or less genuine types of personalisation which can take endless forms : simplifications, or creation of more or less simple original forms, or acquisition of a particular form, which can be conventional or stylised.

Personalisation is not a quality in itself. Its value lies in the choice of the elements of which it is made. It derives from the natural capacity of an individual to express, or accentuate how different he is from others. But it also derives from the need to create an appearance, even if this is based on convention. The personalisation of handwriting can therefore bear witness to this fact, as much by showing a high level of natural evolution and a freedom of inventiveness, as by revealing a real constraint imposed by the writer upon himself, at least to start with.

Whatever the type of personalisation may be, it must remain within the limits of legibility; this implies that the capacity to reconsider the taught forms and their connections, or even to create new forms, is allied to the retention of clarity and homogeneity; one should bear in mind that what is revealed once again goes beyond the writer's expressive intentions and his conscious awareness of them [26].

Too early a personalisation of writing often goes hand in hand with a little confusion, and this is why an adolescent writing that is both personal and clear, is a very positive thing.

SIMPLIFIED

SIMPLIFIED writing moves away from the model, inasmuch as the writer, far from reinforcing the form, removes certain elements from it : loops and bows, for instance. The personalisation is done through a shedding of the unnecessary elements of writing. Along with this, the vertical dimension may be reduced, and the progressiveness of the writing can increase the horizontal dimension. This is accompanied by a modification in the continuity, which turns out to be to more or less connected, but this is not a rule, for one can find many simplified, connected writings.

To simplify is to make a choice, to grade, to retain only what the writer considers to be essential. If the choice is judicious, that is to say, moving towards greater speed and efficiency, the writer shows initiative, intelligence and a critical mind. The mental agility which follows, predisposes the writer to make the best of use of facts, especially if the stroke is of good quality and if there is a good distribution of space. It is a sign of an evolving personality which is more directly goal-oriented.

The inherent danger of this approach is a lessening of legibility; what is a simplification for the writer, becomes obscure for the reader; it is all a matter of degree. The choice of the simplifications is therefore more questionable if the forms are merely implied.

This choice, which tends to favour certain movements, is revealing of the writer's preferences.

Although simplified writing does not necessarily conflict with fullness of form, there is a tendency not to use the form as a means of expression, and this gives an increasing importance to the quality of the stroke. A simplified writing associated with a thin stroke, reveals that the writer tends to remove himself from reality; his thought processes can lead him towards theories, abstraction and austerity.

It can happen that the simplifications apply to certain letters, while others remain complicated; two contradictory gestures which attract the graphologist's attention, and will reflect on the real efficiency of the writer.

In children and even adolescents, simplifications are more related to evasion, since, most of the time, they are not accompanied by good structure of the writing; the simplifications are more due to neglect than to an elimination of unessentials and they do not arise from a deliberate choice.

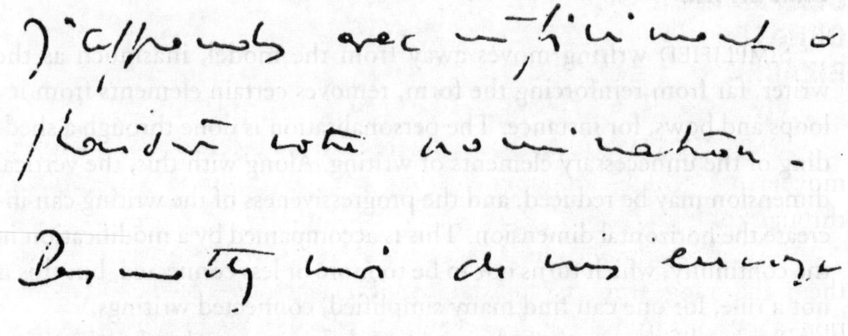

[handwritten sample]

Man, 50 years

Simplified writing, progressive, connected, light, with a filiform tendency, small and wide: that of a lively, intelligent and sensitive engineer. The individualisation is achieved through an elimination of unessential forms for greater efficiency and speed. Vibrant and dynamic movement; rhythmic writing.

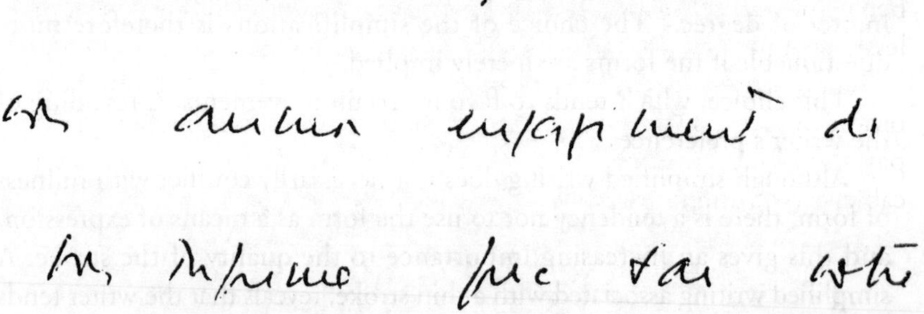

43

[handwritten sample]

Woman, 30 years

Simplified writing, personal, rhythmic, precise, with flying strokes, strong pressure, and spaced out, in an intelligent, determined and active young woman. The majority of the movements lead to greater efficiency; closely connected to this, the irregularities, the suspensions, in a context strongly projected towards the right, betray a certain tension. The considerable simplifications sometimes make for imperfect legibility, their choice goes together with a stylisation which reveals the writer's tendencies.

44

COMPLICATED
ORNATE
BIZARRE

COMPLICATED writing is encumbered with unnecessary or complex movements. Unlike simplified writing, the personalisation takes place through complications.

All types of complications are possible, and it would be futile to list them; they range from the addition of a few elements, to such an elaboration of movements that the whole writing is modified by the disproportions or the complexities they generate.

The copybook model combines a simple form with a logical trajectory; the opposite happens in a complicated writing whose pathways never cease to surprise.

Faced with a complicated writing, there are good grounds for believing that the writer does not understand himself clearly, that he seeks to find his own rationale, the motives of which are obscure, and which make it difficult for him to reason intelligently. As a result, an uneasiness affects his behaviour; his self-expression becomes unnatural, even clumsy or pointlessly dissimulated. Judgment is subjective, the subject tends to stiffen up.

The more insidious the complications (to the extent of generating bizarre or confused writing), the more necessary it is for the graphologist to pay attention to them, as the writer is a prisoner of a more or less inextricable web of feelings or ideas.

---

spécialisée dans le promotion immobilière et de la gestion de

45 Woman, 25 years

Woman, 25 years

45 *Complications and numerous double-joins in this constrained, precise and obstructed writing. In other respects, there are simplifications and a personal layout showing the good cultural level. In spite of a proper adaptation, everything, in fact, remains very complicated.*

This type of complication produces ORNATE writing where the enhancement of form is evident. The ornaments are most often based on more or less complicated swellings causing disproportions detrimental to harmony, even if they are produced by a creative personality.

If the writing is noticeably ornate, it shows a tendency to lyricism, a taste for pomp, a desire to attract attention or to produce an effect, which is not lacking in ostentation or insolence, and also a little naive. It suggests the capacity to circumvent things. The self-assertion is, partly, artificial.

Ornate writing, nowadays, nearly always affects only capital letters, which are more representative of the social ego, and the signature. It is sometimes produced by writers of modest socio-cultural level, for whom it is a compensation. Ornaments then show a social ambition which can be a motivating force.

---

46 **Man, 60 years** - *The ornaments occur only on the inflated capitals, showing how much the writer values social success; the superelevations point to the same* *meaning. An understandable attitude in this writer of modest socio-cultural level, hard-working, and proud of a success which he owes to none but himself.*

Complicated writing can be so in a way which is exteriorised. The writer gives the impression that he has to prove more, but he does so with gestures which often are skilful, on a basis of expansion and not retraction.

Showy complications of this sort, as opposed to more discreet, but more insidious ones, are easy for the graphologist to spot . It seems that the writer derives advantages in not too obvious a manner from complications which seek to get round other people. Seduction, imagination, mannerisms, dominate a communication which takes place in a way one could describe as playful, but never simple.

The complications may affect only certain letters; maybe the capitals, or some small letters, or the signature only, and sometimes, the diacritics; each kind of complication is significant.

One sometimes finds complicated writings of a theatrical and slightly weird sort in some artists.

47 **Woman, 50 years** - *Large and complicated writing with twists and volutes, thrown, badly controlled, disproportionate. Profuse imagination, need to attract, intense excitement and illusion.*

Complications of all kinds can lead to the oddities of BIZARRE writing: showy weirdness through which the writer liberates himself, but also weirdness affecting some letters only, without the writing being bizarre as a whole, when one first looks at it (see writing no. 90).

The graphologist should be alerted by this sort of weirdness, particularly if the general context is anxious and if the writer is young.

Man, 22 years

48 *Very personal writing, simplified, rapid, a mixture of bizarre and elaborated forms. A highly evolved young man, but with a strangeness which makes him difficult to understand and to help.*

ACQUIRED
ARTIFICIAL

In a writing which is complicated, even ornate or indeed bizarre, the writer may resort to some surprising devices, but nevertheless he remains the inventor of his own forms. The case is quite different for a whole series of personalisations, in which the writers purposely force themselves to adopt a way of writing quite different from their spontaneous writings, and which is inspired by a fashion, by a different code, or, on the contrary, by a marked return to the copybook model.

These are ACQUIRED writings, in which the writers' personalities are expressed under the protection of a chosen front. They contain lasting modifications which are sufficiently marked to give a particular style to a writing, unlike ARTIFICIAL writings, which are temporarily modified for a specific purpose which, according to Klages, only concern the camouflage or the embellishment of one's own writing.

Since handwriting reflects the feeling we have of ourselves, an intentionally transformed writing means that the writer does not follow his natural inclinations, because he is not satisfied with them; he would like to be different from what he is; he has become aware of a real or imaginary inadequacy, against which he needs to react. The writing he chooses to make his own, aims at giving other people an image of himself which corresponds to the impression he wants to make on others[7], but it can also help him to build up his personality.

---

il de soleil et de lumière, dan
rté exceptionnelle. De la neige su
es et autour du chalet mai
bleu de Provence et des écureui
s arbres.

Woman, 50 years
Acquired, controlled, resolute, clear and simple writing. Dominance of a form which is constructed; secondary connections which increase the stability of the baseline; the dimensions concentrate on the middle zone. The writing is low but is aerated. A deliberate construction dictated by having to submit to a strict life-style. At the risk of appearing banal, it is discipline, a sense of responsibility, courage, perseverance and a sense of realism that remain.

49

---

7   This explanation corresponds to the meaning given to acquired writings by Klages and Hegar.

As acquired writings are produced in a constrained way, we find therein what comes from being deliberately careful : increased pressure (and frequently the use of a broad felt pen), rigorous organisation, straightened-up slant, and, with regard to form, its enhancement through the contours and dimension; most often, all these elements are associated with more or less marked stiffness.

In spite of the control exercised by the writer on his graphic movement, some characteristics which largely escape voluntary control, diacritics in particular, connections, some forms of low letters, and spacing, give information without his being aware of it. Incidentally, they are particularly taken into account in document authentication.

Below, we reproduce the table of Klages, who devoted a whole chapter to acquired writing; in it he gives the laws according to which a writing can most easily be intentionally altered : laws of the direction of attention, of the degree of difficulty of some graphic factors and of the side effects which unintentionally increase [27].

A. DIRECTION OF ATTENTION

+

Forms of capitals, long and medium letters.
Largeness, width, position, "tempo", intensity.
Lower extensions.

−

Form of short letters.
All other graphic characteristics.
Inner upstrokes and diacritics.

B. DEGREE OF DIFFICULTY OF SOME GRAPHIC FACTORS

◄─────────

Easily managed : Pressure, slowness, smallness - largeness, rapidity, absence of pressure - verticality - Lack of slenderness - Organisation - Regularity - L. extn. > U. extn. - Narrowness - Disconnectedness - Slant - Width - - - Big D. L^8. - Connectedness - Angles - U. extn. > L. extn. - Arcades - Garlands - Filiformity - Small D. L. - Lack of organisation - Irregularity - Slenderness : *Hard to manage.*

─────────►

C. SIDE EFFECTS

Tending to increase involuntarily: Regularity, narrowness, pressure, disconnectedness.

Table from Klages' book : " Handwriting and Character" [27]

---

8   D. L. : difference of length, i.e. the proportions between upper and lower zone extensions and the middle zone. [T(ranslator's) N(ote)]

If, during the phase when acquired writings have not yet been integrated into the natural script, they are partly fabricated, J.C. Gille points out that the intentional transformation of handwriting eventually becomes second nature for the writer through the introduction of certain features which he likes (what Klages called representation), and which change in accordance with his personality [28].

CONVENTIONAL
TYPOGRAPHIC
STYLISED

CONVENTIONAL writing takes its forms from a fashion, from an era and in a given environment. The writer chooses it because he finds it elegant, or because it is the writing of people with whom he would like to identify; thus his self-confidence is strengthened.

The writer who produces a conventional writing, mostly follows a desire for a good social position, for the attainment of which he is prepared to make efforts, or even sacrifices.

Conventional writings are mostly found in women; respect for that type of form goes together with respect for traditions, a certain need for security, but also concern for efficiency.

Fifty years ago or so, a strictly supervised way of learning the copybook model produced what has been called "Sacré-Coeur" writing, based on angles, covering strokes, and great regularity, associated with connectedness. There was no room for neglect; self-assertion was achieved through severe ethics, which gave support to female writers in frequently difficult tasks, but not without causing a certain amount of intolerance.

Today, conventional writing, more often than not, is based on an increase in the curvedness of forms, which reveals the need to attract, rather than real assertion.

A large number of adolescent girls adopt this way of writing in which seduction has its place, usually temporarily and through their own choice.

Adaptation, however superficial and a bit artificial it may be, is nevertheless efficient.

[handwriting sample]

Woman, 40 years - *Conventional writing with stylisations; a mixture of stiffness and skill, of ethics and affective needs. A sense of her personal dignity, courtesy coexisting with tenacity and efficiency. Conforming to a slightly fashionable attitud, gives support to the writer, rather than making her dependent, since the qualities of the personality here are real. Conventionality does not replace personality, as sometimes happens.*

50

[handwriting sample]

Woman, 18 years - *Conventional writing quite typical of its generation, but, in this case, in the context of an interesting evolution. It originates from a small, stiff, angular, narrow and fragile writing; if traces of effort (deviated pressure) and of blockages (left-tending gestures, double-joins), can be found, the adoption of a fashionable form permits graphic cohesion; along with this, one can justifiably assume that the personality is being strengthened.*

51

TYPOGRAPHIC writing is made of letters close to print types and, like them, disconnected. It used to be taught as basic writing in certain schools, particularly in Switzerland [29], then abandoned, because it slows down the writing, owing to the necessary penlifts. At the present time, it is still given as a model for headings and retained for some children who, for various reasons, may have difficulties in producing a legible cursive writing.

Typographic writing has the merit of being clear and orderly, but it runs the risk of introducing a stiff, even stereotyped writing.

It indicates a desire for good presentation, socially correct and stable behaviour, self-control, but the dominance of constraint shows how much the writer watches his step, which puts a brake on his adaptability. When deliberately chosen by an adult, it shows an attitude deliberately adopted; the subject probably finds extra self-confidence therein.

In some professions, e.g.. architects, draughtsmen and project managers, typographic writing is readily used, in which case it falls into the category of designing or drawing plans, to which such writing belongs, and it then loses part of its artificial character.

Among pre-adolescents, one can often observe a typographic period, a transitory stage between copybook and personal writing.

---

complémentaires que vous pouvez désirer.

En vous remerciant de l'attention que vous voudrez bien apporter à ce

vous prie d'agréer, Monsieur, l'expression de ma respectueuse considéral

Man, 27 years

52 *A predominantly typographic writing, still, disconnected, clear in spite of its smallness. Discipline, seriousness, a desire to be well thought of, characterise this young engineer, but this writing is too perfect as a whole, ought to move, to liven up, in order to denote a dynamic personality. Here, the absence of movement is too much, in view of the writer's educational level.*

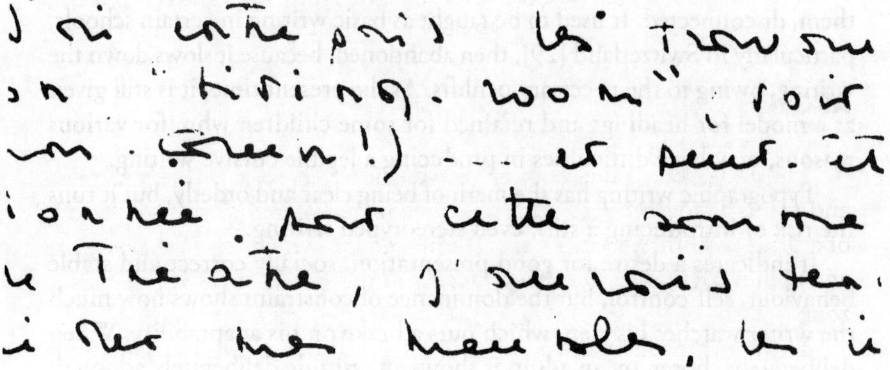

[handwritten text]

Woman, 40 years

53

Stylised, pasty, rather low writing, with some typographic forms and arcade connections, wide but moirée with lapses of continuity, with frequent left-tending movements, flowing as well as reared. Taking the stylisation and the pasty stroke into account, a graphologist can make the hypothesis of an aesthetic sense, of a taste for a studied or original presentation; great need to monopolise others in her contacts, and some seduction too.

STYLISED writing is an acquired writing. Its peculiarity lies in its form, selected for a certain plasticity.

With stylised writing, the writer has the image of a "beautiful" writing in his mind. This concern for presentation and aestheticism corresponds to an innermost tendency; it does not imitate a fashion, it expresses the taste for a form considered more elegant or interesting. To this extent, a stylised writing, although acquired, involves more of the personality than a conventional writing does.

Stylised writing shows a concern for presentation, selectivity, high respect for a frequently simplified form; it is the chosen elements of stylisation which will give their meaning to the writing. The elegance of the form does sometimes limit the vitality of the writing.

2. *The major basic scriptural forms*

ARCADE

The ARCADE is the classical form of the letters *m, n, p* (French style), and *h*; it is a movement towards oneself, which evokes the image of a vault, of a bridge. With *m*'s and *n*'s, it is a movement which leaves the baseline and comes back to it, thus contributing to the stabilisation of the middle zone

The effort made by the child to produce arcades shows how conscious is the application which these require; they are so basic to the construction of a child's writing that, if they are badly done, the writing collapses.

The school arcade is retained in writings which have remained close to the school model. The writer cannot, or does not dare, change the learnt model; he prefers to keep to the security of a known form (see copybook writing).

The trajectory of the arcade, which produces something resembling an enclosure, is not conducive to connectedness; it involves frequent penlifts and it is often found in disconnected writings in which garlands seldom appear;   typographic writing is an illustration of this.   One of the interpretations of arcades is thereby explained : distance kept between the self and others, a distance which is also respect for others.

But, in most cases, the arcade evolves. Carried along by the acceleration of the rightward movement, it opens out and loses some of its deliberately constructed character to become lighter and more supple, and thereby makes for easier connections. It is frequently combined with garlands, or it becomes angular; in so doing, the writing keeps sufficient stability on the line, with no loss of elasticity. Reserve of character, thoughtfulness, discretion, the keeping of what has been acquired, all symbolically contained in the arcade, are present, while at the same time, a more supple participation on the part of the writer is suggested.

The more the arcade becomes expressive of the writing (i.e. the more it becomes one of the major characteristics), the more one is entitled to think that the writer is turned towards his inner world and fears the intrusion of others. He protects and shelters himself, his exteriorisation is very circumspect, even if he remains courteous. The difficulty in being open to other points of view besides his own, can cause isolation and selfishness.

Writing no. 55 shows how little freedom there is in a writing which is predominantly arcaded. This is probably one of the reasons why arcades often appear in conventional writings, and especially in writings marked by stiffness.

Arcades, indeed, belong to the signs of resistance; such writers keep a check on themselves rather than allow themselves to be expansive; in any case, arcades seldom pervade an entire writing, which garlands can do.

Nevertheless when arcades become the rule and are combined with covering strokes and sometimes, with slowness, it means that the writer withdraws into himself and can dissimulate.

The prolonged presence of arcades in the writing of adolescents, especially of girls, needs particular attention [11]. By facilitating legibility and order, it gives the writing an aspect of correctness, which is an omen for good socialisation and the capacity to resist influences. The notion of precise and respected standards is related to moral conscience; it is noticeable that one seldom finds arcaded writings which are slack.

By its presence in emotionally very laden words (I, mother), arcades indicate sensitivity to the repercussions of inner conflicts which cause inhibitions; in the writings of depressive people, one can sometimes observe a difficulty in producing *m*'s and *n*'s which can even be so narrow that the arcade becomes a mere stroke whilst the other letter forms are kept; this precedes any other deterioration.

Conversely, there can be reinforcement of *m*'s and *n*'s through stiffness and narrowness as well as through the increase in the number of downstrokes; *m*'s with 4 downstrokes and *n*'s with 3 can appear temporarily in children and adolescents; this is not a good sign of psychic equilibrium if it persists in adulthood.

M's and *n*'s are small signs among others, but repeated modifications become significant.

There does seem to be a relationship between *m*'s and *n*'s and the writer's feeling of his own identity.

There is a form of arcade, called regressive, in which the third downstroke of the *m* or the second of the *n* goes towards the left, which interferes with the connection to the next letter : this is a retracting movement which can show inhibition or mistrust, but also possessiveness, or calculation.

Exaggeration of normal curves into the shape of an arc produces a over-curved, affected and slowed down writing. In some cases, the writing shows no straight lines; the hand seems to turn with the pen; one says that the writing is OVER-CURVED, thus indicating self-searching.

The LOOPED ARCADE is produced with a left-tending movement, in the form of small rings at the base. According to the elasticity, or the stiffness of the writing, it can be considered that the looping enables the movement to bounce, or, on the contrary, that it accentuates the closed aspect of the arcade. The graphic context will therefore help the graphologist to decide whether it is a matter of effective savoir-faire, of tenacity, or if the looping is related to double-joins (see writing no. 90).

The connections between letters, taught as garlands, can be made as arcades. (Thus the writer favours the top of the middle-zone, with a tendency to cover the writing, which proceeds from an arcade-like movement). These are called overhanging connections (see writing no.247).

54

Man, 30 years - *Writing with angular arcades with a few garlands. These are supple arcades which do not hamper the connections; the writing is also connected and rapid, and the movement is dynamic. Preservation of what has been acquired, and solidity, as well as a good capacity to evolve in this young engineer.*

54

ressources et empen,
protéger la propriété, fruit de l'effort et
de l'intelligence,
développer le sens et donner les moyens
de la responsabilité partout où les hommes

Man, 60 years - *Writing in arcades, and even arched, in the sense meant by Crépieux - Jamin [14]. Heavy, pasty, black, narrow, restrained and resolute. The very structured personality of a tenacious writer with strong convictions. A calculating mind, fiercely keen on his independence.*

55

GARLAND

Unlike the arcade form, the GARLAND form evokes the symbol of a cup. A writing is said to be in garlands when 'm's and 'n's taught as arcades, are executed in garlands; the connections are in garlands too. This transformation can pervade the whole script, particularly the 'o's and 'a's.

A garland is a curved and open gesture; it joins the next letter spontaneously, which made Klages say that, out of the various forms the garland is the only one where expectation of what is ready to be linked is expressed [23]. It is also a gesture, the central part of which rests on the baseline. The garland makes for easier rightward movements and facilitates the acceleration of handwriting.

Crépieux-Jamin notes that the garland arises from a gentle, sinuous, easy movement, hence its meaning of gentleness and suppleness [14]. It is one of the best elements of suppleness, provided it is performed with sufficient firmness. Indeed, because it facilitates movements to the right, the garland can easily introduce slackness.

Corresponding, symbolically, to genuine adaptability and to friendliness to others, a supple and firm garland, or even a garland with slightly lightened pressure, has taken on the significance of receptivity, naturalness, frankness, good capacity for relationships, seduction and tolerance. A small garland in a supple, simplified and rapid script, is related to a receptive intelligence and an agile mind.

56 **Woman, 50 years** - *Firm and supple garlands, simple, with balanced proportions, precise stroke with slight relief, flowing movement. Sensitivity and an open intelligence, but also dynamism and commitment in this harmoniously constructed personality*

If the writing lacks firmness and if the tension of the stroke is insufficient, the garland becomes flabby and flattens down on the baseline. The slackness favourable to emotional lability sets in together with a tendency to be easily influenced and dependent. Openness becomes impressionability, trust becomes anxious expectation of other people's affection, and adaptation takes the easy way out.

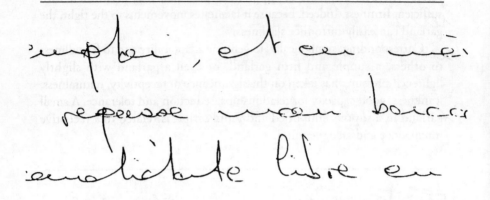

57 **Woman, 40 years** - *Wide, slack and reared garlands, tending towards filiformity. Thin and precise stroke. Obvious lack of structure; dependent, changeable and whimsical, nonchalant and demanding, impressionable and anxious. Here, the garlands have nothing to do with receptivity (notice the double-joins). Adaptation is quite superficial.*

If the tension of the stroke increases, garlands become harder, lose their original suppleness for a different reason. That is why the study of garlands is of interest for the understanding, right from the outset of graphological studies, of the importance of the concept of elasticity, which introduces that of suppleness. If garlands lose this elasticity by becoming too slack or stiff, their classical meanings are profoundly modified.

With only one more step, we find a garland which is both stiff and acquired. This is the SQUARE GARLAND, the name of which evokes its inherent antagonism.

If garlands sometimes lose their elasticity, they can also lose their lightness. It is common, especially with the use of felt pens, to see a heavy garland appear, associated with very rounded forms in a connected continuity.

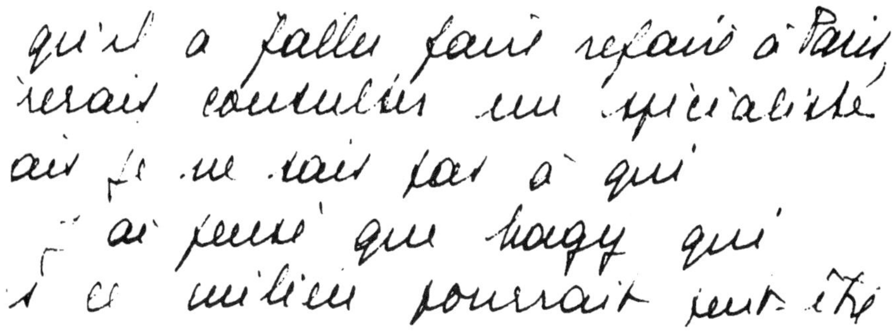

[handwriting sample in French cursive]

Woman, 45 years - *Tense, looped garlands in this courageous and upright woman; the capacity to listen to others is linked to a sense of duty, more than to natural receptivity.*

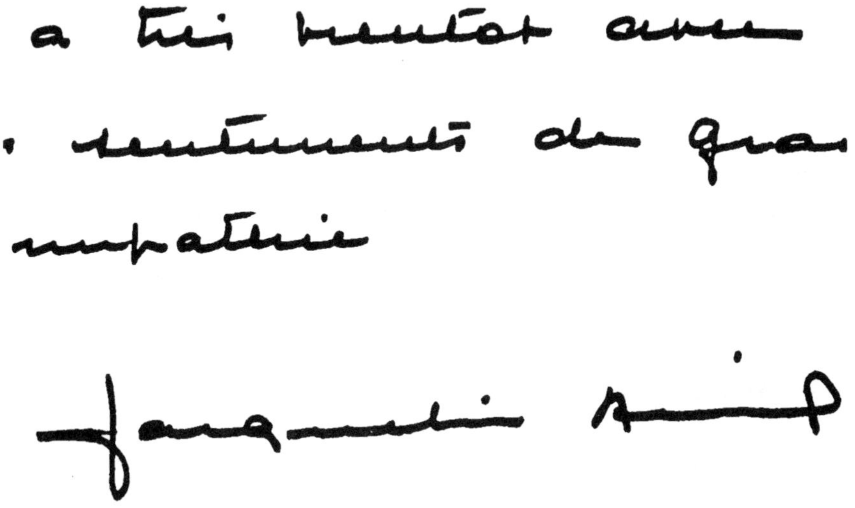

58

[handwriting sample]

[handwriting sample - signature]

Woman, 40 years - *Angular, square, crushed, heavy and very wide garlands; deviated pressure, but resolute, connected, heavy, aerated and orderly writing. Probably there was receptivity once in this woman pilot, a victim of a serious accident, but what is left here is the fierce and painful will-power of someone*

59

energetic and determined. Through this practically automatic movement, the garlands take on an acquired character.

LOOPED GARLANDS, more frequent than looped arcades, are also based on little rings. If they restrict the lightness and the rightward direction of the garlands a little, they also allow a skilful movement which can be quite free and rapid and which reinforces the continuity, usually already connected. Looped garlands, in a supple and rhythmic script, indicate skill, efficiency, savoir-faire and civility.

But looped garlands can also be seen in constrained or monotonous writings, where the stroke, heavy or stiff, does not permit the bouncing quality of a skilful gesture. The looping is then more related to the secretive and sometimes tormented disposition indicated by the double-joins; the notion of tenacity implied in the looping can become a tendency to stubbornness or a propensity to brood over one's preoccupations. If the graphic milieu is pervaded by dominant left tendencies, by stiffness, slowness and lack of rhythm, looped writing suggests calculated amiability, possessiveness and selfishness.

Looping is a good example of the determining influence of the graphic context on the significance of a sign.

. vide que pauait creer la dispoaition alheureusement qu'un jour , il faud tes parents, mais la peusse que ce, L demain ou même celui que l'on est e

Woman, 30 years - *Heavy, looped and almost square garlands, low, connected, strong pressure. The receptivity is put to the service of her capacity for work, skill, and unfailing tenacity. The looping is just as much part of her attitude never to lose track of objectives, as it is part of her secretive personality. This young woman has fairly heavy responsibilities in her business. Worth noting are the concentration and density of the middle zone.*

60

CUPPED GARLANDS are those forming a deep and, more often than not, narrow cup; the movement is restrained and stiffened. Receptivity is painful, especially if the writing is monotonous. The subject is easily affected, but is unable to react adequately; he is on the defensive, and this guides him in his choice of relationships.

This lengthy consideration of the garland, which can range from a sign of supple adaptation to superficial, laborious or tense adaptation, shows once more how different movements can be grouped under the same terminology.

As we noted in the case of arcades, an arcade-garland mixture is frequent during adolescence. Although some adolescents, boys mainly, often adopt a small, light and supple garland, one notices that garlands acquire real suppleness only progressively; this is quite logical : suppleness and autonomy go together.

I M² + J A² est une constante qui ne dépend
Donc la médiatrice △ est contenue dans
Démontrons maintenant qu' il n'y a que le
qui convient: l'ensemble des points M. ayo
par rapport à {A} et {B} est l'ensem

Boy, 16 years - *Small writing with supple garlands, concentrated in the middle zone, very skilfully and soberly connected; a few remaining arcades, slightly double-joined. Concentration of mind, suppleness of intelligence and early maturity in this young boy, who is equally brilliant in both arts and sciences.*

61

*Notre impossibilité de livrer tou
qui nous sont demandées est déja
sérieux pour la rentabilité de nos
certains ne cachent pas leur im
même leur découragement*

Man, 50 years - *Undifferentiated curves in an overall inhibited context, with stick-like, broken and atrophied gestures, and a devitalised stroke, which speak of the dominant anxiety of a depressive writer. His identity fades away as he loses self- confidence. Here, the double curves reconstitute the ambiguity of behaviour which seemed well adapted while, in fact, the personality was already very much affected.*

62

Given the name of DOUBLE CURVE, is a curved form (arcade or garland) which is not differentiated either at the top or at the bottom of letters. This mainly affects 'm's and 'n's which show no difference of form at the top and on the baseline.

It is a sign of intellectual agility and of resourcefulness in a good graphic context, but it is also an ambiguous form which does not give a very definite feeling as to its identity. If it is important in a writing, the graphologist is led to seek other possible signs of imprecision.

The slightly ambiguous aspect of a double-curved writing has given rise to meanings of elusiveness, of dodging and, in a weak context, of a tendency to take the easy way out, of indecisiveness, and of wavering attitudes.

ROUNDED
INFLATED

A round shape implies a circle, and it is one of the first forms small children try to produce. The clumsy and tenacious attempt at a closed form, which they generally wish to be round, although it is widened owing to clumsiness[9], is rather moving when one considers that this closed form later becomes the little man, that is to say the child himself and all those around him.

ROUNDED writing is where the normal copybook curves are accentuated or where normal angles are replaced by curves. It is called "curvilinear". Mostly the letters involved are those with a round middle zone, *a, o, d, g, q,* that is those which encompass white space, but straight strokes also can become curvilinear. This term is used in contrast to writings dominated by straight strokes, like angular writing, for instance, which one calls "linear".

Up to the age of 11, rounded shapes are more present than linear ones. They are frequently found in adolescence, especially in girls, due to their overriding interest in the affective side of life.

In adults, rounded writing is closely related to affective demands, femininity, narcissism, captivation, as well as to the world of fantasy and, more particularly, that of childhood. It correlates with the idea of good social behaviour, and sometimes with a helpfulness from which not all secondary personal advantages can be excluded; it also goes with a taste for life.

In the context of a small script with linear tendencies, the presence of decidedly round middle zone letters is interesting, due to the compensation or the contradiction which these forms, called "full" in Klages's terminology [23], bring to forms which in other ways are narrow or retracted.

If rounded writing is found in a flabby context, the graphologist has good reason to think of lack of initiative, of passive adaptation to the environment.

---

9   This type of round form, widened through clumsiness, is called PLUMP [8].

me concernant surtout aux concernant la maison en patois quelques exceptions produits "Beauté" ou tout

Woman, 30 years - *Rounded, looped garlands, pasty, heavy on the baseline (permanent choice of black felt pen), rather large, fairly clear; this writing shows narcissism and authority, good apparent sociability, but little real interest in other people. The egocentric movement denoting captivation is reinforced by the looped garlands, the double-joins and the reared movement. Very short lower extensions.*

63

vous dérange pas trop, nous die un certain nombre de choses qui pourraient nous éclairer par rapport à la

Woman, 50 years - *Rounded writing, but totally free of unessentials, light, simple, clear, aerated, a little wide and with an almost flowing movement which tells of adaptability and spontaneity. Feminine sensitivity, open and understanding mind, sociability made up of intuition and altruism. The independence of the writer is preserved.*

64

In INFLATED writing, essentially curvilinear, the exaggerations of curves affects, besides the ovals, the upper and lower extensions and the capitals.

This amplification of the curves goes beyond what is expected from strong affective needs. Expressed here is a showy attitude, sometimes quite vain, aiming at capturing attention; others are manipulated, they are objects more than subjects. One notes a tendency to excessiveness and bluff, allied to lack of discrimination.

If inflated forms are to be expected in an already rounded, large and wide writing for instance, one can also find some in a small writing, which reveals an aspect of the personality in contradiction to the overall context. The graphologist should be especially on the alert, as the inflated forms are less blatant.

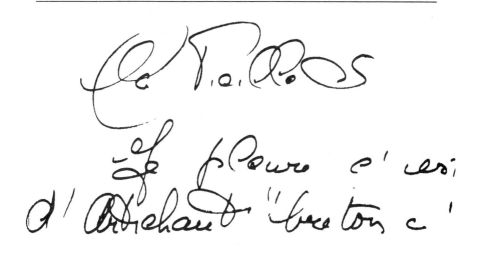

65 **Woman, 40 years** - *Much exaggeration in this large, inflated, inharmonious, superelevated writing with left-tending lasso gestures. Exhibitionism, seduction, subjectivity, wild fancies, lyricism and warm - albeit invasive - affectivity. Reality appears only via her own way of looking at things; the feeling of self is probably less confident than would appear. It is also a complicated writing.*

ANGULAR

An ANGULAR writing is a linear writing which uses chiefly straight strokes; it is characterised by the accentuation of angles, by the replacement of curves with angles; the connections can also have an angular trajectory.

Far from the conciliation symbolically implied by garlands, severity is suggested by angles. One finds the analogy of the archetypes : curve - femininity, and angle - virility.

The angular gesture corresponds to a definite change of direction. It is more intersection than continuity; it is a movement of retraction, which may be firm, but soon becomes affected by stiffness, and it belongs to the signs of constraint and tension.

Hence the meanings of combativeness, courage, sense of duty, obstinacy, and therefore of an adaptation involving struggle, because more energy is needed to produce angles than curves. But this energy is costly in terms of effort and there comes a time when resistance is what prevails. This is why angles also have the meaning of abruptness, stubbornness, intransigence, pigheadedness, contradictoriness and aggressiveness, especially if the overall context happens to be a disharmonious one.

Crépieux-Jamin remarked that the significance of different angles can can be deduced from the timeliness, the naturalness and the happy combination of forces which produce them [14]. This is true of all the signs, but particularly of angles, the interpretation of which could easily be on the negative side.

What is specific to angles, when they are part of a dynamic script, is the resolute and wilful aspect of a writer who reasons things out and makes choices for which he takes responsibility. It is true that these choices are based more on refusal than acceptance; they also reject accommodating attitudes and it is often more difficult to say no than yes, when one has responsibilities. Besides, in this case, angles arise from a movement that is firm but not stiff, and if they are expressive of the writer, they are not his only means of expression. Here, they act as support, they reinforce the firmness of the other elements.

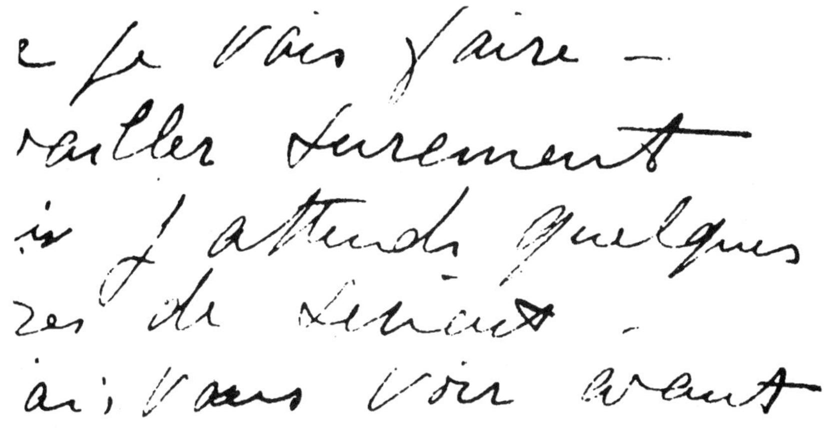

[handwritten text]

Woman, 55 years - *Angles, but also arcades and garlands in this large, thrown, connected writing, with a propulsive movement, superelevated and with irregular pressure. Ardour, combative will, determination, tenacity of this strong personality which imposes its own rhythm. Endowed with a lucid intelligence and a critical mind, the writer acts and reacts like a woman of action, whatever the cost may be. This is the writing of Coco Chanel.*

66

In writing no. 66, the angles are part of a very dynamic overall context which retains enough elasticity and curves. The absence of straightness is proof of skilfulness in the appreciation of reality. One can resist other people, but they nevertheless remain partners, and the effort made renders one worthy of authority.

The less angles are combined with other forms, and the more the linear characteristics take over, the less elasticity there will be.

There exists a particular angular form of lower extensions called "triangles' (see writing no. 174); it is a sign of an authoritarian, even sometimes a tyrannical character, if this form is very pronounced.

[handwritten text]

Man, 60 years - *Small, angular, simplified, personalised, connected, precise, precipitated and wide writing with a tense movement. The angles show both effort and stiffening of behaviour. In spite of the liveliness of the intelligence, the writer does not control his underlying dissatisfaction well. Difficulty in finding a trusting relationship within a group.*

67

If the presence of angles becomes altogether dominant, in a context where tension is badly controlled, relationships with others are conducted in a confrontational mode, possibly to the point of more or less violent aggressiveness. One can observe reactions of strong touchiness, impatience and a lack of impartiality.

However, if the writing is lively, although marked with a jerky rhythm, the writer remains aware of others, even if they are roughly treated. It is a different matter in the case of automatic writings with no rhythm, where angles lead to serious restrictions, or with inhibited scripts which are both weak and stiff, and from which all elasticity is excluded (indeed one should be aware that weakness and stiffness are frequently found together in disharmonious writings).

It seems that more often than not (with the exception of writings of the above type), one finds that angles originate in a combined feeling of intensity and dissatisfaction; this can be a motivating force, provoking challenge and successful compensations; this explains why angles are often found together with obstructed movement.

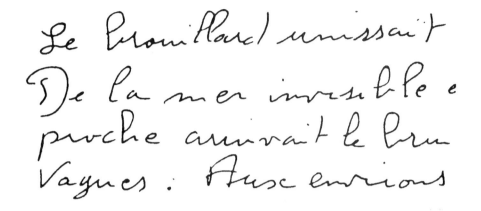

Man, 35 years - *Angular, inharmonious writing, both weak and stiff, heterogeneous, with a fluctuating baseline. The broken-up and hesitant movement shows great difficulty in living, and a feeling of failure. Relationships with others are broken off, no interest in others is taken, with ensuing frantic selfishness.*

68

What matters is the association with elements which allow sufficient elasticity. This is essential, otherwise the feeling of helplessness causes reactions of opposition.

Some professions make better social use than others of the drives implied by angles.

In children, "one should not be surprised to find that those whose writings have an angular contact with the baseline, have difficulties in adapting to their immediate environment, and in the same way, those who have dented curves, have a vulnerable sensitivity" [30], which, to a lesser degree, is true of adolescents. Angles do not facilitate communication, especially in girls' writings, where angles are certainly not a typical feature.

Angles, owing to the impossibility of maintaining a supple script, belong to the signs of aging and of fatigue (see writing no. 27).

Woman, 75 years - *Small and personal writing, in which the forms and the stroke are spoilt by illness. Owing to effort, angles have replaced the garlands which were normal in this writer. The trembling and broken stroke show difficulty in achieving goals. However, the sobriety, simplicity and the rhythm of distribution show the quality of the intelligence and sensitivity.*

69

FILIFORM (Thready)

The writing line in FILIFORM writing is like a graphic thread where precison of form is more or less evaded; form becomes less important or is impaired, particularly in the middle zone ('m' and 'n' especially) which, as we know, best reflects the awareness an individual has of himself.

There are strong and weak filiform writings, as has been verified in the case of other major basic forms.

Through its representative aspect, clear form, related to clear self-awareness, offers protective points of reference enabling the subject to fit in better and those around him to perceive him better. Deprived of such support, the legibility being mostly secured by the upper and lower extensions, filiform writing must be interpreted according to the quality of its stroke, the dynamism of its movement and the organisation of its space [31].

The graphologist must be able to recognise whether the freedom shown by the writer in relation to the copybook model comes from the desire to keep up with rapid thinking, to reach his goal more quickly and directly, or from a weakening of the form owing to lability, passivity or dissimulation, in which case the stroke lacks strength and the writing, rhythm.

Indeed, one finds filiform writing linked to a high graphic level in writers with a rich personality, who may either hesitate, or do not wish to make a choice, among multifarious possibilities, which, for people around them amounts to a slightly ambiguous attitude.

In a rapid, simplified, sober and efficient writing, filiformity goes together with the liveliness and the intuition of an unprejudiced mind; an overall, sometimes rather hasty grasp of realities, is compensated for by a capacity for understanding and renewal of approach. The quality of the stroke informs us on how strong the writer's self-assertion and convictions are. In the case of writers well versed in complex thinking, filiformity at the end of words - resulting from a great progressivity of the graphic gesture - constitutes an abbreviation and is related to the meanings of diminishing writing : subtlety, capacity to read the mind of the person one is dealing with, or skill in discussion (but also difficulty in reaching conclusions).

Filiformity combined with good pressure and a solid stroke, belongs to writers who have sure instincts and need concrete achievements.

Due to the fact that form is eluded - not counting the cases where filiformity is caused by the rapidity of an evolved mind - those with filiform writings will often share some uncertainty regarding their own worth. They react to this with individualistic behaviour, or with hesitation and sometimes with abrupt reactions, showing the discrepancy between intelligence and emotions.

In a light and filiform script, where imprecison steps in and disconnectedness becomes important, emotional vulnerability is no longer offset by sufficient commitment. The writer sometimes protects himself from this by seeming detached, by a faculty for conciliation which produces an illusion concerning his real participation. The seemingly simple writing covers complex emotional interactions. The lessening of the rhythm in the writing will give the graphologist the clue.

In a slack writing where tonicity is lacking, filiformity suggests that the writer's doubts can no longer be resolved and that his subjectivity is considerable.

Owing to the ambiguity which filiform writing suggests, it can be one of the signs of dissimulation.

The erosion of the forms sometimes is the cause of filiformity in depressive writings which are also very monotonous; here the filiformity results from neglect in forming the letters; it reflects passivity and discouragement.

---

70   **Man, 55 years** - *Filiform, simplified, sober, rapid, light and rhythmic writing, with a vibrant to flowing movement, good distribution of the graphic groups. Sensitivity, sharpness of a fine intelligence. Emotivity and inner uncertainty can, however, cause clumsy reactions.*

In children and adolescents, the emergence of a filiform script should not be put down to rapidity, but to a dodging of the forms. It is a movement indicating inner conflicts, or a lack of structure in the personality. Filiformity generates a confusion which augurs bad school results.

The fact that, in adolescence, it is practically impossible to combine filiformity with a clear layout, makes us think that a lot of maturity is needed for this type of form to be really successful.

Woman, 30 years - *Filiform writing, elastic in spite of small angles; very wide, with strong pressure; a black felt pen is always chosen. The connected aspect has something relentless and is related to the possessiveness implied in the lassos and the capital 'A'. How can one escape from the overwhelming influence of this imperious and mysterious personality who is sure of herself, adroit and tenacious? Yet, the almost total lack of white in the ovals shows the extent of what the writer means to preserve.*

71

SIMPLE

Simplicity is one of the components of harmony; by virtue of this, it belongs to the signs of balance, naturalness, uprightness, which were part of Crépieux-Jamin's ethics.

It is true that a SIMPLE writing is always a positive sign, but its significance becomes clear in relation to its association with the other elements of the writing.

The same quality will not be attributed to simplicity, for instance, in an evolved, rapid, combined and simplified writing in which the writer's model has evolved alongside the evolution of his intelligence, or in a writing which has remained simple because it has stayed close to the school model, that is to say without much alteration of the form.

Simplicity can also be characteristic of a writer with only limited abilities; it is then associated with poor forms (but poor forms could also be found with complications and confusion which could affect the writing negatively).

Whether the writing is lively, the quality of the stroke, the treatment of the space, will help the graphologist in this examination.

On the other hand, the simplicity of a writing must be studied in accordance with the socio-cultural level of the writer.

One says of a simple writing that it is economical because there is no wastage of movement; the same is true of sober writing.

Ayant jeté tous mes brouillons, j'ai choisi de vou deux feuilles de mon cours d'anglais de l'année dernière qui peut-être plus intéressantes que des équations pour la grapholog J'espère que vous pourrez en tirer parti.

72

Woman, 22 years - *Simple, clear, orderly, connected and restrained writing. Capacity to see the essential and to act thoughtfully, prudence, discipline, seriousness and tenacity in this young woman, who had just come top in a competitive entrance exam to one of our foremost "Grandes Ecoles"*[10].

10 'Grandes Ecoles' are very selective, even elitist, higher education establishments in France. (T.N.)

CLEAR
CONFUSED

Clarity, like simplicity, is a major quality of handwriting and belongs to the components of harmony.

A writing is CLEAR when it can be read easily, thanks to the precision of the forms and to the good black and white relationship at all levels; in the letter, between letters, between words and between lines. Margins and the general layout also contribute to clarity.

The precision of the forms corresponds to words with well-structured contours and good proportions, forming clearly individualised wholes. Words, also, are distinct entities because they stand out in the space[11].

This definition of clarity shows how far-reaching it is. If Crépieux-Jamin used to consider that clarity is the essential mark of the best qualities of intelligence and character, it is because it derives from a harmonious relationship between the fundamental elements of handwriting such as firmness, form structure and good distribution of space, thus making a decisive contribution to the other elements of handwriting.

Like simplicity, clarity is independent of the type of writing. However, the quality of clarity differs according to the graphic milieu to which it belongs : it is more logical to find it in a typographic writing than in a simplified, more evolved writing.

On the other hand, although clarity is always a positive sign, it comes into its own in a lively script (the same was true of simplicity). But it is also found, for instance, in regular and monotonous writings which confusion would make worse.

In a lively graphic context, clarity indicates a clear mind, logical thinking and intellectual honesty; it bears witness to the equilibrium of the writer, his genuineness, his uprightness. Clarity, as it involves firmness and self-control, brings in balanced adaptation.

---

11 The terms 'words with well-structured contours' and 'words standing out in the space', each correspond to component 9 of the degree of firmness, and to component 3 of the degree of organisation, among the components of personality listed by H. de Gobineau. These terms have become current in graphological language [19].

In a graphic context of a more modest standard, it indicates the tendency of the writer to keep to what is obvious, while at the same time remaining controlled and precise.

In a monotonous context, clarity prevents the discordances with which it is incompatible, thereby showing at least a minimum of common sense.

Since there are two levels of clarity, the legibility of the word itself and the quality of the treatment of space, it is possible that one is more successful than the other, or that one compensates for the other. Among intellectuals, for instance, a good distribution can make up for a merely relative clarity.

---

inir une voiture tres rapidement la leur de la voiture nous est tres indiff nous n'y tenons pas specialemin · autres teintes n'etant pas mal du to même nous n'avons pas command · fort ouvrant mais s'il y eu avai

Woman, 35 years - *Clear through its legibility and the good distribution of the words in the graphic space, rounded, light but precise, connected. The mixture of arcades and garlands attests to savoir-faire. Good self-awareness without conceit. The controlled movement and the balanced layout suggest a good use of aptitudes.*

73

Unlike a clear writing, a writing is CONFUSED when it is difficult to read due to anomalies involving either the structure of words (imprecisions, disproportions, excessive complications, overdone combinations) or the distribution of space (arhythmy, compactness, bad layout).

In both cases, one is dealing with fundamental elements of handwriting which, for the writer, are related to the feeling of his identity, his relations with others, the clarity of his mind, or to the desire to dissimulate, in the case of the heterogeneous writings of unstable people or of crooks, who form a fringe population.

Confusion in a writing is always a negative sign whose significance must be sought in the signs which generate it, and in the associations of signs of which it is part. Confusion due to tangled lines does not have the same meaning as confusion due to imprecision, disproportion or precipitation. Speed is relevant in so far as the confusion is more noteworthy for the graphologist in a context which is slow overall, for example, than in a rapid and simplified one.

As with clarity, confusion is found at the levels of both form and space; here, we are more concerned with form; the confusion due to bad distribution of space is easier to detect (see Chapter 9).

If one makes an exception of polymorphism due, in a good graphic context, to a creative writer, one can distinguish the confusion caused either by the similarity of different letters, or by the polyphormism of similar letters or by the 'bad forms'[12] (see sample no. 75).

The poorer the graphic milieu, the more derogatory the meaning of confusion in form will be.

12 Term used by Ajuriaguerra in his scale of dysgraphy for component d22 [8].

Woman, 45 years - *Confusion due to imprecision and ambiguity: 'a' like 'o', 'e' like 'c', 'u' like 'i'; bad proportions, badly differentiated zones, irregular dimensions, suspensions and bad space distribution. The words, chopped up and illegible, lose their coherence. One guesses, however, a good socio-cultural level. A depressive personality.*

74

Boy, 15 years

Boy, 15 years
An inhibited, emotive and vulnerable boy, doing badly at school, in spite of his high level of intelligence.
   The writing, with a movement which is both vertically chopped up and weak in its rightward progression, is particularly ambiguous in its forms.
   The confusion of the o's and a's is evident, a frequent happening in childhood, involving affective letters, which hardly matters when there are no other confusions in the writing.

75

But, in this writing, there are a good many other ambiguities and bad forms: 'v' like 'r', when 'v' should be in the shape of a cup[13], the top of 'g' similar to the top of 'y', 'b' looking like a large 's', 'f's always made like 'j's. etc.

The writer is passive, hesitant in his choice of identification; he aspires to an autonomy which he feels he is incapable of reaching. The affective relationships he has with other people are just as likely to take place in an aggressive and antagonistic manner, as they are in a passive one, and with a lack of resistance.

Ambiguity, when still present in an adult, expresses difficulty in communicating in a responsible manner, in accepting a code.

3. Emphasis on closedness or openness of forms

A. CLOSED FORMS

Closed forms are based on movements going back towards the left and called left-tending (see Chapter 7). They may consist of an exaggeration of the copybook left-tending forms, in the creation of forms going back to the left when the cursive progression makes them go to the right, or of superfluous forms enhancing left-tending movements, or of exaggeration of the spirals in initials, final letters and free signs.

All these forms have in common a movement coming back towards oneself, the ego of the writer being his main landmark in making judgements.

This closing movement goes against the normal rightward progression of writing.

It can be found in some writings which retain a good level of suppleness, but it tends to introduce stiffness and heaviness into the script.

---

13 French copybook 'v' is cup-shaped. (T. N.)

DOUBLE-JOINED
LASSOS

In DOUBLE-JOINED writing, ovals are locked , as it were, by small loops, obstructions, or scrolling. Double joins are facilitated by starting the letters on their left. They are perhaps more frequent in feminine writings where form dominates. Incidentally, they are one of the elements of acquired writings in fashion today.

If there is always egocentrism and subjectivity in double-joins, they can also express seduction and pleasure in living. The writer takes more than he gives, but he exudes a warm presence. In this case, the script is supple, adroit and lively. Double-joins can also express tenacity.

In a writing which is too right-tending, double joins sometimes show a salutary reaction, applying brakes against the thoughtless impetus of writings in which one can guess a possible lack of prudence.

The heavier and the stiffer the script becomes, the more expressive it is of someone prone to brooding and who is totally wrapped in himself, to the exclusion of anything else. It is the sign of a withdrawn, distrustful and often selfish character.

In a slow writing, double-joins belong to the signs of dissimulation.

LASSO writing is thrown to the right, and comes back to the left with a greater or lesser amplitude. It is easy to detect in signatures, where it is quite frequent, and in texts when it is part of an ample movement (writings which are also inflated or expanded, for instance).

It is a different matter when the lasso is produced by a small left-tending gesture well integrated into the middle zone where it can go unnoticed.

The significance of lasso writing can range from adroitness to calculated friendliness and even go as far as intrigue; but it can also show resourcefulness, or the more or less acknowledged desire to seduce or captivate, especially in the small lasso quite often found in adolescence.

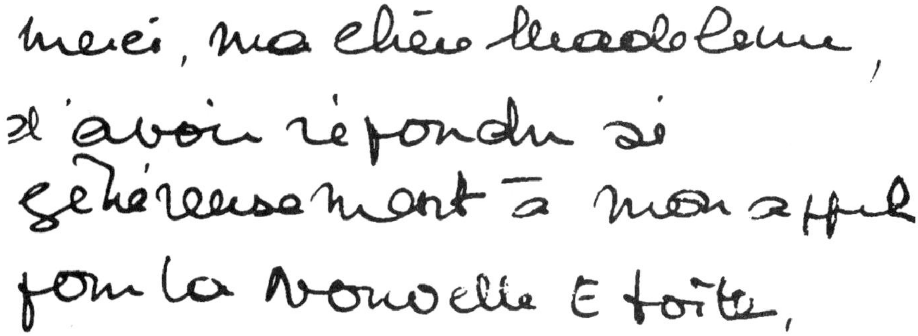

[handwritten text]

76 **Woman, 45 years** - *Double-joined, looped, rounded, rhythmic, rapid, well-nourished, pasty and supple writing. If there is captivation, there is also adroit activity in this script, social ease, a certain cheerfulness and even spontaneity, allied to the capacity to keep quiet if the writer wants to keep things to herself.*

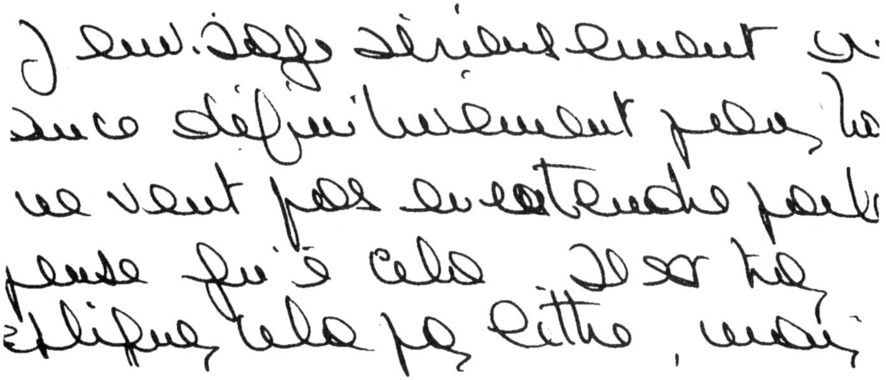

[handwritten text]

77 **Woman, 45 years** - *Rounded, inflated, left-slanted writing, which groups together double-joins, looped garlands and small lassos (on 's's); one also finds reverse movements ('p') and supported strokes (other 'p's). The egocentric circular gesture is the favourite one. The writing is curvilinear, but stiff in its progression. Seduction and unfailing tenacity to reach a goal (aiming at self-interest). Although they are in contradiction to the concentric movements of closedness, the bowl-shaped lower extensions (an open, right-tending gesture) indicate general skilfulness.*

Angular and reverse lower extensions, covering strokes, whip-like upper extensions are closed forms, but they will be studied together with left-tending forms, to which they belong (see Chapters 6 and 7).

Closed forms are important to spot, for they reveal a tendency to possess and a refusal to share, which leads to looking upon others as immediate rivals, and this does not make group work easy.

B. OPEN FORMS

Open forms include all the handwriting transformations based on rightward tendencies (see Chapter 7 on Direction), i.e. the forms normally going towards the left, tend to be cancelled, and replaced by forms going towards the right. They also include the forms characterised by an opening at the top of the letter.

They move in the direction of graphic freedom, and facilitate greater speed. They are found in a good many simplifications.

They are therefore more frequent in the scripts of writers who are very used to writing, especially in the writings of intellectuals.

This is why both closed forms, like open ones, must be considered in relation to the socio-cultural level of the subject.

OPEN
PROGRESSIVE

OPEN writing has an opening at the top of ovals which should be closed.
It can be an efficient simplification in a firm, right-tending script where the continuity shows that leading ideas are carried through. It can also, however, be a refusal to change the movement to produce circular letters, starting them on the right or left, generally without lifting the hand, either because one does not want to make the effort, through nonchalance, or because one more or less surrenders to events.

In a sufficiently structured and rhythmic context, open writing indicates openness and agility of mind; it is related to intuition, spontaneity, easy and rapid adaptation and social ease.

In a weak and slack context, it belongs to the signs showing that one is vulnerable, easily influenced, that one gives up easily, is scatter-brained and tends to opt for easy solutions. This right-tending movement lacks quality.

Some lower extensions can be regarded as open forms : bowl-shaped lower extensions that go up to the right instead of forming loops to the left, and V-shaped ones which also go up to the right, but more stiffly. These two forms of lower extensions are conducive to a faster movement across the page, and thereby are often associated with progressive writing (see writings no.77 and 134).

PROGRESSIVE writing is a global and qualitative sign, often studied with Direction because it is based on right-tending forms (see Chapter 7). If progressive writing is definitely oriented to the right, with all that this implies symbolically, there are in addition, other notions also which give a lot more value to it than that of a merely right-tending writing.

In particular, notions of sobriety, of simplification and combination of forms come into it. Progressivity facilitates a greater degree of openness of forms, and so the stroke should in general be sufficiently firm for the letters to remain structured.

Crépieux-Jamin says that progressive writing constantly aims at the most intelligent and rapid progression. This is why progressivity enables one to spot the qualities of intelligence and understanding belonging to people with good maturity.

Moreover, the efficiency of the Form-Movement relationship it achieves, which is both dynamic and balanced, suggests good power of adaptation and an active character. Initiatives are taken with progress in mind.

*victoire - Fat de leur
confiance, je ferai de
ma vieux pour le vie
la France.*

Man, 60 years

78

*Writing with forms open owing to progressivity; personalised by simplifi-
cations, very rhythmic, dynamic, simple, sober, thrown and wide. The openness
indicates receptivity and intelligence, a forward-looking attitude and sensitivity.
It is not detrimental to convictions, to personal commitment, because the writing
is firm. The signature - as dynamic as the text - shows the unity of the personality.
This is the writing of Georges Pompidou who was President of the Republic.*

4. *The notion of homogeneity of form*

Homogeneity is a global factor which indicates the concordance between all the elements of a writing, which Crépieux-Jamin made one of the fundamental conditions of harmony; in view of this, we have included it in the components of harmony.

HOMOGENEITY OF FORM, in a wide sense, is independent of the type of form, but its quality is dependent on the graphic context to which it belongs.

All configurations are possible, provided they have a formative element in common. That formative element itself can generate cohesion, through a personal writing or an acquired writing. By preventing, in either case, all discordance of form, of movement or of distribution, it provides a natural or calculated unity.

The writings of people well adapted to life have this homogeneity, showing inner cohesion; this is why its absence reveals a precarious inner equilibrium.

The quality of the writing's rhythm enables one to distinguish homogeneity founded on the subject's equilibrium and freedom, from the homogeneity of constraint.

The concept of homogeneity also covers the different writings which a particular writer may produce, according to the subject-matter he deals with while writing, or according to the paper size, the recipient, or what his circumstances happen to be.

One may make an effort to write more legibly to fill in official papers; one may write smaller or spread out one's script when taking notes. A piece of work done in rough reflects the uncertainties, or the application of the writer.

The different writings, then, show basic similarities which, while testifying to the double purpose of handwriting, both as a personal instrument of work and a means of communication, also show how the writer adapts to what he is doing.

The changes from one writing to another should, however, be contained within certain limits, even if one knows that these changes occur for a specific reason.

These limits themselves are interesting for the graphologist, who asks for several documents to do his analyses. There is a notion of the stability of maintained forms in the concept of homogeneity.

Finally, it happens that certain states such as fatigue, illness, mourning, or cold, temporarily modify the writing, although without the personality being modified; it is, however, necessary to distinguish between a mechanical cause and a psychological one whose repercussions are, besides, quite significant.

The concept of homogeneity also covers the relationship between text and signature (see Chapter 10). Although the signature is a free and eminently individualised movement, the form may remain the same as the text, or differ from it.

Not counting a few superior creative people who can have several writings, each one being homogeneous (as was the case with Balzac, Jules Verne and Victor Hugo), a writing which changes for no apparent reason in the course of several documents of the same type, or even in the course of the same document, is lacking in homogeneity; it is heterogeneous.

The frequency and the importance of its variability of form relate it to an element of instability. There is, specifically in this case, no structuring force to ensure the cohesion of the personality, hence unpredictible behaviour occurs where the force of emotions is not contained by a mental structure, or by a sufficiently strong superego. The difficulties in structuration can be seen, in any case, mostly in the signature.

However, it can happen that some scripts are marked by changes in the appearance, essentially involving direction (changes of direction[14]), but form also. This modification may be quite temporary in children or pre-adolescents. The writer seeks to break away from the copybook model, by finding a personal writing; the movement records his hesitations in finding his way. It is for a similar reason that, at the same age, a typographic style is temporarily adopted. In behaviour, this is shown in no more than a few changes of mood.

---

14 See Chapter 7.

3

DIMENSION

The overall dimension of a writing is a relatively easy element to assess immediately; it is what delimits the writing and gives a first picture of the expansion - considerable, moderate or insufficient - a writer allows himself in his graphic space.

Dimension is closely connected to form; to start with, form is produced within certain limits and according to given proportions, and its significance is partly derived from the modifications of these proportions.

Dimension is assessed according to the amplitude of the movements, first and foremost to a vertical and a horizontal axis[1], in relation to the movements of flexion and extension, and the movement of progression, which are affected multifariously by the writer's vitality, emotions, intelligence and way of exteriorising.

Although the observer, when he sees a writing, perceives the overall dimension, that is to say in relation to the three zones of handwriting, the term, Dimension, in French graphology, is reserved for the middle zone, the zone of the Ego in its affectivity, relationships and activity. The horizontal dimension of this zone is defined by other signs. A writing which is small in height and large in width will be called 'small and wide' and not 'small in height and large in width'. The upper and lower zones, which give the whole span of the writing, are studied separately and in their relation-

---

1 The graphologist, Jeanne Dubouchet, has produced a method of observation of handwriting in which she integrates all Crépieux-Jamin's signs in a synthesis of two axes : vertical and horizontal. This approach to handwriting is particularly suitable for dimension [32].

ship to the middle zone; the extent of the variability within the same zone is also an important element.

It is accepted that dimension is linked to the feeling of self and consequently, to the kind of relationship the writer has with others and with reality.

Before tackling the different signs of dimension, we shall state the following norms:

a) **Height** :

Middle zone :   In French calligraphy one distinguishes between :

"la grosse" (large)	:	8 mm
"la demi-grosse" (semi-large)	:	6 mm
"la moyenne" (medium)	:	4 mm
"la fine" (small)	:	2 mm

In classical graphology, the norm for medium size writing is 2.5 mm, a dimension also adhered to by Ajuriaguerra in his Children's Scale [8], but one should mention that as soon as children use squared, lined paper[2], the interval between the small lines is 2 mm only.

On unlined paper, children write big, due to clumsiness, until a fairly late stage, but they soon learn to respect the interlinear spacing used in schools.

Upper and lower zones : Their dimensions vary according to copybook models, and specially according to work books or to teachers' writings. The dimension is usually one and a half times, or twice the height of the middle zone. The unlooped upper and lower extensions are, normally, shorter than the looped ones.

b) **Width** : Models, in work books, show a *'u'* placed either in a square or a slightly high rectangle. The connection between two letters is about 1mm, that is about half a *'u'*. We should note that the width dimension is freed from constraints sooner; teachers do not notice it so much, unless it is exaggerated, and its standardisation is not helped by the small spaces between the printed lines, as in the case of height.

---

2   The standard paper which schoolchildren use in France. (T.N.)

1. The middle zone

A. The vertical axis

LARGE

A writing is LARGE when it clearly goes beyond medium copybook dimension, i.e. beyond 3.5 mm; it is fairly large between 2.5 mm and 3.5 mm, exaggerated beyond 6 mm; the extent of the amplitude of the movements goes beyond what is necessary. Under what impulse does this development take place?

Emphasis on dimension is related to emphasis on the feeling of self under the influence of very different motives, but all of which involve a need for expansion; the latter may be connected to the writer's vitality and can encourage, at the start, an elan capable of giving the writer confidence in his potential and a taste for exteriorisation.

The emotional character of this self-estimation may reduce objectivity, and hence entails risks, but it may also enable someone to surpass himself with an ardour, an enthusiasm, a radiance, or a scope which are often stimulating and creative.

Because of its capacity for expansion, large writing, when associated with firmness and good proportions, suggests the capacity to play an active part, and desire for a field of action sufficiently broad for the writer to be able to express himself fully. It finds its best expression in a genuine, resolute and supple context.

The writer's spirit of conquest, his presence, will benefit the group to which he belongs, as a whole.

Large writing is related to freedom of action, to an audacity sometimes needed in new or difficult commercial transactions, as also to the inherent limelight given by professions where a public figure is of particular importance (public relations, politics, professions involving communication or entertainment).

Yet, largeness of writing is no sufficient indication, for one can quote many an example of people in the limelight, whose writing has remained medium or even small. One can notice, however, that in such cases, the signature is frequently amplified (see Chapter 10).

---

mu , je m'en garde

pour l'instant ! je

? tendrement ,,

l a Kreme

Woman, 40 years - *Large, a little narrow in relation to the size, in relief, rhythmic, garlands, clear, rapid, but also irregular, lapses of continuity, spaced out and sharp-pointed; signature like the text. Energetic, enthusiastic, ardent, no subservience and yet anxious, impulsive and controlled; wit and repartee are strong. The large size indicates the importance of self-awareness, the need for a vast field of action, keenness, presence, but not to the exclusion of self-questioning and doubts. The simple forms reveal the genuineness of the personality.*

79

It is a different matter if the feeling of self gains importance without being backed up by real potential and self-confidence, thus causing presumptuousness or compensation, overexcitement or vanity.

In a left-tending context with bad proportions, demands increase along with emotional needs; egocentricity and lack of judgement are detrimental to group work.

In large writings with a dominance of form, often acquired or conventional (they mostly are feminine writings), one notices the presence of round forms, more or less coiled, which show strong self-awareness, but without signs of good relationship with others. Narcissism, or the feeling of belonging to a privileged social group, induce these subjects to boast about their actions, to captivate the attention of those around them, making real dialogue impossible.

Woman, 35 years - *Large, reared, precise, closed (double-joined, looped, reverse, left-slanted, compact) as well as rounded, and inflated. The concentric movement of captivation is paramount, and the middle zone is not well balanced by the other zones. Self-interest dominates. Biased and authoritarian character lacking in genuineness of this bank official who, in other ways, is hard-working and tenacious. The intellectual level is hidden by the imperious nature of the narcissistic demands.*

80

Contradictory associations such as large and narrow, large and left-slanted, large and weak, indicate a difficulty in relationships, despite a self-awareness which is real, or which compensates for a feeling of insufficiency.

In adolescence, although one finds mostly medium size writings, one notices above all that the dimension of handwriting is related to the writer's sex; girls, generally, write larger than boys.

This observation holds true for adults also. In spite of the change in the social status of a large number of women, the dominance of feelings which tends to increase the dimension of a writing, remains a feminine component.

Finally, it can happen that some words, in a text, more heavily charged with emotional meaning, are written larger.

SMALL

Handwriting is SMALL between 2 and 1.5 mm; it is exaggeratedly small below 1.5 mm. Reduction of dimension is related to a different kind of self-awareness from that of large writing, or to a reduction of the feeling of self, for various reasons. It is also related to the work of thinking which causes a concentration of movement, through the attention that this entails.

There is not, in small writing, that potential for natural expansion which one finds in large writing; the feeling of life, the Ego impulse, are somehow interiorised; the writer's power to sustain effort is, none the less, just as high.

When dimension is smaller than average, the graphologist may wonder whether smallness, for the writer, is connected to the sense of his relativity, though without reducing his self-confidence, or to a feeling of deficiency, whether this be physical, psychological, intellectual, or to do with relationships, thus causing a feeling of underestimation. Here the graphologist is helped by the quality of the form-movement relationship, that of the stroke, or of the space distribution, for instance.

If small writing is found in a context which is also simple, sober and personal, where smallness is allied to skilful connections in order to increase the speed and the life of the writing, we can conclude that the personality being more cerebral, the concern for objectivity, reflection, concentration and a self-awareness more sensitive to self-criticism, limit the amplitude of the movement.

These elements introduce a relationship between smallness and intelligence. Furthermore, there is a strong correlation between smallness and the writings of intellectuals [33]. The tendency to introversion also goes in that direction.

This does not mean that smallness signifies restriction of action. The subject acts differently from the writer with a large writing and gives preference to reflection, management and foresight. Smallness is not detrimental to the precision of writing, showing as it does, the writer's precise mind.

Moreover, involvement in action, the self-assurance that knowledge of his potential gives him, even the will to be strong, although interiorised, can be surprising in someone who writes small. The script may be smaller, but is solid, rhythmic, often connected, and has strong pressure.

81

Man, 50 years - *Small, personal, rhythmic, simplified, firm, progressive, well-nourished. A lively and subtle intelligence pervades the balanced script of this engineer. The dense, connected, rapid writing, regularly right-slanting, with no stiffness, shows decisiveness and stability in his objectives. One can assume a realistic self-estimation and a simplicity which enable him to adapt easily. Humility, modesty, spontaneous acceptance of what he feels is his duty; receptivity and conviction give the writer his strength and his humaneness.*

In a simple, sober, clear and balanced context, smallness can be related to genuine humility; this is probably more frequent than one might think, particularly in those who give themselves to their work, not for personal gain, but so that their enterprise may succeed.

If a small writing is allied to narrow, angular and jerky forms in a context which is generally inhibited and either too light or too heavy, restriction prevails over concentration; communication is hindered by a critical mind, or too much selectivity; the subject no longer puts limits upon himself, but withdraws into an anxious and lonely attitude which may well have an element of selfishness.

In a very small writing, one can go as far as including reactions of opposition.

Small writing associated with spoilt, crushed, or badly-proportioned forms, shows the uncertainty of the feeling of self. In a not very homogeneous graphic context, with slack movement, there is, quite clearly, a feeling of self-depreciation and powerlessness, when facing a situation felt as too much of a burden.

---

82 Man, 40 years

82
Small, but prolonged and superelevated, angular, narrow, connected, heavy, narrow spaces between the words: intransigent and painful ethics mark this stiff writing. Communication takes place mainly on an ideological level, but in spite of a desire to be rigorous, ideas run the risk of being clumsily formulated. The writer endeavours to suppress an acute sensitiviry and a demanding self-respect. But there is so much inner tension and such a defensive aspect in this priest's writing that one wonders if smallness here is not reactive.

As far as children are concerned, it is just as normal for a young child to write large, before the age of 8, on unlined paper, as it is necessary for a graphologist, in the case of a child who writes small, to look for the causes of what amounts to a reduction in dimension related to a feeling of inferiority. Excessive smallness, in an overall constrained, angular and slack writing associated sometimes with ambiguous, poorly-shaped forms, can express opposition and even behavioural disorders.

However, in an overall clear and well organised script, smallness suggests a dominance of the intellect in children, particularly from the age of approximately 9 -10.

In adolescence, sexualisation of handwriting becomes clear and one can observe that boys, on the whole, write smaller than girls.

Depressive conditions, fatigue and old age cause a restriction of the movements and a reduction of writing dimensions, which are associated with a bad quality, jerky stroke.

Smallness of the signature, especially if more pronounced than in the text, is very significant (see Chapter 10).

83
Woman, 30 years - *(see opposite page)*
Small, irregular, filiform, crushed, light, slack and wide. Not a very well-structured script and the right tendencies derive from resignation. The writer has lost her self-confidence and the obstacles she meets only increase her feeling of powerlessness. Discouragement, fear and a feeling of insecurity dominate her relationships with others. Smallness, here, adds to a negative accumulation of the other signs of fragility.

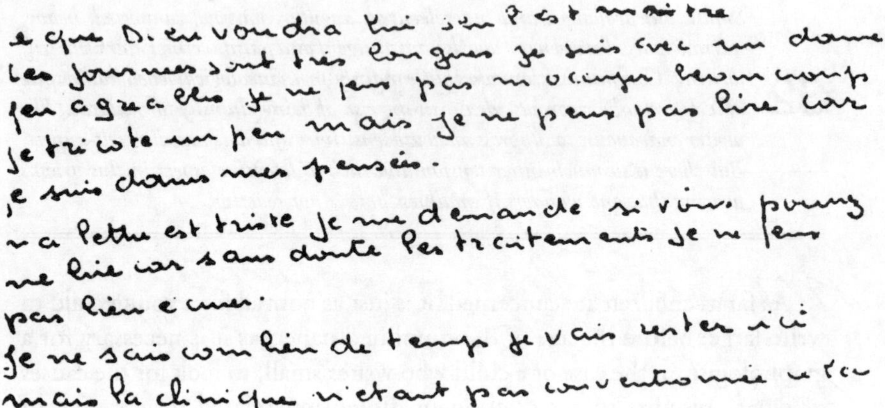

83

ENLARGING

Crépieux-Jamin saw as ENLARGING a writing which progressively increases in size at the end of words, or lines, showing the writer's desire to have the last word or to conclude his action with a special effort[3], in a slightly crude way. Enlarging writing can also be found, logically enough, in a context which is animated or expanded in other ways.

But it is not always so; the enlargement may not necessarily be progressive and may occur suddenly and by choice on the final letter alone. This particularity seemed interesting enough to Müller and Enskat for them to make it one of the essential variables to look for in a writing [34].

---

3 For Crépieux-Jamin, this was a characteristic of children's writings, as he thought it to be expressive of their effort. We do not think it desirable to retain this observation, as recent studies on whole groups of children have not sufficiently corroborated this finding, statistically.

Indeed, the final letter of a word is particularly important, inasmuch as it prepares for the next word. It can also be considered in relation to action and relationships.

---

84 **Man, 45 years** - *Large writing, animated and clumsy, angular, connected, jerky, imprecise and enlarging. Obstinacy is on a par with the irascible and rapacious nature of this second-hand goods dealer who has managed to acquire several shops in the same street. The enlargement is in keeping with the overall context of this combative and badly controlled writing.*

Stressing a final through enlargement causes "a jump which breaks the normal continuity and the harmony of the writing", all the more so as it goes against the progressiveness of the writing. It is the unexpected use of energy which holds the attention, especially if it happens in an otherwise sober and controlled script. Stressing the dimension of a final often goes together with an emphasis on the form, with the elaboration and effort which that supposes.

In a generally well-controlled writing, an enlarged final is unexpected and therefore creates a contradiction which the graphologist should note. It suggests both possible reserve and not very consistent behaviour. The writer may prove to have an interfering character, which leads him to take initiatives without due consideration for others, and to justify himself, or simply, to show himself more assertive or courageous than one world have thought possible.

There is therefore both an instinctive and a reasoned impulse which can reveal itself as aggressive in an arhythmic, tense and irregular graphic context. The subject's personality is in the grip of dislikes and prejudices which generate imprudence.

The graphologist, having been put on the alert by an enlarging final, should check whether it alternates with a diminishing final, thus revealing a contradictory alternation in the way the writer behaves.

Man, 50 years - *Lively but uneven writing, disconnected, wavy, a thin, jerky stroke with strong, slightly deviated pressure. The emphasis on finals comes as a surprise and supports the contention of less natural behaviour than the apparent freedom might lead one to suppose.*

85

DIMINISHING

DIMINISHING writing gradually decreases in size at the end of words, lines or even paragraphs. As this decrease of dimension goes in the direction of progressivity of handwriting, it is less unexpected than emphasis.

What matters is to know whether diminishing is an effectively economical movement, in which case it is justified as a sign of abbreviation in combined writings, the rapidity of which is then facilitated, or whether it is the result of a movement unable to maintain a given dimension.

In either case, however, such a writer does not wish to assert himself in an obvious manner : his attitude is different; he prefers to keep small, to work his way in gently. In a rhythmic, sober, combined and often small graphic context, diminishing writing means subtlety, finesse, a critical mind when the stroke is precise, even if it suggests a little impatience to bring actions to their conclusion. Allied to elements of suppleness and to the motivation for conquest, it belongs to the signs of cleverness or opportunism.

Allied to bad continuity, arhythmy, slack movement, labile forms, or to a heavy overall context, diminishing writing indicates difficulty in asserting oneself, the attitude of abdication, and discouragement. Owing to the weakening of tonicity that it may show, it belongs to the signs of fatigue, depression and ageing.

Man, 50 years 86

Diminishing, thrown, precise, connected, sharp-pointed and spaced out writing.
A critical intelligence, rapidity of decision and involvement, but tension
showing difficulty in keeping up with a level of activity which is probably great.
Relationships with others are marked by a certain distance and, at the same time,
a somewhat aggressive attitude.

87 **Woman, 45 years** - *Diminishing writing in a filiform, very stretched out context, with bad space distribution. Adaptation is difficult and painful in the face of well justified obstacles.*

Due to the imprecise forms to which diminishing writing can lead, one is inclined to think that the writer tends to escape via this reduction of amplitude. If this is rather disconcerting and sometimes offhand, the interpretion of cunning and dissimulation which is sometimes given, would be correct only if many other imprecisions were present, with or without a lack of speed.

Diminishing writing is an interesting sign; it may express the qualities of a negotiator, but it may also express the risk that, when the writer faces too arid a task requiring peristent effort, he is less interested in completing his action than in starting it.

The decrease in dimension may occur on final letters only, causing a surprise, as in the case of enlarging finals, if this decrease is very marked. Then it indicates the possibility of unpredictible reactions.

B. The horizontal axis

In tackling the horizontal axis, we shall study the width of the base of letters, called primary width, and the width of the connections between the letters, called secondary width[4]. These two aspects of the horizontal dimension are prescribed at the beginning and determined in relation to the height of the middle zone. Both participate in width and narrowness; other elements, too, may be involved with regard to continuity and space.

WIDE

A writing is WIDE when the relationship between width and height is greater than the copy-book norm[5]. From these two types of width (primary and secondary), several forms of width can develop. All have expansion towards the right in common, the quality of which depends primarily upon firmness.

1. Association of primary and secondary width : this is the most widespread formula and probably the most homogeneous since, as far as the two aspects of width are concerned, it proceeds from the same expansion to the right.

---

4   The German graphologists Müller and Enskat [88] make a distinction between the variables 'ample' and 'thin', which describe the width of letters, and 'wide' and 'narrow', which they reserve for secondary widths. We have not used this distinction because of the ambiguity of the term 'thin', which is a sign of pressure, in Crépieux-Jamin's vocabulary.

5   As we have mentioned in the last chapter, our observation of handwriting , inspired from children's writings and developmental psychology, makes a special point of discriminating between letters and letter-connections.
    This distinction is also respected very well by Italian graphology, deriving from Father Girolamo Moretti. As far as width is concerned, it emphasises the width of letters and space between letters, and letter-connections [35].
    The Swiss graphologist Max Pulver [24] also distinguishes primary width, the distance between downstrokes, from secondary width , the distance between two or more letters.

When width is moderate and sufficiently firm, Pulver's words come to mind; that the You is symbolically situated to the right, signifying the outside world, the future. The writer who expands in that direction shows he is prepared to assimilate what is foreign to him (people, facts, experiences). He feels the need to widen his knowledge, and to get hold of other people. Width reveals a need for conquest, an enterprising spirit, a certain faith, whether justified or not, in the value of spontaneity, a readiness to involve oneself, a desire to be needed and sometimes, avidity.

In a large writing, where expansion is already obvious, width noticeably increases the space taken by the subject, but it comes as no surprise, as it derives from motives inherent in largeness and reinforces them.

In a small writing, where expansion is only slight, width is a significant compensation. Reasonable self-awareness is allied to a desire to have a field of action, or even a social sphere, which measures up to a desire for

88 Man, 40 years - *Very small, wide, thrown, progressive, simplified and rapid writing. Mobility of an agile mind resolutely turned towards the novelty of events, quick to grasp arguments put to him. The rightward slant reinforces the wide gesture.*

conquest, inadequately expressed in other ways. The reserved aspect of communicativeness is broadened by a capacity for sociability which can be seen in the width.

If firmness is lacking and width is coupled with badly-controlled, slack movement, weak filiformity, and often with diminishing size, one can deduce a tendency to let oneself be easily influenced, to have difficulty in pulling oneself together and to ineffectual hastiness.

---

89 **Man, 24 years** - *Unevenly wide, light, poor relationship between form and movement, arythmic spacing. Association of stiffness and slackness. This student does not really know where he stands, tends to be emotionally unstable, to let things go, to improvise. At the same time, the quick, sharp-pointed gestures with deviated pressure, show the reactivity and the uneven quality of his effort.*

---

2. Primary width only : more easily observed in large, and often rounded writings, in which case the impression of inner comfort is reinforced; it is also found in small writings. This type of width may affect some letters more than others : round letters, or *m*'s for instance.

3. Secondary width only : all the more noticeable in that it lends itself to tense gestures, giving an artificial aspect to the expansion; the resultant forcing is often revealed by deviated pressure. It is not unusual to find narrow letters associated with this type of width. Constraint appears in the behaviour, and affects the way one adapts and socialises (see Chapter 5).

A wide and left-slanted writing indicates a contradiction between an attitude of withdrawal and a desire for expansion. In some graphic contexts, one can really consider secondary width as a positive compensation for a defensive character; it then indicates the wish of the writer to go beyond his inhibitions.

Man, 50 years
90
Acquired, double-joined writing, with looped garlands and arcades, static, strong pressure, stiff and straight-lined. Flagrant contradiction between narrow and double-joined letters, and the secondary width whose tension attests to the complexities of the personality. Heavy progression across the page. Inner tension and strong constraint in this writer who relentlessly forces himself to achieve concrete, successful results, and - not unskilfully - manages it. On the other hand, almost total defensiveness of a closed and personal world.

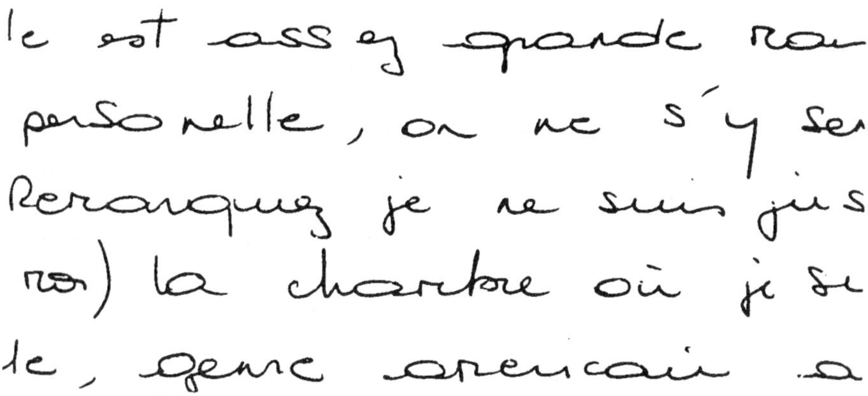

[Handwritten French text sample]

Girl, 15 years - *Considerable emotional needs, inhibitions and expansion combined, trust and mistrust, clumsiness and skill. The overall writing is tense, but lively. The association of width and narrowness affecting only certain letters, amounts almost to a system; there are good reasons to believe that this is temporary. Notice the importance of the middle zone (shortened lower extensions) and the ovalisation of the round letters (plump).*

91

In adolescence, it is not unusual to meet with the combination wide-narrow, affecting mainly certain words and certain letters, especially wide *o*'s and *a*'s, and narrow *m*'s and *n*'s; this probably reflects the uncertainties of a young person (more often girls), an ambiguity which can be considered normal, and which, in any case does not affect the homogeneity of the writing.

It is a different matter when this association is found in adults, where it becomes an anomaly.

NARROW

NARROW writing is characterised by a narrowing of the bases of letters (primary width) or of the connections between letters (secondary width); both types of narrowness usually go together. The writer is loathe to progress towards the right, with all this implies by way of restraint and pulling back. To compensate for this decrease of horizontal amplitude, an increase of vertical dimension, or superelevation, often occurs.

If narrowness is not exaggerated and the writing is also sufficiently supple and genuine, one can deduce that the subject draws his strength from reflection and restraint. Priority is given to self-control, prudence, concentration and the importance of strict principles.One can see a tendency to preserve and strengthen values considered as safe; the way one

écoulement intra et extra muros hexagonaux.

Les jars de Fiat n'ont rien inventé. Mais ils le remuent!

92 **Man, 60 years** - *Narrow, firm, connected, well-nourished, in relief, supple, in spite of arcades and angular garlands; the spaces, a little large, although irregular, compensate for the narrowness. Restraint and discipline,but no inhibition; the writing is fairly large and the finals are enlarging. The writer completes with vigour and firmness, what he has decided to do, and his refusal to be influenced strengthens his team-work without limiting it. The narrowness, more primary than secondary, suggests good social contacts, free from any familiarity.*

manages things is careful, prudent, one's independence is preserved through close calculation of the risks involved. One notices difficulty in delegating, fear when faced with the unexpected, and a tendency to retreat into an attitude of dignity.

The constraint implied by narrowness easily causes tense writing and monotony, especially when coupled with angular forms, arcades and a dry stroke. Self-assertion is not free and takes place in an excessive, or clumsy way with intransigence, a spirit of contradiction and authoritarianism. Risks, calculated with too much apprehension or mistrust. lead one to selfish behaviour, or to ill-timed aggressiveness. Sometimes, assertiveness gets nowhere. Narrowness in an inhibited graphic context shows the extent to which constraint is dominant.

---

93 **Woman, 60 years** - *Writing so narrow that it produces covering strokes; angular , dry, sharp-pointed, obstructed, but resolute and conected, as well as right-slanted. Critical mind, parsimony, argumentative disposition. Nothing escapes this distrusful but authoritarian and determined woman who, however, controls her aggressiveness.*

Narrowness can be such that the writer cancels the space between the downstrokes, or else goes over part of the downstrokes; in the first case we have the COVERING STROKE or, in the second, the SUPPORTED STROKE (see Chapter 5).

In adolescence, the significance of relatively frequent narrowness can be limited to apprehension about the future, to a lack of freedom and ease in relationships with others, or to a certain shyness. Most often, this is a temporary narrowness which, although indicative of a tendency of the personality, will nevertheless not necessarily become a major constituent. Narrowness can arise from constraints felt too strongly by adolescents or children.

2. *Proportions between the zones*

Crépieux-Jamin states that the proportions of a writing are the main condition of harmony, and that they are closely connected with order and clarity [14]. Klages, discussing the formlevel, gives great importance to proportions [23].

Whilst the different elements of handwriting are involved in these proportions, the relative dimensions of the zones play a crucial part in the equilibrium of a writing. This is why some graphologists [32] say that, even more than absolute size, one should consider the relationship between low letters and upper and lower extensions. Moreover, this relationship is usually constant in the script of a specific writer.

The middle zone, being the central core of handwriting, its centre of gravity, will acquire all its strength only if its dimensions are in a balanced relationship with the upper and lower zones, and if it maintains sufficient regularity.

Good upper and lower proportions strengthen the middle zone; bad proportions throw it out of balance and therefore weaken it. All the same time, this is no argument for too much regularity. The life of a writing lies in the infinite variety of its nuances. Slight variations in the proportions are even desirable, but always within the limits of sufficient equilibrium with the middle zone.

Good proportions are connected to self-confidence, to the ability to participate and to acknowledge the value of the outside world; they show that there is nothing lacking, nor any exaggerated predominance in the main functions of the personality. Self-mastery, common sense and good judgement, are thereby reinforced.

Balanced and nuanced proportions are related to the subject's autonomy and his good integration within the social group.

Conversely, proportions which are too personal must not be detrimental to the homogeneity of the writing, so that individualism is successfully assumed, and discordant proportions, which break up homogeneity, bear witness to difficulty in adaptation.

Children very quickly acquire the sense of the proportions of the zones when they first learn to write, even if these proportions are imperfect[6]. They tend to settle for proportions close to the copybook model between the ages of 7 and 12, yet with slight differences (lower extensions, a little too short, or upper extensions, a little too large, in particular).

In adolescence, the difficulty of finding one's place, and deeply felt dissatisfactions, do have repercussions on the proportions of handwriting; these will, however become personal at an early stage. Whilst one need not pay too much attention to the negative aspect of bad proportions, the solidity of the middle zone should always be observed by the graphologist.

The symbolism of space, a table of which is given in Appendix 1, can give us indications, which need to be very carefully shaded, on the meaning of the variations in proportions. Indeed, we would warn our readers against the fact that the symbolism of the upper and lower zones is less well

---

6   In Ajuriaguerra's Children's Scale, it has not been necessary to list errors in proportions.

   As for the difficulty in differentiating between the zones, if it has been the object of a developmental item in the same scale (F14), it must be mentioned that this particularity very soon disappears (only 12 % of children aged 8 still show some letters which slip into another zone, *t* like *i* or *i* like *t*, for instance).

   In fact, big errors in proportions, or lack of differentiation of zones are not often found, except among dysgraphic children.

   A confusion of zones in adults is therefore all the more unexpected, and difficulty in making objective judgements is involved.

defined, as far as interpretations are concerned, than that of the left, the right and the middle zone, to which we subscribe, and which has been validated by experience.

SOBER

A writing is SOBER when it is free from superfluous movements, while at the same time remaining legible and keeping to moderate dimensions. The middle zone is balanced by the other zones in an economical manner; there is no dispersion of movement, but balanced proportions are maintained.

Sobriety is one of the components of harmony and Crépieux-Jamin considered it as a qualitative sign, one of those which profoundly mark a

[handwriting sample in French]

Woman, 50 years - *Small, sober, simple writing, both simple and simplified, comfortable, rhythmic and a little wide, mainly owing to the white spaces. Genuineness, great simplicity, selectivity, seriousness, ability to serve others or causes with great modesty and dignity. Clear, thoughtful and intuitive mind.*

94

script. It was also, for H. de Gobineau [19], a component of autonomy predicting the maturity of the writer. On this point , she is in agreement with Pulver.

Sobriety expresses self-control, simplicity, moderation and attention; it tends towards introversion. Owing to its reduction to essentials, sobriety is associated with the signs of intelligence insofar as it shows the capacity to grasp the essentials and to see things according to their importance; it therefore originates from some sophistication. In a writing which is not very personalised, sobriety shows common sense, probity, and the prudence of someone who knows his limitations.

The restricting of movements in sober writing, is more or less consciously meant or desired; this occurs in a lively graphic milieu and is distinct from the restricting of movements which can occur in an inhibited context, where it impoverishes the writing.

PROLONGED UP AND DOWN

Increased amplitude involves both upper and lower zones, and the more the outer zone extensions are prolonged, the more imbalanced the middle zone becomes.

If we remember Pulver's remark : the greater the personal maturity, the more the upper and lower extensions tend towards central balance, and the more one's consciousness concentrates the interplay of possibilities towards what might be called, broadly, "realisation" [36]; prolongation up and down indicates a personality seeking satisfaction. For Klages, our extensive movements are related to the degree of distance between ourselves and the aims we pursue.

There follows, therefore, a discrepancy between the aspirations of the writer and his capacity to fulfil them, with all the dissatisfactions which this may cause. The joining of upper and lower extensions to the middle zone, the solidity of the latter, the suppleness of the writing, its mode of continuity, its spatial distribution, will help the graphologist evaluate the real possibilities of achievement.

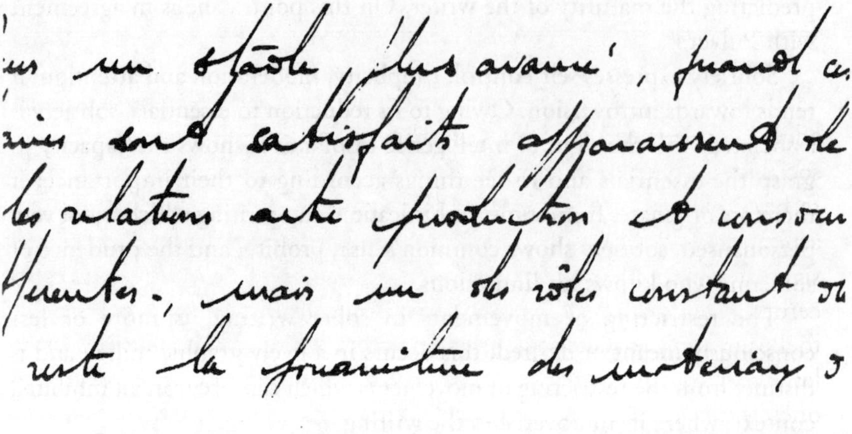

[handwritten French text]

Man, 18 years - *Prolonged up and down writing, superelevated, strong pressure, in relief, clear and connected. The prolongations which show both aspirations and anxiety, are all joined to a solid middle zone which, there is reason to believe, will end up by being balanced by the other zones. The feeling that there is still some way to go, and the considerable self-respect, are evident, but so is the capacity for personal realisation.*

95

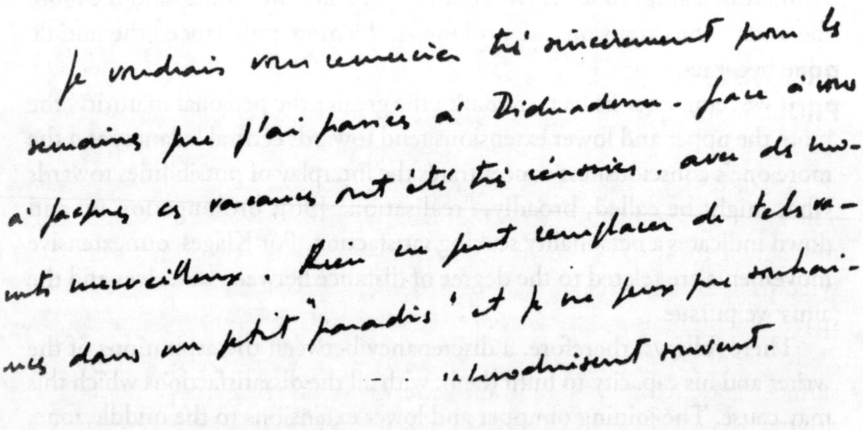

[handwritten French text]

96 *The handwriting of the same writer aged 26, after he entered professional life. This sober, dynamic, well-proportioned writing is a good illustration of*

Pulver's words: "Maturity, when it has reached a certain point, is incompatible with any sidestepping".

Prolongations up and down, especially up, are frequently found in adolescence, especially in boys, perhaps owing to their more demanding social ideals, but also in girls who do not feel they are what they would wish to be. Prolongations can prove to be generators of progress, owing to the aspirations and the desire to participate which they represent. But they are signs of effort, rather uneconomical, as far as graphic movements are concerned. Too much prolongation, even in adolescents, shows a propensity to illusions and to acute touchiness. In adults, where evolution is necessarily less likely to occur, prolongations up and down show difficulty in accepting oneself for what one is, possible dispersion, indecision, utopiansim and illusory self-assertion.

One should note, nevertheless, that prolongations up and down, if they are firm, can form a kind of positive anchorage and compensation for a manifestly poorly structured middle zone.

PROLONGED UP
PROLONGED DOWN

A handwriting may be prolonged only upwards, or only downwards. The gesture of abduction, more difficult to produce, shows effort and the movement towards the lower zone shows affirmation. Parallel with the symbolism of movement, one notices, in accordance with the symbolism of space, an emphasis on the upper or the lower sphere (see Appendix no.1).

If the writing is not excessively PROLONGED UP and starts in a sufficiently solid and lively middle zone, the prolonging can prove to be a driving force, insofar as it is likely to inspire the writer with the desire to do better, hence the interpretations of high ideals, ambition, and perfectionism. This is true only if the upper extensions are well connected to the middle zone; one can then assume that the critical mind remains vigilant.

If the upper extensions are excessively prolonged, either with a weak middle zone, or in a context where there is a bad relationship between form and movement, irregular space distribution, or a precarious stroke, the graphologist is entitled to think that the writer's aspirations belong to the world of illusions, escapism, exaltation and irrationality; all this causes dissatisfaction and dispersion.

Woman, 28 years

Very pronounced upward prolongations in this writing, which can also be described as soaring, with a relatively structured middle zone, disconnected, narrow, rounded in some letters, imprecise and twisted. Irrational thought, which only follows the norm through necessity, in this young woman, a painter who also has a doctorate in law. Reality cannot be perceived as it is; mediocrity and banality are refused.

97

Prolongations can be stick-like or inflated. We should mention also inflated upward prolongations of children who are going through a period of day-dreaming.

PROLONGED DOWN, in the same way as prolonged up writing,can exist within a whole range of different gestures involving form, firmness, tension and the quality of the stroke, as well as the joining with the middle zone.

One can indeed note big differences between lower extensions; some are weak and dangle, indicating poorly controlled self-assertion; some are in sticks and driven down like posts, which is a sign of activity, but where self-assertion is in danger of being tense or systematically oppositional. Some are angular and firm, which signifies authoritarianism and determination, the opposite of lower extensions which dangle downwards.

The form of the lower extensions should be interpreted closely together with the stroke and the general aspect of the writing. One should note the frequent emphasis on lower extensions in writings of average socio-cultural milieu (see Chapter 1, second part).

Woman, 40 years - *Inharmonious writing, disturbed in its form and rhythm due toirregularities of all sorts. Lively but feverish writing. Tension, dissatisfaction as well as obstinacy.*

98

We should pay more attention to either prolonged up or prolonged down writing, if the lower extensions in the first case, or the upper extensions in the second, are atrophied.

The less balanced the proportions, the more it becomes necessary to find somewhere else in the writing, elements of strength and suppleness capable of compensating for the disproportions.

LOW

In LOW writing, lower and upper zone letters have reduced dimensions to the proportions of the copybook model. In very low writings, these letters are hardly differentiated from the middle zone ones. It is in this zone that the writer expresses himself, whatever its dimension may be.

If the orientation towards a central equilibrium of the writing is to tend towards maturity, proportions must remain within certain limits, which in low writings, is no longer the case. First, it is the composition of the middle zone, then of the writing as a whole, which will enlighten the graphologist as to the reasons for the decrease in the amplitude of the upward and downward extensions.

There are indeed some almost low, but very rapid and rhythmic writings which, nevertheless, do not emphasize the middle zone. This happens among intellectuals who write a lot and whose precise thinking leads to this economy of movement.

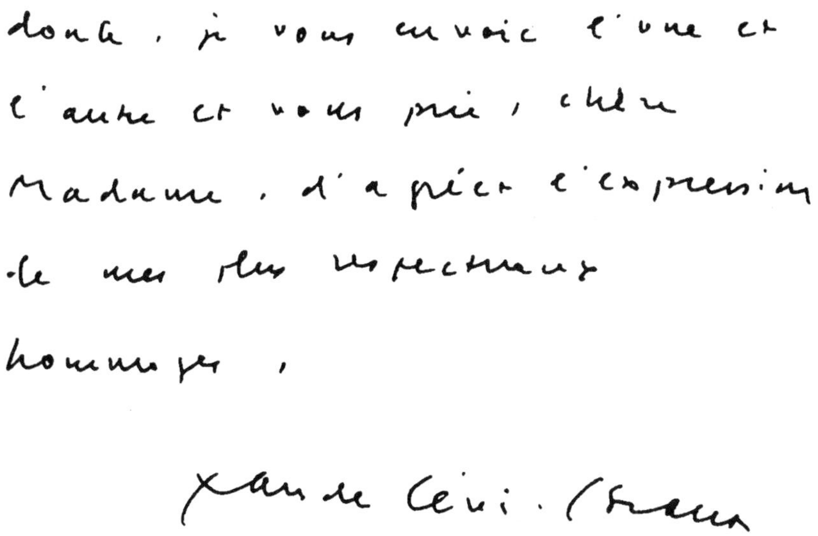

[handwritten letter in French cursive]

[signature]

99 **Man, 72 years** - *Modest, discreet and prudent aspect of the man and the scientist. Simple, simplified, aerated, sober and almost low, disconnected to grouped, vibrant and tile-like. Even though the writing concentrates in the small middle zone, it nevertheless is a zone open to the world.*

With this example, one understands to what extent low writing takes its meaning from association with other signs, and chiefly from the genuineness of its forms and the rhythm of its progression

100 **Man, 40 years** - *Small, low, while respecting the zones, stylised, condensed and compact, precise forms, clear, nuanced regularity, well-nourished stroke with slight relief; insular layout. Not much movement here, aesthetic pursuits are deeply experienced, the intensity is given by the quality of these rigorous forms. The low dimension indicates total commitment of an author to his work, his profound reflection, a concern to find the closest possible "mot juste", and the resistance he expresses against any unexpected incursion.*

voilà qu'à mon tour je n'ose plus vous écrire : vous exercez un art redoutable. Et pourtant, merci pour cette analyse étonnante. On m'avait fait incidemment des "remarques" sur mon écriture, mais rien qui m'ait jamais paru probant ou convaincant. Alors que vous — ni moi ni mon entourage n'en sont encore revenus —, d'emblée vous touchez loin et juste : pour tout vous dire, je suis d'origine calviniste et je dois bien me résigner à voir, passé 40 ans, que malgré tous mes efforts, c'est le genre de chose qu'on n'efface pas. Cela ne fait pas tout, bien sûr, mais que vous releviez la subordination à une éthique, la "contrainte intérieure" remontant à une "éducation traditionaliste", "un Surmoi avec sévère et exigeant", personne, hormis ceux qui me connaissent de très près et me pratiquent quotidiennement, n'a jamais pu le "diagnostiquer". Même chose en ce qui concerne la "défense contre toute incursion inopinée", la "réserve" — bref, vous ne le dites pas en ces termes mais j'en sais un peu quelque chose, ma tendance à l'autisme. Je ne vois rien, dans tout ce que vous dites, à quoi je pourrais redire : c'est "ça"! Freud, Benjamin et quelques autres n'avaient pas tort — et à vrai dire, je m'en doutais.

100   Man, 40 years

101   Man, 30 years

Man, 30 years - *Large, almost low, cylindrical, looped, double-joined, connected, strong pressure, pasty and static. Inflation of the self, and lack of genuineness, in this acquired, almost feminine, compact and ensnaring writing. Excessive importance of a middle zone expressing narcissism. No rhythm. Limitations in exchanges with others.*

Writings with shortened lower extensions are no longer sufficiently rooted in the lower zone, if one thinks of its significance as the zone of assertion and of rootedness.

If shortening of lower zone extensions is part of concentration of thought in a simplified, rapid and condensed writing, it can also belong to the signs of reduced capacity for assertiveness, and sometimes also, of difficulties in integration into reality, particularly if this shortening is found in an overall inhibited context, thereby reinforcing the negative meanings.

Woman, 50 years - *Numerous signs of anxiety in this inhibited, left-slanted, light and disconnected writing, imprecise mostly owing to unfinished and suspended letters. Difficulty in sustaining adequate lower extensions, which increases the fragility of this suffering writing. The simplifications and the extreme sobriety show the level of intelligence and the intuition.*

102

In a perturbed and weak graphic context, where lower extensions do not rejoin the middle zone, the negative significance of the shortening is reinforced. The personality of the writer is lacking a solid basis, is cut off from its foundations; efficiency and realism are hypothetical.

SUPERELEVATED

Superelevations in handwriting consist of abnormal lengthening of some letters, either due to increased dimension, or to the addition of a stroke underneath letters, giving them pedestals, or above the letters, which increases their height [38].

Superelevations are a complex sign which takes very diverse forms, their meanings deriving from their associations with other elements of the writing.

A graphologist should consider the gesture of superelevation as a small sign - meaningful in itself if it is repeated - since very different interpretations are involved, according to the letters, owing to the very nature of the movements producing them.

Some lower- case letters, *p, j, s, q, g, r* and *t* and all upper-case letters, capital *m* in particular, lend themselves to superelevations. We must see in which zone of the writing they occur and from which zone the movement producing them starts. Besides, a letter can be superelevated in very different ways.

The meanings of a superelevated small *p*, for instance, will not be the same in all cases. The simplification of *p* into a stick drawn from the upper zone, if it is firm, belongs to the signs of assertiveness slightly marked by susceptibilities which may push the writer to surpass himself. The firm stick of a superelevated *p* provides the anchorage of a weak middle zone, or participates in the emphasis of the upper zone, in someone slightly hot-headed. The superelevation of a small *p* can also result from a movement rising up from the baseline.

The example of the small *s* is quite different, because it is based on a left-tending copybook movement which is emphasised by the superelevation and often reinforced by a small lasso at the base[7].

Capital *m* lends itself to numerous versions ranging from all the variations of lengthening of the three downstrokes in the upper zone, to a movement ending in the form of underlining, or quite simply, a movement of lengthening into the lower zone.

In spoken French, *j* is the initial letter of the most frequently used pronoun and concerns the writer as the active subject. Consequently, this letter is loaded with very profound expressiveness, and is graphologically very reliable; so the graphologist should note, extra carefully, in what way it is superelevated.

We shall limit ourselves to these examples, recalling the importance of small signs which are repeated in an obvious way and can become distinct features of a writing.

We shall retain the meanings of slightly excessive self-respect, with its corollary of touchiness, but also the desire to do more and to be more, or rather haughty domination, ambition, pride, pursuit of prestige, quest for consideration, or the attraction provided by high objectives. The graphologist should investigate through which associations of forms the superelevations are expressed, and through which type of movement they take shape. A small, superelevated writing sometimes indicates the strength to put oneself forward, in a writer who is modest in other ways.

In adolescence, the small or capital *j* is certainly marked by the personality of the writer; superelevations indicate both his egocentricity and his aspirations.

---

7   French copybook '*s*' is like this: ⟋𝓈   (T.N.)

---

103   **Woman, 45 years** - *Numerous kinds of superelevations in this rhythmic, stylised, soaring, aerated writing, in relief, also very uneven, particularly in the middle zone. The superelevations do express the relationship between an elevated ideal of the self and the fear of not reaching it, despite the originality of the personality. Note the descending lines.*

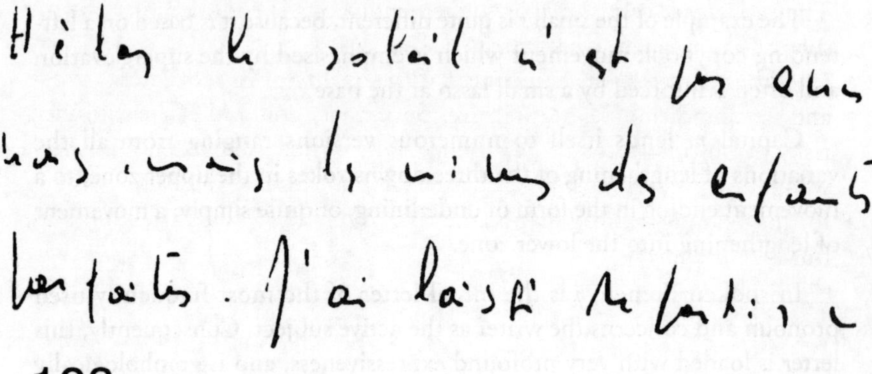

[handwritten text in French]

103 Woman, 45 years

We shall now discuss two signs in which the overall proportions are modified.

EXTENSIVE MOVEMENTS
EXPANDED

A writing with EXTENSIVE MOVEMENTS, is lacking, to a greater or lesser degree, in medium dimensions. Movements are increased in all directions, mainly in the outer extensions, and there is a great risk of drifting into discordance, for the harmony between the different elements of the writing is distubed, and the middle zone can no longer play its role as the centre of gravity of the writing.

A writing with extensive movements indicates excessive need for expansion and, more often than not, the need to captivate, by means of a rather theatrical presentation of oneself.

However, if the writing remains genuine, supple, and has a sufficiently solid middle zone, one sees an easily triggered-off capacity for participation, sociability founded on simple good-heartedness, and the need to play a role.

The capacity for illusions, or to create illusions is considerable, but the subject has a dynamic presence.

If the writing loses genuineness, if the quality of its movement, stroke and spacing disminishes, extensive movements then indicate excitibility, risky overestimation and impatience. The writer is a burden on others, whom he considers more as objects than as full partners. He is always asking for more, and as a result, runs the risk of dispersal, dissatisfaction and, finally, closedness.

Man, 40 years - *Thrown, carried away writing, with extensive movements and a very irregular middle zone, angular, sharp-pointed, but a pasty stroke almost blurred in places. Lively and enterprising personality, but excessive, impulsive and imperious. One wonders how well founded the initiatives are.*

104

EXPANDED writing shows increased expansion in its forms, especially in its curves and spacing.

Handwriting, a psychomotor activity involving the feeling of plenitude one experiences, may be temporarily expanded under the influence of a state of euphoria.

If the expansion is habitual, it expresses expansiveness of feelings, love of life, cheerfulness, provided the writing remains proportionate and firm, and has a supple baseline.

If the forms are original and genuine, and if there is movement, the graphologist can diagnose artistic imagination.

But if the graphic context is slack, too left-tending, or insufficiently structured, expanded writing is likely to express talkativeness, thoughtlessness, extravagance and dependency.

Expanded forms are quite often found in the signature, even when they are not present in the text (see Chapter 10).

We shall end this chapter with the global notion of stability or variability of dimension.

REGULARITY
UNEVENNESS
IRREGULARITY

Unlike the copybook model whose regularity, however exemplary it may be, is not lively, handwriting is made up of a whole interplay of variations specific to the personality of its author.

A writing has regular dimensions when the outline of words fluctuates only slightly. Growth of handwriting has a lot to do with this regularisation, a stage more or less reached between the ages of 8 -9 and 11-12.

Nuanced regularity [39], that is to say regularity which preserves the homogeneity of a writing as well as its life, belongs to the components of autonomy [19]. It indicates self-control, discipline, and stability; it goes together with a controlled movement.

Regularity should be interpreted according to the educational and professional level of the writer, insofar as one knows that the need for speed or for rapidity of thought is not conducive to regular writing. The relationship between form and movement must be good if regularity is to go hand in hand with speed.

The positive meanings of regularity decrease to the extent that a writing becomes more monotonous or more rigid. The writing as a whole will reveal whether its regularity shows an aptitude for repetitive tasks, or if it is related to emotional deficiency, which disturbs responsiveness and slows down adaptation.

Slight unevenness of dimension, which can also be called nuanced unevenness, is part of the vibration of a writing; this makes the writer's sensitivity perceptible, and enriches it as long as it does not damage the writing's cohesion and concurrently, the writer's self-confidence.

If variation of amplitude increases, especially in the middle zone, the writing, by becoming decidedly uneven, records the subject's uncertainties. The graphologist will find out whether such irregularity of dimension is associated with irregularity of pressure, continuity and spacing. Difficulties in assessing oneself, and emotivity, appear together with the imperfectly controlled reactions thus caused : touchiness and responses unsuitable to the circumstances.

The greater the variations of amplitude, both vertically and horizontally, the more a writing becomes irregular, to the point of being discordant, and therefore inharmonious. Any flagrant irregularity has a repercussion on the firmness of a writing, indicating the writer's inner discomfort. The graphologist should look for elements which might compensate for this irregularity, or for elements which, on the contrary, make it worse.

Moreover, all irregularities which contradict the major components of a writing (large and very narrow writing, for instance, or a large writing with a small signature), make such writings heterogeneous if they are very pronounced.

4

MOVEMENT

French graphology is often accused of considering handwriting from a static angle, neglecting the aspect of "movement". The reproach is exaggerated - even unjustified - and is founded mainly on a question of terminology.

The great French pioneers did indeed constantly refer to graphic movement, and all the graphology of Michon and his successors is an interpretation of this movement, following a symbolism of "the psychology of movement"[1], even though the word 'movement' is not mentioned.

This is probably why Crépieux-Jamin did not think it necessary to make movement a separate category. The term 'movement' appears in his writings only as a sign which he calls 'animated' where "the mobility of the writing is striking", and in another which he calls 'extensive movements', in which both form and dimension "exceed normal movements". But if one considers his descriptions of, for instance, 'sober' or 'effortless' or "inhibited" writings, one is struck by their expressiveness, as far as movement is concerned.

Sober writing is that in which "the movements are contained within moderate dimensions".

Effortless writing is recognised by "the harmony of its movements".

Inhibited writing "is characterised by a lessening, or a more or less abrupt cessation of the movements".

---

1   An up-to-date treatment of the psychology of movement is given in a still more explicit way by Suzanne Bresard [40]. For the author, it is movement which shapes forms, and the interpretation, in graphic syntheses, is made according to a psychology of movement founded on an original theory of personality. The book, very much geared to psychology, necessitates a basic knowledge of classical graphology if it is to be properly understood.

In analysing the characteristic factors of these signs in this way, Crépieux-Jamin makes the role of movement stand out clearly. The fact that he confines the use of the term to the two signs where excesses are conspicuous, confirms the extent to which, for him, the notion of movement is inherent in writing itself.

Movement represents a complex notion which includes several others - one can see this straight away by the actual description of these signs. It is not easy either to grasp movement, or to break it down into components. The approach to it is less concrete and less quantifiable than the approach to dimension or slant, for example, or even than the approach to form, which can be gauged according to a definite yardstick.

The same will of course apply even more strongly to rhythm, perhaps all the more so in view of our Cartesian minds[2].

Here one should note the influence of nationality and of the times on each one of us, including our great masters. Harmony, a very French notion, which has amongst its components, 'sober' and 'effortless' (comfortable), dates from an era which paid tribute to logical intelligence and to the will, and tended to hold up as an ideal, a writing which aimed at order and proportion, but was effortless, the result of supple movement.

It should also be noted that depth psychology has widely explored the driving forces and the motivations underlying each handwriting, these being very closely connected to movement, to what impels the writing forward or holds it back; this is the movement Pulver is referring to when he states that the graphologist is a "translator of movement" [41]. It is also that very movement which Crépieux-Jamin proposed to "re-experience in order to define a writing" [42].

We have therefore thought it useful to add an extra chapter on movement to those dealing with the classic categories, and to study its relationship with form in a separate chapter of its own.

This study of movement has been undertaken to improve and update teaching, although that does not make it any easier; the graphic act is one

---

2   Relating to Descartes and by extension: rational, logical (T.N.)

which involves all the signs simultaneously. Without pressure, writing would leave no trace; without movement, a letter would be a mere dot.

Movement is expressive in a relatively direct manner, more so than other categories such as form or layout. It is more closely related to motor behaviour and the difficulties of learning how to write; it is awkward movement which spoils the form and the handling of the graphic trail.

Dysgraphia, in its various forms [8], gives us an illustration of awkward movements; the results are informative, since they look like caricatures, magnifying the difficulties which some writers have in acquiring a free-flowing movement.

To write with ease, one has to integrate the forms and dimensions learnt at school into one's own writing movement. When this movement has been properly mastered, a positive evolution of the form will then be possible in accordance with each individual personality.

If one goes back to the early stages of learning to write, it is easy to distinguish one movement involved in the actual setting down of the letters and another involved in the graphic progression (from left to right in our handwriting model), commonly known as cursive movement. In adults, these two movements are integrated into the total graphic gesture; it is this movement, in its broad sense, which will be examined here. It is also the very same global movement that German graphologists study in what they term 'rhythm of movement'.

Whilst the mode of progression is particular to specific types of movement - controlled, propulsive, obstructed, for instance - the setting down of letters, with its integral relationship to progression across the page through linking of letters (continuity) and speed, participates in the type of movement.

Hélène de Gobineau, who to her great credit, has studied movement by observing it separately [19], seems to have been tempted to base her study on cursive movement. She was probably influenced by her research into children's handwritings. Her 'still movement' links up with the 'absence of movement' (i.e. of progression) which is usual in children who are learning to write. Her 'flowing movement' (with 'cursive' as a subtitle) is that which gives the best flow from left to right.

We shall retain Gobineau's signs of movement inserting those signs which will enable us to describe movement as a whole, needed as much for transcription of letters as for their progression. However, we shall not keep the same order, which ends with dynamic movement, the highest grade in her quantitative scale[3]. Without wishing to follow a developmental approach, the order we follow, starting with still movement and leading finally to movements where antagonism appears, describes each movement and then its pitfalls (e.g. excessive control bringing constraint).

We shall thus study :
- still movement (Gobineau),
- controlled movement, resolute writing (Crépieux-Jamin),
- inhibited, restrained, constrained writing (Crépieux-Jamin),
- floating movement (Gobineau), slack writing (Crépieux-Jamin,
- flowing movement (Gobineau), or effortless writing (Crépieux-Jamin),
- dynamic movement (Gobineau), dynamic[4] writing (Crépieux-Jamin),
- propulsive movement (Bresard), carried-away and thrown writing (with flying strokes) (Crépieux-Jamin),
- vibrant and effervescent movements, animated writing (Crépieux-Jamin),
- reared and obstructed movements (Gobineau),

Some of these Jaminian signs are among the important qualitative signs, because they encompass the essential aspects of a writing : effortless, inhibited, restrained writings[5] are among these. Their names are almost interpretations in themselves, and can help the graphologist to form an initial impression.

We also intend to identify, through the different kinds of movement, the essential features of inhibition, progressiveness, rhythm, or absence of rhythm.

For Crépieux-Jamin, RHYTHMIC writing is one sign amongst others; he stresses this notion of alternation. Present-day French graphology has extended this notion of alternation to the very life of the writing. Movement, an eminently personal matter, is above all a factor of rhythm.

---

3   Scale measured in 5 grades, in her graphometric study of personality.
4   'Dynamic' here translates both Gobineau's 'Mouvement dynamique' and Crépieux-Jamin's 'Ecriture dynamogeniee'. (T.N.).
5   See chapter on methodology.

STILL MOVEMENT
(absence of movement)

When the child starts to write, he places his letters on the line without 'apparent movement', says Hélène de Gobineau [19] and, following her, Ajuriaguerra [9].

The child appears to act as if he were setting a line of printed text, although his forms are clumsy, his dimension and direction irregular and his lines badly maintained. He tries mostly to respect a coded form (in terms of form-dimension-proportion), so much so that Gobineau calls this difficulty in integrating form with movement, 'dominance of form over movement' [19].

Learning to write takes a long time, and Ajuriaguerra's scale brings out the persistence of this item in 68% of twelve year-olds. The graphic act is seldom mastered before the age of 14. For a handwriting to move freely across the paper and be effortless in an activity requiring very delicate motor control - Ajuriaguerra [9] says that of all the various actions of the hand, writing is the one that allows it least freedom - the psychic state should be liberated, but training and practice are also essential.

Frequent writing practice, therefore, is a factor which must be taken into account with every graphological approach and especially with regard to the problem of movement, which is mastered, in a positive way, only late and laboriously. This is obvious in the case of children; here, even months matter, and it would be fair to be acquainted with what is expected of the child, and what models he has been given. This is important also in adolescence, where for long periods, practice in writing will vary a lot according to the writers, and in the case of adults, whom the graphologist must always place in their socio-cultural[6] and professional context (certain professions, for instance that of a draughtsman or a school teacher, may influence their writing).

Some people write only from time to time after leaving school, and although the school-leaving age has now been raised to 16, the degree of graphic maturity at this age shows considerable variation.

---

6   See Chapter on Organisation.

However, with adults and even adolescents, STILL (STATIC) movement (the term is often replaced by 'absence of movement') demands the graphologist's attention.

The static appearance of the writing gives rise to a monotonous expression from which life, desire, and plans seem missing, or prevented from realisation. It can also indicate contradictory, unresolved aspects of the personality, which manage to bring any lively movement to a standstill. At best, these elements adjust temselves within the narrow confines of repetitive tasks.

The graphologist should concentrate on understanding the writer's motives. One can control one's writing, concentrating so much attention on oneself that projection towards the outside world cannot take place; whether this is due to excessive self-satisfaction or to its opposite, the effects are the same, because the self-preoccupation in both cases creates paralysis. One can feel the need to fabricate an arbitrary or artificial image of oneself, in order to protect oneself, or to appear exemplary.

There is no reason why the setting down of letters should not be both animated and associated with a lively progression, thus giving an individual tempo - or even a rhythm - to the writing. Animation, in whatever degree, is synonymous with life; movement is succession and diversity, and through its capacity for adaptation, becomes a positive factor towards evolution. This presupposes a desire to start moving and the strength to do so; it allows a different, and above all, a more complete mode of expression.

One should therefore pay attention to the first signs of movement in the evolution of a writing. When the first indications appear among people who write only rarely, one will be in a position to understand such signs : they may simply show some positive tension in the handling of the written trail. Even some writings which remain very close to copybook, or typographic models, can show positive tension if they are in keeping with the writer's graphic attainment, or with what he experiences, perhaps temporarily or professionally. For instance, people whose writing is static, can find a niche in some professional areas where technical execution demanding regularity and patience, are important .

If this animation is not present in an adolescent's writing, one can surmise that he is going through a phase of stagnation or even regression[7].

Les hommes de cette planète cesseront enfin de ne d'eux-mêmes; du jour où ils lèveront les yeux ! la nature au point, de comprendre que c'est ... il leur est permis de vivre, à partir de ce ? seront délivrés de toutes servitudes et leur commencera .

Man, 21 years - Secondary education, computer operator

105

Despite the rightward slant and an attempt at connections, which however are uneasy and amended, the writing scarcely progresses; it is very hesitant, the stroke is almost shaky. There is not much tension, the expansion to the right is very much reduced, the letters are fragmented, suspended, and the accents are a little heavy, all adding up to a strong picture of inhibition.
He carries out his work very seriously and scrupulously. He finds relationships very difficult to establish, owing to a lack of self-confidence.

Generally speaking, whether there is passivity or indifference in an inert and frequently poorly structured writing, or inner tension causing inhibition, or dominance of constraint, making the writer regard any novelty as a potential risk, or artificial constructions, uniformity prevails above all and rhythm is therefore impossible.

---

7   Kestemberg talks of the prolonged hyperlatency period which can occur in this age-group, at a time when specific reorganisation should take place [43].

Woman, 30 years - Married, 2 children

There is very little apparent movement. The concentric gestures in light blue ink proceed neither toward the right nor towards the baseline in a continuous way because of the suspensions. The reverse letters create no link at all with those that follow (the disconnectedness, with some grouping, is static), whereas the general roundness, the small curved starting strokes, the selected forms and the absence of margins in this context, which has retained plump, inflated childlike forms, all cry out for tenderness and attention. The rhythm is broken by the stops, the gaps, the large and uneven spaces, and the chimneys.
Deep-rooted inhibition, in spite of a superficial appearance of social ease and well-managed activities.

106

CONTROLLED MOVEMENT
RESOLUTE WRITING

A writing with CONTROLLED[8] movement implies a firm and organised progression to the right, resting firmly on the line. In general it is a movement marked by discipline, and a certain restraint. The writer has good mastery of the graphic movement, but he watches himself carefully; The conscious dominates, the will intervenes to control possible impulses; there is some underlying resistance to events.

Experience, recorded statistically [11], has shown that in adolescents, controlled (or poised) writing is a factor of a reasonable and desirable development towards adult writing: the majority of good school pupils, 'good' whether in terms of social behaviour or academic results, produce, while still in the sixth form, a writing which is controlled in its movement. A higher percentage of girls than boys retain this advantage. One wonders if this is due to certain demands (even in our present-day society) or to differing constitutional factors, as far as certain forms of activity or aggressivition (in the broad sense of the term), are concerned.

It would be detrimental to miss that logical stage in the evolution of handwriting. The dysgraphic writer is precisely the one whose writing, not evolving according to the normal laws, remains very clumsy and does not attain a good mastery of motor impulses and movement, nor, consequently, of form.

An adult who seldom writes, produces, logically enough, a writing whose movement is controlled. It is rare, practically contradictory in fact, for a writing called crude or elementary, to have, in a positive way, a dominance of movement which is efficient, as the graphic ease needed to master movement is acquired only with training and practice. One should therefore not depreciate control, even if it constrains the writing a little, in those types of writing which can become individualised through their stroke, rhythmic spatial distribution and suppleness, and which then be all

---

8   By controlled movement, we mean here a writing ruled by a positive control because it seems in keeping with the nature of the writer. We reserve the connotations of brakes on expansion and of inhibitions, to RESTRAINED AND CONSTRAINED writings.

the more worthy of notice. We must also be prudent when faced with an ill-controlled movement which would affect the structure of the writing.

If the general aspect of a writing with controlled movement is poised, its apparent calm does not necessarily imply indifference; intensity can coexist with control.

This type of movement shows a determination, a more or less acknowledged decision on the part of the writer to move within chosen and accepted limits. This choice could be due to ethics, prudence, conservatism or experience.

Daily matters are undertaken with discipline and tenacity. The future is envisaged with prudence, but without apprehension, and risks are well calculated. The writer tries to be objective in his emotional life, but also in his judgements; his adaptation is reasonable and related to his potential.

Controlled writing is kept in check, but is still lively. It has rhythm, sometimes a relatively strong one which is well sustained, for if there is control, it usually implies energies requiring control. The layout is usually conventional, but a good graphic distribution is helped by mastery of movement.

The force of controlled movement can be the foundation of RESOLUTE writing.

Resolute writing is a resultant; it is an important sign which defines a graphic context well, and places it under the auspices of directed homogeneity. Its determined and well-sustained pace goes together with a solid stroke, clear forms and proportions, and a speed which attains its goal. Its antonym is hesitant writing.

The writer involves himself unreservedly and is fully independent. He devotes himself to a project because he has chosen it and thinks it feasible.

Intellectually, resolute writing generally indicates a positive, clear and concrete mind, yet more or less subtle.

The character of such a writer is reliable, responsible. On the other hand, he may lack suppleness and refinement. He is someone who is active in terms of strength, rather than finesse.

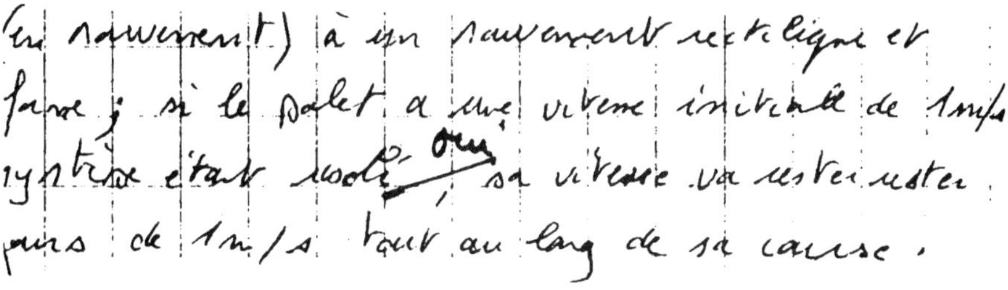

[handwritten text in French]

Boy, 17 years - Technical secondary education, average school results
*Irresolute writing. Badly controlled movement. In this writing, fairly typical
of boys in his age group, neither movement, direction, baseline (the paper is
lined), spacing, nor the very irregular dimension are well mastered. The
writing is fine, lively and reactive, jerky, tense with angles and crushed forms.
The lower extensions are unfinished. The relatively consistent connections,
and the pressure, give a certain cohesion and a certain strength to the words.
Sensitivity, finesse, but emotivity, vulnerability, difficulty in finding just
what is wanted. There is tension, but it is directed towards as yet ill-defined
objectives : the inner attitude remains uncertain and a little sceptical.*

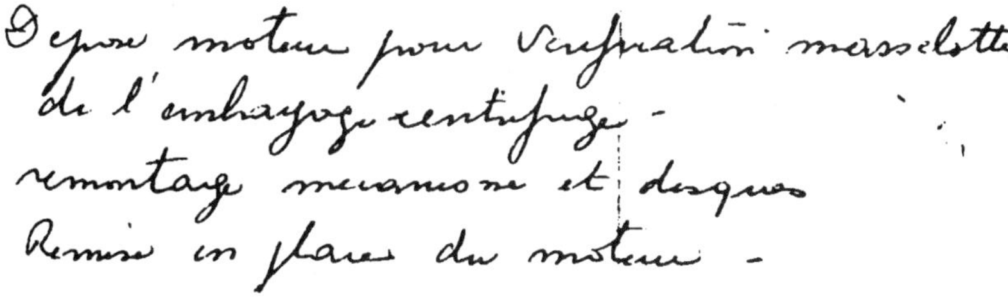

107

[handwritten text in French]

Man, 50 years - Garage mechanic
*Small, connected, very homogeneous and condensed writing which progresses
to the right with firmness and ease, especially if one takes its socio-cultural level
into account. The forms, simple but skilful and with a few simplifications, the
dimensions, the connections and the finals, contain and control a movement
which one feels is strong and determined. One notices, however, the unevenness of the left margin, accompanied by lower extensions slightly pulling
leftwards on the one hand, and the accents placed much ahead of the letters
(and very high) on the other. The writing is resolute. It has rhythm.*

108

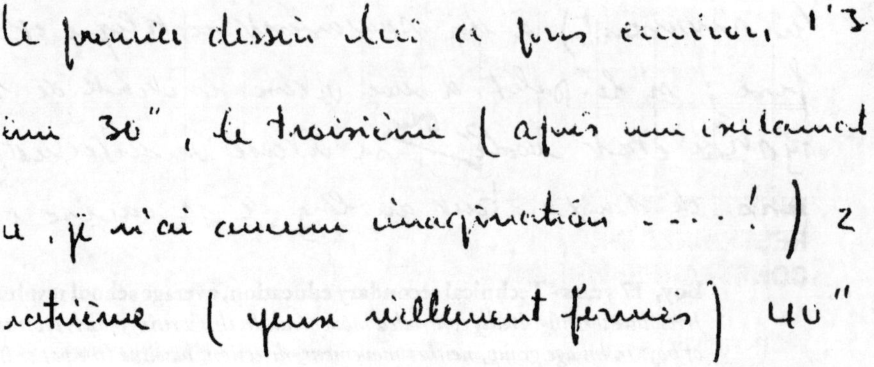

[handwritten text]

Man, 40 years - *Overall firmness in a controlled writing. Verticality, a dense stroke, well-kept lines, very structured spacing, giving a poised, but quite strong and sustained rhythm. Concentration and efficiency in relation to concrete, well defined and precise plans. Good balance between curved and straight strokes, small irregularities, a few slightly open ovals, wise letter-bases on the line, yet quite supple : realistic receptivity goes hand in hand with determination.*

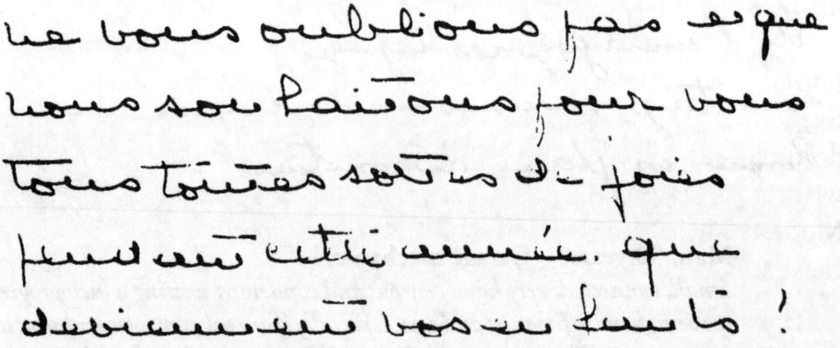

109

[handwritten text]

Woman, 45 years - *numerous social activities*

110

Resolute and compact writing with a predominant middle zone. A constant rhythm imposed by control, close to moral constraint. The writer does not allow herself to relax much. The square garlands, slightly looped and with

secondary width, stick to the baseline which the deviated pressure intensifies
and makes even darker. The line is emphasised, as it were, by the t-bars.
Much constancy and continuity in activity, strong personal commitment in
this respect, as in human relationships also. Sense of effort, stability.

INHIBITED WRITING
RESTRAINED WRITING
CONSTRAINED WRITING

INHIBITED writing is indicated by a lessening, or a more or less abrupt stoppage of movements [14]. It includes numerous signs, because inhibition is shown by all sorts of graphic signs. A writing can show its inhibition quite plainly, in a direct manner, or by way of compensation, in an indirect manner, for example by an increase in dimension or pressure.

In restrained and constrained writings, brakes are applied to the progression of the written trail. A writing can be RESTRAINED in various degrees; the brakes applied to controlled writing, depend on the writer's will, but those applied to restrained writing originate more from a more instinctive apprehension. The control becomes very important.

If a little restraint (and even a little inhibition, according to Crépieux-Jamin) is necessary in all social life, its excess interferes with spontaneity, freedom of expression and action. An attitude of circumspection definitely dominates the progression of the movement of a writer with restrained writing, as he feels the environment as not very friendly, even coercive. Modesty, social and moral demands, the strong prevalence of self-control, cause stiffness or great reserve.

If the movement of progression is even less free, then the writing is called CONSTRAINED. Inhibition is stronger. Feelings of inadequacy or guilt, principles which are constraining, or which go against the writer's tendencies, can cause this strong restraint which is felt as an obstacle.

A writing is restrained or constrained because of a whole convergence of signs: if, for instance, a writing is a little suspended or a little narrow, or shows a few slightly stiff forms, it is simply not classified as belonging among these important qualitative signs (which are very fundamental to the graphic milieu), and one would simply say that there are some signs of constraint, of inhibition, or of restraint.

One must group together all the elements that have contributed to putting a brake on the course of the writing.

If the graphic milieu is neither homogeneous nor clear, if it has little spontaneity, restraint can indicate dissimulation, and constraint can indicate deceit.

The lack of freedom of inhibited writing, restricts self-expression in our relationships with others, but it also limits the expression of imagination and can encourage a person to remain confined to what he knows and has experienced, to restrict himself in order not to expose himself to criticism, or to the scrutiny of others, which, he feels, would amount to intrusion.

Adolescence is a period when inhibition is frequent, and one can start suspecting the writer of being blocked when his writing becomes too static, too monotonous, or too stiff. Oversensitive reactions to the outside world

111

Boy, 17 years - Upper sixth former
Very restrained and constrained writing. The middle zone is very small, closed, with narrow primary and secondary width, touching letters (addossata), a stroke too heavy for this reduced dimension. Affective and sensual tendencies are causing embarassment and are not expressed very much. Connected, vertical writing, dash-like accents not in proportion with the writing, on which they weigh heavily.

bring about defensive vigilance, non-involvement, and often hold back the writings of this age group. Diffidence in expressing oneself is sometimes quite a burden, as far as communication within one's circle is concerned, and it also interferes with schoolwork. One comes across individuals who may well have more to say and do than what they, in fact, achieve. A graphologist can help them to become aware of what holds them back, and they are then in a better position to make use of their resources.

---

112 Woman, 55 years - *General stiffness of form, connections, line, starting and final strokes are constraining the writing. This woman forces herself to play a successful part in the field of activities and human relationships.*

113 Woman, 44 years - *A more unusual constraint here, partial but real. The stroke is hypersensitive, the ovals are dented and sometimes open; the lower* *extensions are short and hesitant. Connectedness seems to have been rejected, while the upstrokes, when they appear, are supple. The emotional vunerability (probably the price of a successful social and professional life) finds protection in these stops, these wide spacings, in the forms which seem to be very clear, simple, almost thin[9] and fleshless, in order not to be exposed. Yet the disconnectedness is not static.*

FLOATING MOVEMENT
SLACK WRITING

FLOATING movement is the result of an uneven and uncertain progression; the writing does not stand sufficiently solidly on the base-line, the handling, or the graphic trail is not firm enough for the script to move definitely towards the right-hand side of the page. The general structure which ruled controlled writing is lacking here since, clearly, control and rational order are relatively wanting. Affectivity dominates.

In floating movement one recognises components of Gobineau's 'surface writing' [19] which were taken up to form item F1 of the E scale [8]. This item characterises children's handwritings in their uncertainity; that is why this is also called 'children's clumsy writing' because of its overall clumsiness, which affects all the categories. It persists in 2/3 of children aged 11, and one can still see traces of it in adolescence. This type of movement goes well with certain aspects of the 'mental landscape' of that period in life, and may be preferable, provided it is not too emphasised, to general stiffness and excessive straightness of the baseline.

All the same, one should not equate floating movement with immaturity : the graphic milieu in which it appears is paramount and enables the graphologist to form an opinion.

The level of intelligence is not in question; receptivity, intuition, imagination, ability to improvise, a sort of floating attention - a sign of

9   'Thin' in Müller and Enskat's sense [88].

receptiveness - are often present. Absolute rigour, close analysis and assertiveness of character are what is lacking, plus convictions which are necessary if thought is to be authoritative.

Personality-wise, desires and aims (as well as the means of attaining them) are not immediately obvious to the writer, his self-perception is not always clear, which makes him feel insecure and uncertain.

The writer with a floating movement makes a pleasant partner, amenable, accomodating, young at heart, but he can be bewildering, due to his unpredictible moods; he is fairly dependent on his environment.

Such writers will therefore be suited to certain types of employment only, for their lack of certainty could be a hindrance in jobs where the capacity to take responsibility and the ability to make decisions, matter. On the other hand, they fit easily into a team which is stimulating and gives them guidance; because of their adaptability, their capacity for tolerance and negociation they are efficient elements in such teams.

Balanced layout, good space distribution and the quality of the stroke which are always elements of an efficient structure, are particularly important with these types of movement.

The type of writing called SLACK has a weak stroke[10], its movement is markedly floating and affects the writing in all its categories; the layout is poor, the form not well structured and the pressure, generally light.

The writer is evasive, either through indifference, or through the inability to direct his efforts towards a goal, to take things in hand. He gives up or becomes discouraged. Tiredness can temporarily have that effect; when faced with a slack writing, the graphologist should ask for further documents.

Slack writing is never positive, and to find it in the scripts of children or adolescents is always a pity, due to the lack of motivation it indicates.

Inhibition can be the cause, as it can also, to a lesser extent, with floating writing; whereas the latter may have some rhythm, probably of an uneven sort, in slack writings the elasticity is insufficient for them to be rhythmical.

Slackness is not suppleness; nor is floating movement, if it is pronounced.

---

10 See Chapter on Pressure.

Je suis entrain de vous utilisant un guide, car seulement j'ai honte de e'criture, mais je su peu capable d'ecrire droi que cette défaillance puis

Man, 32 years - *Floating movement, slightly reared at times, arhythmic. The writing incorporates a lot of white in the drawing of the letters; it shows residues of surface writing with slightly stiff forms; the directions, proportions and spacing are not well mastered, the cursive movement has moments of both suppleness and jerkiness. The baseline is wavy. The left margin, quite well kept, the rather precise stroke, and the straightening up of the slant, serve as anchor points.*

114

A very uneven personality, difficulties in making decisions, with arbitrary choices sometimes, but a faculty of adaptation, imagination; contacts with others easy on the surface (more reticent deeper down).

FLOWING MOVEMENT
EFFORTLESS WRITING (COMFORTABLE)

Handwriting with a FLOWING movement progresses freely, using the space and the baseline with suppleness. There are few impediments in this flow, which is unhurried and thus well controlled.

The ease observed here is the result of an inner equilibrium enabling the writer to remain natural.

It is quite obvious that the flowing movement, because of the skill and the autonomy it involves, does not exist in children, and is rarely found in adolescents. In adults, however, if a copybook writing is perfectly effortless, it has a flowing movement[11].

Flowing movement shows good resistance to frustration, reactions which are in proportion to events, and an adequate use of one's potential. The elasticity of the graphic movement gives rise spontaneously to a balanced rhythm of distribution, although often conventional. This means that adaptation to reality takes place smoothly, that the writer communicates with others in a considerate and easy manner, without reservation. This gives those around him a feeling of security, which can also be felt in the way he gives orders.

Pressure and horizontal dimension should be observed, inasmuch as strong pressure is rather infrequent here, because it would impede this type of movement. The pressure is usually medium, rather light, which is part of the general skill of the flowing movement. But by emphasising suppleness and rightward tendencies, this movement runs the risk of excessive width, which could make the writing lose its density. It is possible, with too much ease, to verge on facileness, opportunism, dithering, or lack of conviction.

Excesses, lack of proportion in one category or another would disturb the course of the flowing movement. It is the small irregularities, the polarities, factors of rhythm, which give it a positive meaning.

Writers with a flowing movement have a whole array of professions to choose from. However, they would be suited to jobs where adaptability and cooperation are needed more than strength, audacity or confrontation.

The writer's intelligence is open and supple, there is enough tolerance (convictions are not absolute and create no obstacles) yet there is sufficient firmness. Thought processes and method are adaptable. Common sense and a concrete logic guide the judgement.

The flowing movement is regular in its progression : it is the antonym of inhibition, with its braking effect. Rhythms which are very strong, very intense, or very vital, do not belong here.

---

11 See writing no. 40: the copybook writing is in harmony with the nature and the profession of the writer.

H. de Gobineau [19] points out that while flowing movement is usually found in well-adapted and active individuals, it is never found in those suffering from mental illness; this movement is closely linked to self-confidence, to a good balance between motivating needs and their fulfilment.

The free course of flowing movement logically gives rise to EFFORTLESS writing : the harmonisation of the essential qualities which make this movement possible, shows the simplicity and the spontaneity which dominate this sign. There is indeed no need to compensate; the personality is expressed and fulfilled according to its nature and its social surroundings.

Je vous envoie, comme vous me l'avez demandé un spécimen de mon écriture actuelle, une page de mon cours de phil,

Girl, 17 years - Upper 6th

The tendency is towards flowing movement in spite of a slight hesitation between some restraint (some smaller letters and straightening-up, enlarging final 'e's, strong apostrophes, incipient angles) and a bit of slackness in its progression (the forms and the garlands collapse a little, the widths stretch out).

115 *Effortless writing and maturity for her age, a well-balanced and receptive intelligence. She is adaptable and participates, but does not accept everything : there is an urge for independence which may be a little aggressive, a need for elbow-room, a need to live without constraint and a need to dream a little.*

See also writing no. 31 which has a flowing and firm movement.

Man, 50 years - Paediatrician

116

The writing is rapid, right-tending, combined, fairly effortless, rhythmic, but the slight deviation of pressure on the baseline, the slight crushing, the incipient sharp-points, show the need to channel a lively emotivity and sensitivity (which are part of the rhythm), but can also be a little disturbing. Intuition in his diagnoses, common sense, subtle and adaptable in his contacts. A little pessimism and impatience.

DYNAMIC MOVEMENT
DYNAMOGENIC WRITING [12]

DYNAMIC writing is lively and energetic, which includes elan but also control. It contains active strength which is goal-oriented and aggressive in a positive way. Dynamic writing is firm, due to its stroke and its movements, to the space it structures, and the stability of the line. Its form is progressive : it advances rapidly and efficiently towards the right (clever linking and arrangement of letters, and simplification produced by right tendencies).

---

12 Crépieux-Jamin's sign: 'écriture dynamogéniée' is distinct from - although close to - Gobineau's dynamic movement. (T.N.)

The whole writing is penetrated by a movement - in the broad sense of the term - implying the ability to channed one's energies into projects, and in which there is an underlying desire to push things ahead and attain one's goal. The subject is ready to act on his convictions, but his combativeness is organised, his good judgement saves him from exaggeration and his perseverance allows him to maintain his efforts. The dynamic movement is handled in an individual and decisive manner implying a good level of autonomy[13], and qualities of intelligence and sociability.

The efficent and rapid movement producing dynamic writing implies an active mind, quick at perceiving situations and giving answers, confident as to the future. The above, however, needs to be enlarged on and qualified a little.

Whilst the writer is a discerning and realistic person, he may also have set, rather narrow ideas and be a little subjective. This is why the proportions of the writing, its suppleness, its ampleness, the diversity of its forms and connections, and the overall firmness will have to be assessed.

People who write like this are best suited to professions where a taste for action, the spirit of enterprise and mental dynamism are necessary. They are persuasive, they mobilise their own energy and that of others, towards achievement, creating new objectives.

The rhythm of dynamic writing is rapid and does not suffer from too many disturbances in its tempo. It has a less supple rhythm than writing with flowing movement, and is less disciplined than that of controlled writing.

As to Crépieux-Jamin's DYNAMOGENIC writing, which he describes as one of the most important signs in graphology, it is not often met with if one is looking for its pure form. Crépieux-Jamin defines dynamogenic writing as having elan, extra power, rapidity, an ascending direction, a well-nourished stroke free from any constraint, and vibrant activity.

---

13 It is, in fact, an almost complete synthesis of the components of autonomy.

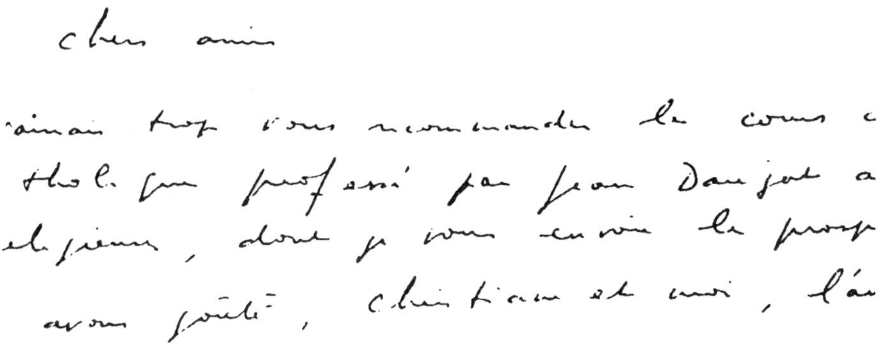

[handwritten text]

Man, 45 years - Engineer

117 *Small, wide, progressive, dynamic and rhythmic writing. The lower extensions widely opened towards the right at middle zone level (they are a little restrained with a left-tending movement at their base), the open ovals, the considerable width of spacing facilitate an increasingly rapid progression and with a progressively rising baseline. The writing is dynamogenic : ardour, convictions, openness can be accompanied by a desire to take over from others and act for them. Enterprising mind, easy and subtle communication.*

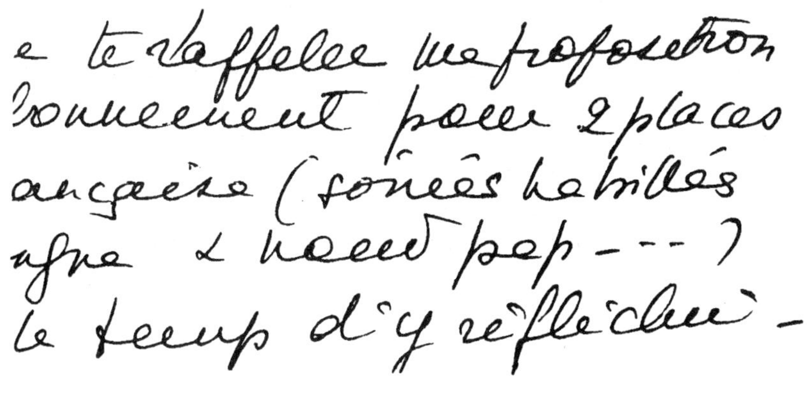

[handwritten text]

118 **Woman, 50 years** - *Dynamic writing with dynamogeny and rhythm .Less free rhythm than in wriiting no.117, the precise and very connected graphic* *thread is taut, and the spaces between words and lines are narrow. Here activity is a protection. The writing rises, the looping and the skilful, rapid double-joins create the motor of dynamogeny; at the same time, they serve as brakes in a writing which tends to live at rather too fast a tempo.*

Practical intelligence concerned with relationships. In this writing, authoritarianism is not far off either, but in a different and more concrete manner.

PROPULSIVE MOVEMENT
CARRIED AWAY WRITING
THROWN WRITING (FLYING STROKES)

PROPULSIVE movement[14] is based on a spontaneous stimulus which projects a writing forward, progression taking place with a thrown movement. The level of being, or of having, is high; the emotions full of ardour and the impatience to achieve goals, reinforce the natural dynamism. Such a writer immerses himself immediately and totally his projects.

The whole quality of propulsive movement lies in its limits, in the adjustment which is made between elan and realisation. The initial elan should not be mere impulse, but must be sustained and helped by reflection and sufficient awareness of the environment, without which it would get lost in illusions and be deflected from the intended goal. The propulsive movement is indeed expressive of forces which sweep people along, greatly helping them in applying themselves, in being enterprising, giving them creative audacity and the ability to stimulate people to action. But this excitement needs to be counterbalanced.

---

14 The term is owed to Suzanne Bresard who makes this movement one of her four types [40].

119 Writing (a) (man of 45 years) is a lot less well channelled in its rightward propulsion than the second. Despite the impetus, homogeneity is not achieved due to the very big irregularities of the middle zone and the width, the impetuous, thrown movements, the capitals within words and the uneven spacing. Strongly emotive, he drives himself (steeply rising lines and strong tension). Restlessness, but also activity and commitment.
Writing (b) (man of the same age) is also uneven, but the counterweights are better distributed (spacing is therefore more regular).

In CARRIED AWAY writing, the counterweights prove to be insufficient. The movements are not sufficiently curbed and do not control either the speed or the force of the movement very well. Excitement dominates and with it, excesses in the personality, as well as in the judgement.

The way the graphic space is occupied, the proportions of the writing, the general tension and the quality of the stroke will help to evaluate the range of these excesses, the strength and the persistence of their effects, and perhaps, where they are most likely to occur.

THROWN writing (writing with FLYING STROKES) has something of the nature of several types of movement; it is characterised by numerous

Woman, 68 years - Shopkeeper

Carried-away writing with flying strokes and restrained movements : the flying strokes are clubbed, the capital letter is narrow, the punctuation is precisely placed and small. The angles resist and obstruct the movement, but the overall context is strong, owing to the pressure, the dimension, the rising lines, the right slant which prevails, in spite of some straightening-up and disconnected initials, stressing the impact of what is felt.

Presence, strength and unyielding authority.

120

strokes, briskly projected beyond the limits observed by the rest of the word, generally upwards and to the right. Finals, t-bars and accents, particularly, lend themselves to flying strokes, but so do capitals, some initial letters and upper extensions.

The writer is very quickly stimulated, so quickly that , more often than not, he defends himself before he is attacked : he is very reactive. The graphic context will show the extent of his impatience and irritability and the vigour of his reactions.

For all these reasons, thrown writing is found especially in combination with carried-away writing, but it can also appear with other types of movement; for instance, in constrained writing, of which it is the antithesis, thus indicating conflict.

Woman, 30 years - Secretary

121

The writing is constrained (due to narrowness, the movements returning to the left, the considerable spacing between words), as well as superelevated, and has flying strokes also. The demands and the mistrust are great. Demands on herself and the environment, and a lot of touchiness. The character is difficult, but most often controlled. Relaxation follows constraint.

VIBRANT MOVEMENT
EFFERVESCENT MOVEMENT
ANIMATED WRITING

The subtle animation of VIBRANT movement involves discreet antagonsim between what impels and what restrains the writer; the movement nudges the writing towards the right without really propelling it, yet without immobilising it. The writing progresses by means of light touches, by vibrations, the writer moving forward almost without appearing to do so. It is a writing of emotive people with average activity, of nervous types. Sensitivity creates an alertness which nurtures curiosity of mind, and yet never strays outside the limits of order.

The writing moves in a subtle rather than forceful way. This is why we should watch out for anything that could mar the structure of the writing, whether it be lack of firmness, too much relaxation of pressure, too much white space in relation to black, too many prolongations in relation to a generally nuanced middle zone. The less structure and cohesion in the writing, the more impact the vibrations will have on the writer, and the less resilient he will therefore be.

People with this type of movement are better off in positions as number two, where their subtle vigilance is appreciated. They generally adapt quite well within the framework of a company, which they find reassuring, even if they are never quite for or quite against it. Research may suit them, also work in which they could stimulate ideas and activities. They like to be near young people.

Vibrant movement is often found in the writings of adolescents; it is frequently associated with the uneven stroke found in over 50% of sixth formers [11]. It suits the personality of boys better than that of girls; girls with this type of movement are searching for an identity with some uneasiness and show more inhibition than boys of the same age, who cope with this antagonism more easily.

Vibrant movement has the merit of giving a writing suppleness, often within a rather short rhythm, which allows the writer to bounce back and to carry on in "his own sweet way" with efficiency and modesty.

If the vibrations go so far as to make the writing look slightly feverish, and the irregularities and alternations are not smoothly integrated, then the movement can be described as EFFERVESCENT

Emotivity is stronger and less well channelled. These writings are often larger: the vibrations are amplified, reactions at all levels are strong, out of proportion to whatever caused them, and often unpredictable.

Man, 55 years - Work notes, scientific training

122 *Small writing, vibrant and light, with frequent irregularity in all categories: right-tending, with suspensions, width and narrowness, straightening-up movements, small angles and irregularly firm lower extensions. The weight on the line is medium, the spaces are wide between words and lines, the forms are simple and sober.*
Exteriorisation is discreet, the thought subtle, intuitive, future-oriented.

Woman, 40 years - Secretary

123 *Animated writing, large, well-nourished, with flying strokes; a little effervescent, connected.*

Intelligent, active and lively, the writer wants to study music and become an impresario. She has potential and a definite need to expand.

Woman, 30 years - Literary training

124

The effervescense of the movement, the tension of the stroke, the considerable overall unevenness have the effect of amplifying one another and give an irregular, insufficient degree of emotive control as soon as feelings become involved. The writing is large, with some tangling lines, the accents are strong, the lines are sometimes rising, sometimes convex and sometimes sinuous. Liveliness, vitality, some excitement. The writing seems to 'trample', seems impatient, dissatisfied and imperious.

How the writer will adapt to, or fit in with professional life is not clear. Such writers wish to be independent, but at the same time are dependent on the environment. They are active, yet poorly organised, quickly motivated into doing one thing or its opposite, both more or less at the same time. They are lively, often somewhat excited, or they are anxious and do not easily find answers to their incessant questions, and are not very satisfied either with themselves or with others.

Also, this movement is rather uneconomical in terms of progress and efficiency.

ANIMATED writing could be placed in between vibrant and effervescent writing. It is very animated and mobile. The irregularities are numerous, but do not interrupt its course. It is lively, although a bit too much so. Its overall degree of sobriety and discretion will lead to interpretations commensurate with those given for the other two movements whose characteristics it shares.

OBSTRUCTED MOVEMENT
REARED MOVEMENT

In writing with OBSTRUCTED movement, the progression of the graphic gesture is impeded as if by the presence of an obstacle. The writer appears to go forward "against the current" and most of his energy is mobilised in this confrontation. Inhibition is fought against.

Intensity and constraint are in a contradictory relationship and produce a clashing writing, often narrow and dense. In addition to the overall tension, this impression of resistance, yet assertiveness, is given by the emphasis on vertical movements, which are frequently prolonged, and by the adoption of a definite and fairly rigid direction.

The writer is self-motivated (apart from cases where the writing is both obstructed and devitalised). He has a constant need to triumph over his defences, a liking for opiniated effort and the idea of a challenge in relation to himself (there is conviction, an inner need for success, so as not to be submerged by his inner confrontations). He gets deeply involved and takes on responsibilities. Initiatives are taken decisively, and sometimes too boldly; far from trying to please, his reactions are expressed forcefully and sometimes abruptly so.

These insistent vertical gestures, although symbolic of rather forced assertiveness, are also symbolic of separation, choice, of an attitude which is "against" rather than "for". They are also a way of distancing oneself from inner factors which are felt as being too influential.

If obstructed movement is often met with among people whom one describes as 'fighters', because they are not put off by difficult tasks and want to win, it also indicates that contacts with other people can be a trifle rough, which must be taken into account when considering team-work, for instance. Relationships are neither supple nor always well-adapted. Writers with obstructed movement are touchy, sometimes imperious, arousing feelings of support or rejection, sometimes both at once, but never indifference. They are tenacious and convincing, for they are affective types. They are not generally afraid of responsibilities.

Having a mind of their own, with strong convictions, they do not easily share other people's point of view. It is therefore of the utmost importance that they should have good powers of judgement.

It is necessary to pay particular attention to homogeneity, proportions, and spacing between lines. On the whole, the layout will have to be fairly classical; since obstructed movement introduces stiffness, the layout, in order to compensate, will need to bring in positive elements through a rhythm of distribution indicating successful social adjustment, and the possibility of cooperation in communal projects. Indeed, this strength of resistance, in order to be an element of success, needs to be adapted to what is at stake and to the human factor.

Rhythm is strong in the obstructed movement; it is contrasted, strongly articulated and sometimes imperious.

Man, 50 years

125

Quite a large obstructed writing, with strong pressure, precise, connected, enlarging, with narrow garlands and angular arcades, prolongations, superelevations, scrollings, right-slanted, and orderly. Structured forms whose narrowness and vertical elongation betray inner strife as well as solidity. Intensity which might not be able to find an outlet in this stiff movement. But, numerous signs of self-assertion, tenacity, pride and even savoir-faire. One can perceive stable goals in this regularly right-slanted writing. All these elements lead the graphologist to conclude that this type of clash between a form and a movement that are equally strong, as well as a little unpolished, eventually results in successful activity. Communication is always dictatorial. Rhythm of movement marks the writing. There is also a personal rhythm of distribution.

J'ai été particulièrement sensible à votre message qui nous a profondément touché tant par ses mots de réconfort que par son contenu de chaleur personn.

REARED movement is a variant of obstructed movement. It indicates mistrust, an attitude of rejecting things altogether and at the same time more deeply felt claims. The dominance of constraint is greater here. Signs of defence appear very clearly in the left slant in particular, but equally in the form, the narrowness and the restrained gestures. Progressiveness is very much held back. Rhythm of movement is rare if the reared movement is very dominant (it can also be associated with other types of movement)

The graphologist should look for compensatory signs in the continuity, in the absence of left tendencies and in the stroke; the latter in particular gives life to the graphic trail.

Sobriety lends this writing a certain quality.

This type of movement is also found during adolescence; the subject has a difficult character, but is generally motivated.

*justifications. Je me permets de vous rappeler que c
conforme aux dispositions et à l'esprit du Droit du tr
J'espère que vous aurez à coeur de vous acquitter l
à mon égard - Je vous joins non arrêté de compt au
Veuillez agréer, Monsieur, l'expression de mes cl*

Man, 32 years

A man "enslaved" by his numerous diplomas which he constantly and clumsily displays in order to protect and reassure himself.

Reared movement, constrained writing, thin[15], narrow with arcades, superelevated capitals, vertical to left-slanted, with strong punctuation, sharp-pointed, reversed letters, descending, squeezed between words.

126

Aggressiveness, a low threshold of frustration in relation to his pride and what he feels are his rights, stiffness; a kind of haughtiness, based on an inner embitterred dissatisfaction, but well-sustained activity (the writing is connected, combined, with a few, rather dynamic juxtapositions) and an ethical sense. There is sobriety in the form (restrained owing to the superelevations) and the uneven stroke, slightly spasmodic, is not dry.

---

15 In Müller and Enskat's sense [88].

5

CONTINUITY

Continuity deals with penlifts and the way in which letters are joined to one another as a handwriting moves across the page. It is this movement which makes it possible to guide the writing towards the right of the page in our writing models, the direction of which is from left to right.

In France, the prescribed model of cursive movement results in producing connected writing, as the penlifts, if any, leave no space between letters.

These possible penlifts are taught in various ways, according to different methods and teachers. A good method is one which recommends lifting the pen before the letters *a, d, g* and *q* which can thus be started from the right, which avoids covering strokes and dissociations. These penlifts are good and logical breaks, as are those needed for adding dots and accents.

Joining letters is difficult for children to manage, and the main signs of continuity[1] are not suitable for defining their writing. They use means which are within their grapho-motor ability and, while trying to keep their letters correctly joined, they attempt to conceal their penlifts by attaching their letters one to another with what are called false connections, or stuck-on connections [8].

Finding one's own connections is an important graphic and psychic act of autonomy, and a good number of the characteristics listed in evolved writings[2] are related to continuity.

---

1 Continuity is sometimes presented under two aspects: the form of connection on the one hand and the degree of connection on the other. The forms of connection being, in fact, forms of handwriting, have been dealt with in the chapter on Form. By degree of connection, we mean the number of graphic signs which are joined together, that is, connected, disconnected, grouped or overconnected.

2 See chapter on Organisation.

Words initially taught as being connected from beginning to end, cannot ultimatly remain like this; each person has to find how to articulate his or her words, the right place for breaks, and how to manage connections. Klages [23] says that no human activity continues in an uninterrupted flow.

One can appreciate just how much continuity matters when one sees the number of signs that Crépieux-Jamin has classified in this category (starting with organised and disorganised writings), and the importance of some of them, regarding the main aspects of handwriting. Indeed, one finds among them, for instance, homogeneous, stable, nuancée and rhythmic, as well as discordant, monotonous and inhibited writings.

Here we shall not deal with all these signs, as, for us, some belong to other categories - e.g. homogeneous, proteiform - and others belong to all the categories - e.g. regular or irregular. We have attempted to stress the importance of signs such as inhibited or rhythmic and to show this throughout the study of movement. Other signs, finally, such as trembling, dotted or senile writings, have not seemed to us worth mentioning in a teaching manual of modern graphology, although, as far as the last one is concerned, one does notice the difficulties of the elderly in maintaining that connectedness and cursive movement which were once so hard to acquire on first learning to write[3].

Continuity must be given its place as part of the whole graphic movement. It is a determining factor in the handling and tension of the stroke, the style of movement, the distribution of words in the context of space and rhythm.

Does continuity in a writing help the graphic path from the I to the You, that intentional act towards an aim as mentioned by Pulver (24), or not? and if so, in what way?

We shall study in succession :
- the classical degrees of connection : connected, disconnected, grouped and overconnected writings;

---

3   See Chapter on Organisation.

- writing with secondary connections; combined writing;
- irregular connections; nuancée writing; hopping writing;
- signs describing difficulties in mastering connections, or describing
  peculiarities in the linking of letters to one another :
  fragmented, with dissociated letters,
  with false connections,
  jerky, telescopic, suspended, unfinished, or with gaps,
  amended, supported, with covering strokes, or with shark's teeth.

1. *Degrees of connection*

CONNECTED

In CONNECTED writing, the graphic thread is continuous - or nearly so - for the whole length of the word: there is a minimum of penlifts. A writing is called connected when the desire not to interrupt words is dominant, even if a stop occurs for adding a dot or an accent.

Connected writing is what is taught and the writer can remain attached to the model owing to a lack of real graphic mastery. But when lack of skill cannot be blamed and the writing remains connected in a copy-book manner, it may be due to conformism.

However, connectedness may be achieved voluntarily and personalised for reasons of efficiency : it is then an important sign of autonomy and development. A connected, supple, rapid writing which is progressive in its course, is generally a sign of activity and, on the intellectual level, a sign of dynamic thinking which is conducted intelligently and thoroughly. With good spacing between words and lines, it shows a mind capable of embracing things as a whole.

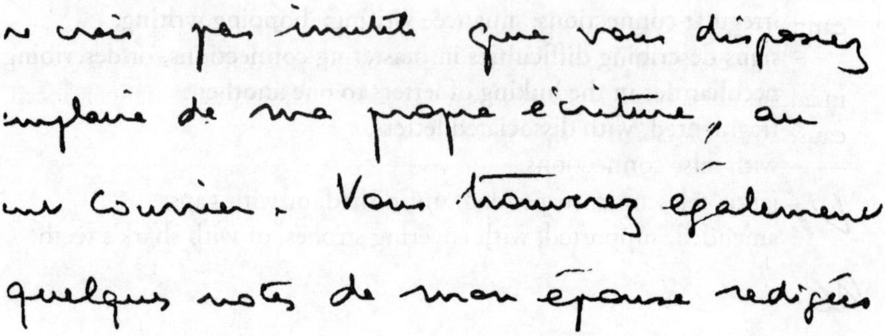

[handwritten French text]

Man, 50 years - Responsible post in industry
Small and connected writing, dynamic with occasional penlifts, progressive,
firm, wide, with a few jerks and occasional restraint.
Ability to synthesise (good spacing), intuition (general liveliness and receptivity),
an outlook turned towards the future (synthesis, intuition and activity, all
associated to changes in direction which "sweep" across a wide field, but with
127   *attention to detail, in a very positive layout).*
A demanding and authoritarian character, with a developed and reactive
critical sense. This sample illustrates an evolved, connected writing, and
brings together many signs of dynamism. It will be found again in the chapter
on Direction and the one on Space (nos. 157 and 197).

Connectedness gives cohesion to words and strength to a writing, thus introducing a notion of cohesion in the writer's identity, and the ability to resist being easily influenced, or deterred. Connected writing is a sign of stability in one's aims, of tenacity and loyalty.

A slightly pronounced degree of connectedness strengthens a writing which has a fragile structure or stroke and suggests that the writer will use his potential well. His personality will be firmer, better defined and more responsible.

A high degree of connectedness is liable to cause tension and monotony. It is desirable then that the context should be alleviated by some differentiated pressure, aerated by spaces and nuanced by small irregularities and a slightly supple baseline. Rigidity of form, regressive movements - looped or double-joined, for instance - overload or stiffen the graphic thread which is already too controlled, and retard its course : the writing can become heavy, not very mobile, and closed.

Connectedness which facilitates cohesion of identity, is a positive sign in adolescence, but if it is excessive and occurs in a stiff, tense manner, it can cause some blockage.

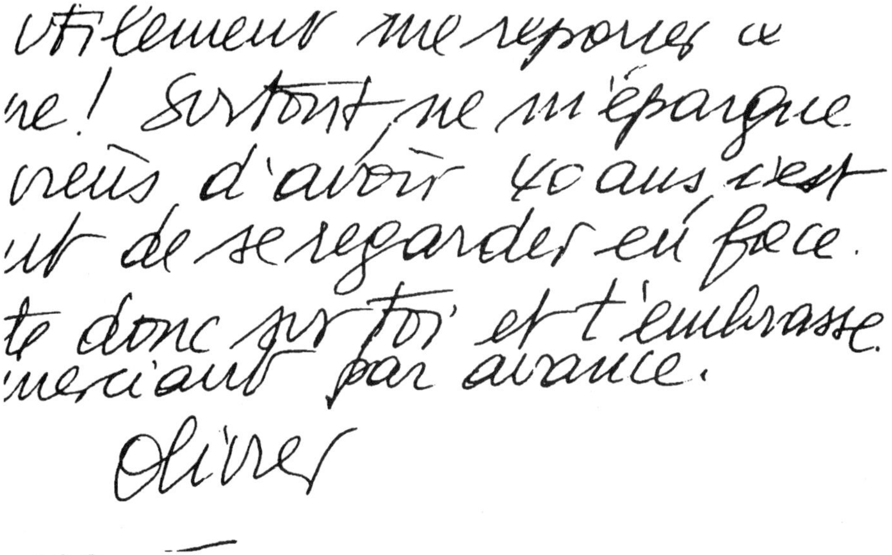

[handwritten text in French]

128 **Man, 40 years** - *Very active and productive progression in a large, very connected, precise, double-joined and narrow writing which leaves litte space between words and lines. The signature, very close to the text, confirms a way of participating which is tense and stimulating in a professional environment, but sometimes oppressive and possessive among people close to him.*

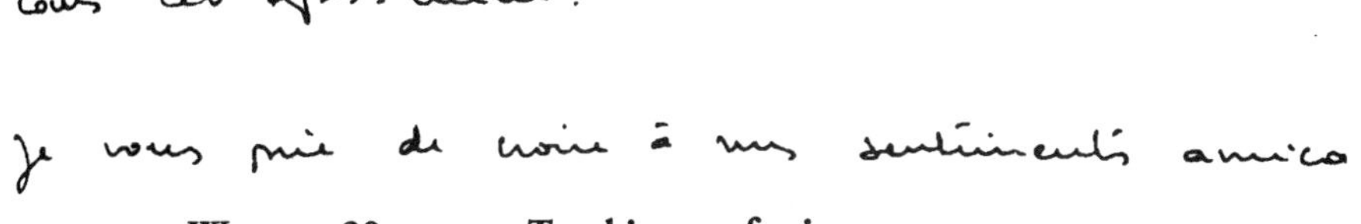

[handwritten text]

[handwritten text]

129 **Woman, 30 years** - **Teaching profession**
Connectedness here strengthens a very small, slightly crushed writing, very spaced out between lines, and with light pressure.

DISCONNECTED (JUXTAPOSED)

A writing is disconnected when the letters are separated within the words.

The graphic method of the writer using this degree of connectedness is fundamentally different, with regard to the taught model, from that of someone with connected writing or even with grouped writing.

In small children, disconnectedness, in the vast majority of cases, is due to graphic inability to connect [44]. At the post-copybook stage, some children (more girls than boys) transform their writing into a more or less skilful script, mixed with cursive writing and, consequently, separate their letters. It seems that this disconnectedness may only be the side-effect of persistence in the choice of form : the form they have learnt seems childish to them, whereas the one in books appears more beautiful and enables them, while retaining legibility, to imagine that they are becoming adults. But, largely unconsciously, this style seems more neutral to them, and is a way of distancing themselves as much from their own problems as from those of the people around them.

Je suis très bien amisée. Je est

130 **Girl, at 9 years**

Petit poisson deviendra grand) pour·

at 12 years

Some soon abandon this disconnected form, others keep to it, or adopt a more classical disconnectedness, mostly clumsy, and leading to an uneven distribution of space. It is disconnectedness based on inhibition in most cases, clearly indicating the changes in this age group, its anxious vigilance, that state of uneasy expectation in which adolescents feel "deprived of what they were and not yet equipped for what they will become" [45].

Successful connectedness is not frequent in adolescence; it is a sign of autonomy.

If this type of connection is generally not detrimental to the purpose of writing, if the letters follow one another giving the impression that they prepare the connection with the next letter, leading to good distribution of the graphic groupings, then the juxtaposition is dynamic [46]. Both behaviour and thought then are free, open, often inventive. Sensitivity, intuition (rapid reactions generally) can be expressed if the stroke is rapid and receptive, the forms simple and subtle and the proportions nuanced.

As soon as constraint or inhibition, conformity or defensiveness appear, the picture is no longer the same, as letters follow one another without a traceable link between them; disconnectedness then is static [46]. Nervous impulses, currents, life no longer flow freely; the breaks are ruptures and have a braking effect.

Stiffness often goes with disconnectedness. Whereas the kind of control implied by breaks can indicate reserve, if the writing becomes frozen, such control becomes a defence which isolates. If the forms are angular, stiffness is accentuated; if they are round, the contradiction leaves the subject disappointed and frustrated. In both cases there is inhibition.

We then no longer speak of intuition (which, in any case, can be found with all degrees of connection), nor even of an analytical mind with the positive meaning of intellectual curiosity : for this, there must be signs of concentration, of precision, of clarity of form and a stroke with precise edges, in a generally well-distributed text.

The adaptation of people with disconnected writing is subject to certain conditions. Those who write with dynamic disconnectedness need independence at all levels, opportunities and renewal of their interests. The others do not easily fit in; their anxiety is a brake on communication, and the fragility which this form of expression often entails [47], affects, according to the context, their autonomy, initiative and ability to adapt to changes.

Worth mentioning is the break after the first letter of a word in a writing which is grouped, or even connected. In this, Michon saw the thinker's pause.

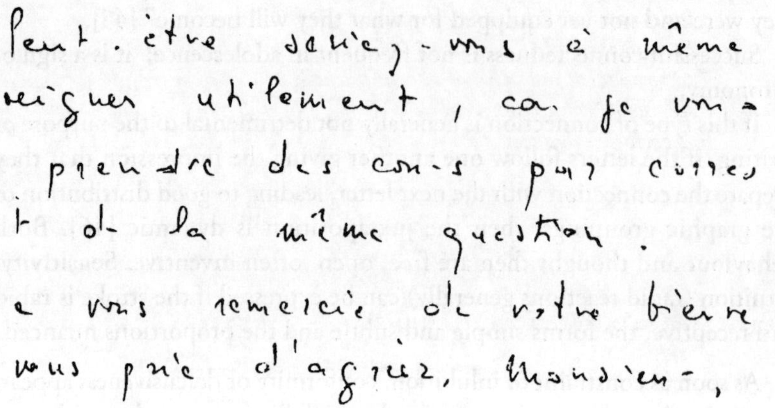

[handwritten letter in French]

Peut-être serez-vous à même
veiguer utilement, car je vais
prendre des cours par cores
+ de la même question.

e vous remercie de votre bière
vous prie d'agréer, Monsieur,

131 **Woman, 40 years** - *Small, lively, fine touches, dynamic disconnectedness. Sensitivity, openness, intuition, receptiveness of mind, but few inner certainties: the spaces are large, the baseline sinuous, the direction oscillates around the vertical, the movement is vibrant.*

[handwritten letter in French]

Mon Bernard Hatler,

Votre spectacle entre aujourd'hui
dans son quatrième mois : nous y pensons
et prenons plaisir à vous lire d'où
nous sommes, loin de vous.

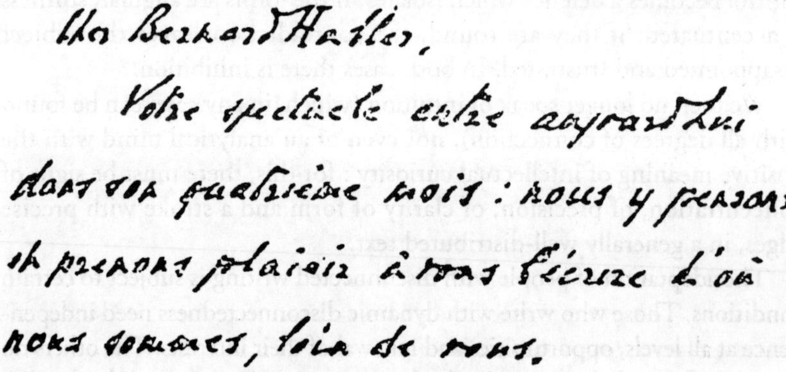

132 **Pierre Fresnay[4] in 1971**
The controlled movement, a little restrained and obstructed, as well as the

---

4   A   famous French actor.   (T.N.)

disconnectedness, control and interiorize the strong emotions in the name of independence, ethics and dignity. Forms are narrow, simple and sober. Spacing is reduced, direction is a little rigid. Here the disconnectedness seems to be adopted in order not to be influenced by the inner tension (as one can see, some connections escape control, others create combinations). It is nevertheless dynamic.

du possible . Actuellement J'ai
qu' il Faut que Je change beau
dans ma manière de vivre pou

Man, 22 years - Male nurse

Large writing with strong pressure, constrained and reared, clubbed, with typographic and left-slanted arcades. Defensive reticence (one can also see the enlarging finals). Spacing is irregular with this cursive movement which does not flow. Lines are a little convex. Character and judgement are excessive. Desire for an independence which is not used in the right way (fluctuating and stiff left margin, uncertain 'J's). Control, presence, pride in his profession facilitate stable contacts which make him feel secure in the practice of his profession. They are more difficult elsewhere.
Static disconnectednes.

133

GROUPED

In GROUPED writing, continuity of words is created by groups of letters, that is to say with a certain number of penlifts. Words are cut into two or three small units or more, according to their length and according to what - unconsciously - motivates the writer to make the breaks.

Some people base their groupings around the diacritics, lifting their pen to make a dot or an accent, or after the t-bar. Others break the words according to the letters they contain, depending on whether their shapes make a grouping easy or not. Yet others simply aerate words in accordance with their personal tempo, which is dictated by reflection, or by a more innate reflex which closely corresponds to their vital rhythm.

There is a rationale in groupings. Some logic has guided them when they are successful, i.e. when they facilitate the articulation of words, which in turn helps good distribution of words and spaces. It is then that one can talk of adaptability, suppleness, ability to vary one's field of activities, behaviour and intelligence.

Groupings cause less tension in the handling of the graphic line than does connectedness, and they indicate less uncertainty - even inhibition, or need for artificial construction - than disconnected writing. They involve interpretive elements less directly than the other two degrees of connection, and their interest lies more in a supple, balanced and mobile continuity, allowing harmonious functioning of the other signs.

Woman, 32 years

A writing grouped in a personal and fairly supple way, sometimes around diacritics, sometimes in a seemingly less logical manner; a few disconnections almost causing lapses of continuity. The writing remains free in its progression, and there is rhythm.

134

On the surface, adaptation is good, but the will is still present, and here the writer keeps her distance: the slim stroke is firmly handled, 'm's and 'n's have angular arcades and garlands, the finals are short. some letters are suspended or straightened up. The slightly rising lines, show some forcing, but also life goals which are not aways very realistic (the double 'l' and the 't's do not reach the baseline). Spaces at the beginning of lines are not regular.

précieux comme référence –
u entendu expliqué que je
connaissais pas personnellement

j'ai essayé de vous
trouver le maximum de
documents.

Woman, 40 years - *Groupings and lapses of continuity break up the words
in a rather disconcerting manner, the signature is on two levels, the Christian
name is very crushed, the family name is in capital letters. More logical*

135 *connections would have brought some cohesion. Dancing words, lower
extensions which do not rejoin the middle zone and are very narrow. Poor
rhythm. Constrained movement, slack and a little obstructed. Wavy and tile-
like lines.*

It will therefore be necessary to judge their quality; good graphic fluency takes a long time to acquire : in adolescence and among people who do not write often, one finds groupings of varying quality more often than harmonious groupings. This is because they are caused merely by a break in the cursive movement.

The term "grouped", which corresponds to a medium degree of connectedness, is often found in the definitions of handwritings. It does not however, always describe successful continuity, and often covers a rather "mongrel" connectedness, either because the breaks do not correspond to any logic, in which case they do not signify suppleness or adaptability, or simply because the writing is more or less successfully connected with a few groupings, or grouped with a few disconnected letters.

OVERCONNECTED

136 **Man, 35 years** - *Overconnected writing, resolute and restrained, precise and sharp-pointed, narrow, prolonged up and down, angular and reaching the baseline with angles, with short, stiff starting strokes, strong diacritics.*

A professor of "Mathématiques Spéciales"[5] , admired by his students for his rigorousness and his clear and powerful demonstrations, but feared for his demanding standards and the intransigence of his character. Strong ethical sense, very selective communication. His very structured and very logical reasoning sometimes gives way to a tendency to paradox when he is not dealing with professional matters.

Boy, 17 years - Upper sixth

137

Very intelligent, but blocked at the moment. Overconnected writing. The stroke is precise, the movement a little effervescent, the right margin large. The loopings, the double-joins, the combinations starting from the diacritics, reinforce the connectedness further and "tie up" the writing to its own stystem. Communication is very difficult.

The desire not to cut words is dominant in connected writing, but excessive in OVERCONNECTED writing. This is, in a way, a caricature of

5   First year of mathemathical higher education in France and leading to possible entry into 'Les Grandes Écoles'. (T.N.)

stiff, connected writing. It involves no interruptions at all within a word, and sometimes even joins certain words in a sentence by linking the final of one word to the start of the next word; or, again, by throwing a bridge (usually by means of a free sign) from somewhere in one word, to the word that follows.

Behind overconnectedness lie strong guiding ideas which have repercussions on behaviour and in the intellectual sphere.

When very marked and reinforced by tension and compactness, the will to attain one's goal and persevere reaches the point of obstinacy and stubbornness. Attachments are intense, with strong likes and dislikes, and risk being dogmatic. The possibly brilliant aspect of hyperconnected ideas should not blind the graphologist to the tendency to lose contact with reality; reasoning could then become sophistry and paradox.

Interpretations will have to vary sensitively, according to the relative suppleness or relative openness which can be displayed by the stroke, the layout and the forms.

One should also be acquainted with the graphic habits of some countries; some foreign writings, English ones in particular, teach over-connectedness in their cursive writings [48, 49].

SECONDARY CONNECTIONS

In secondary connections, the linking gesture is voluntarily stretched towards the right, and, the space thus left between letters is generally greater than the horizontal dimensions of the letters themselves[6]. This widens the writing, making it look rather unspontaneous, taking into account the fact that this type of connection often goes together with reinforced or deviated pressure which arises from the same control, even from the same forcing.

The space which could exist there, is cancelled out; the opportunity for lightening the stroke, for supple articulation of words, is rejected, as if there were a danger or a feeling of weakness in letting things happen, in taking a rest, or in adapting to whatever is coming.

6   See Chapter on Dimension : primary and secondary widths.

The subject seems to have programmed his responses in advance; an ethical standpoint, a courageous will, draw him on in spite of possible mistrust of others, or of events.

Secondary connections frequently create a rigid baseline.

Ethics or principles can be linked to a sense of duty and morality, or they can also be linked to social conventions.

Writing no. 110 in the chapter on Movement can be studied from the point of view of secondary connections, as can also writing no. 9 in the chapter on Pressure.

COMBINED

For Crépieux-Jamin, COMBINED writing represents the highest degree of his first guiding synthesis : organised writing.

A writing is combined when its more or less connected and simplified forms are well arranged. This definition by Crépieux-Jamin [50], more than any other perhaps, highlights the notion of synthesis inherent in the writing gesture; it includes all the categories ("it must have a supple and nuanced movement"), and allows a multitude of formulas, provided the different elements of the writing are found to be in harmony with one another.

The quality of the combinations will therefore need to be examined : "more than the extent of the connections" one looks for "the richness of the associations of movement", "the choice and aptness of the connections, abbreviations and simplifications". It is this quality which gives combined writing its significance in terms of general level, and it seems that graphologists may have distorted Crépieux-Jamin's point of view a little when they see only the positive aspects of this sign, neglecting the restrictions which he himself pointed out (it can be "degraded by various disorders", "clumsy combinations can only point to the writer's lack of intelligence and, if they are ridiculous, his lack of balance").

Combined writing was indeed - and often still is - considered as the main sign of intelligence and culture. Yet we know, and find more and more often, that simpler arrangements than those of combined writing can be signs of a form of intelligence well adapted to present-day techniques and demands for efficiency (see writing nos. 109 and 197).

Combined writing is the one which departs most from the taught model
as far as connections are concerned. Letters are joined to one another with
all sorts of personal links, articulations and contractions, which play with
letters and forms and between them, at times even joining a word to the
next one; accents and t-bars are good opportunities for economy of movement and for progressiveness, but they can also be a pretext for complications and even for monotony when, for instance, all i-dots are systematically
connected to the following letter with a line always having the same slant.

Woman, 27 years - *The very numerous combinations rather complicate
the writing and make it a little obscure in spite of the rich, creative
intelligence. Everything is a pretext for combinations. One finds head to foot
connections (accents bending towards their letters), foot to head connections
('b' of "oublié" towards the 'l', or 'o' towards the 't' of "bientôt"). One also finds
the two forms of lower extensions combined with the next letter : tong-shaped
in "telephone" (activity, efficiency, critical sense), and bowl-shaped in
"pardonner" (productive intuition). These sorts of lower extensions are right-
tending gestures[7], but one can observe here that the 'f' of "faire" and the 'p' of
"pardonner" are identical, which does not make reading easy, also that there
are numerous reverse letters ('b's, 'o's and some 'a's), and that many words are
unfinished. All this in a very rapid context.*

138

7   See chapter on Form.

The quality of the combinations should be assessed according to the improvement brought about in the suppleness and rhythm of the progression.

We can talk of suppleness of mind, inventive abilities, original associations of ideas, of independence, 'savoir-faire' and ingenuity, if the rest of the writing points to this.

If one tends to be cautious when looking at a writing which has become combined too early, it is because one needs to be wary of the tricks of facileness, of elusiveness, and because, more than graphic progression, one can see in it total inability to produce the copybook model, in most cases.

A writing must be decipherable, otherwise it loses its very purpose. If the merit of combined writing "lies in its strangeness" [50], this may be an element of creativity, but communication is doubtful; individualism, even impenetrability, are apparent.

In adolescence it runs the risk of shutting up the writer into his own world (see writing no.137).

139 **Man, 45 years** - *Numerous combinations, personal forms and dimensions, words close to and joined to one another, looped garlands and small loops. The writer's point of view - which he imposes with charm and skill, but also with tenacity - is intelligent, subtle, and does no harm to his numerous interests.*

In the same way as the quality of the connections in Combined writing is a *sine qua non* for that sign to have all its positive meanings, good connections are also those in which, if they are well mastered, the elements of the wrting are successfully interrelated. None of the three classical degrees of connectedness has any value in itself; each one may, or may not, show a good relationship with the rest of the writing, and may, or may not, be positive, helping the easy progression of words with good alternation of intervals.

IRREGULAR CONTINUITY
NUANCED
HOPPING

Like other irregularities, IRREGULAR CONTINUITY can enrich or weaken a writing. Two signs are positive in this respect : Nuancée writing and Hopping writing.

NUANCED writing is characterised by a script which is lightly uneven in all categories, but remains regular in its overall movement; it reflects a qualitative sensitivity and a capacity to experience numerous and controlled emotions, greater than that of uneven writing, and even more so than that of very irregular writing[8].

HOPPING writing is the writing of people who manage their connections quickly and in a varied way, ready to respond to the demands of the environment. The graphic line is lively, the rhythm of thought and action rapid, but such writers, rather than dominating the rhythm, are led by it. Structure of forms and weight on the baseline are generally average, pressure is most often light, direction not very fixed and accents rapidly filled in.

This type of connection often indicates intuition.

---

8   See Chapter on Dimension : Regularity, Unevenness and Irregularity.

Irregularities of continuity play a more active role than irregularities in some other categories, if one thinks of the relationship of continuity to the guiding syntheses of homogeneity and organisation, and if one assesses their influence on the basic graphic gesture.

Adolescencefavours irregularities of continuity; they go hand in hand with all that is represented by the questioning and the doubts one has at that age. It is also because, at that time, the graphic movement is often not fully controlled. But irregularities belonging to that period are rarely rhythmic, unlike those of nuancée and even hopping writings (examples of these two types of irregularities can be seen in writing nos. 122 and 246).

2. *Difficulties and peculiarities of connection*

FRAGMENTED
DISSOCIATED LETTERS

In FRAGMENTED writing, discontinuity applies to letters themselves. It is the extreme degree of disconnectedness, since letters are not just separated but divided into fragments.

We must note whether these cuts appear occasionally in some letters or if the text is mostly (or entirely) fragmented. In the latter case, it would indicate very great hesitation and, more likely, considerable inhibition, the strength of which will be lessened if only a few letters are divided.

Dividing letters can also be a means of devising one's own writing.

The writing as a whole will enable us to distinguish the particular inhibition which is likely to fragment a writing, from the choice of an assumed, or acquired writing which, even though resulting from a constraint, can, however, be well integrated.

Woman, 46 years - Signature similar to text
This seems precisely the sort of disjunction which Klages [23] referred to as one of the signs of acquired writing, which he considered as a means of representation deriving from self-control.

140

The writer has gone through tough ordeals and shows only a happy, cheerful, athletic and active side of her character, which can be deduced from the liveliness of the whole script, from the 'j', 'm's and 'n's. She writes very fast. She has "moulded" herself into this second nature. The spaces are very large, but fairly lively.

It is more usual to come across cursive writings, some letters of which are made up of two parts when they could be made with no penlift; we then talk of DISSOCIATED LETTERS.

These dissociations often occur on round letters (*a,d,g,q*), but can also affect other ones, *m*'s, *n*'s and *p*'s in particular.

This is due to a lack of graphic freedom[9], manifested in a particular way which, if the context confirms it, points to emotional vulnerability; these dissociations are left-overs from childhood.

9   See Chapter on Organisation.

Children quickly get over this clumsiness, especially the *a* in two bits[10]: only 30% of children aged 9 make an *a* like that.

The choice of dissociated letters is not due to mere chance; it is most often round letters, the affective letters, which are made this way, and also *m*'s - very symbolically loaded[11] - and *p*'s which lend themselves to assertiveness, since they can be drawn with no penlift and with vertical pressure.

FALSE CONNECTIONS

False connections correspond to the movement made by children when they lift their pen between two letters going in the same direction, and correct themselves with yet another start. The term "soldering" which Ajuriaguerra gives to children's false connections is evocative, as the joining point between the two parts of the graphic thread can be seen clearly; this joining may be executed with a variable amount of skill, according to the control of movement and the attention given to precision. The term "false connections" is suggestive also, for it indicates the reiteration, the determination not to interrupt a movement which - for some reason or other - one thinks must continue.

As seen, clumsiness is obvious in children incapable of linking those letters which lend themselves to joining. It is all the more so in adolescents or adults, who should have found a simpler and more economical way of solving the connection problem[12].

In writing with FALSE CONNECTIONS, the gesture is tense, the defences, in the broad sense of the term, are badly managed and do not facilitate adaptation. As a result, the rhythm is broken and chopped up.

There is anxious fear, lack of confidence in one's own potential, difficulties in taking action, in entering into relationships, in pursuing one's plans and, at the same time - unless the graphic context is weak and shows

---

10 Item F8. Ajuriaguerra's Children's Scale [8].
11 See Chapter on Form.
12 See Chapter on Organisation, writing no. 234.

that one gives up easily - it indicates the effort made not to give up. Both fear and effort are present, based on scruples, especially when the false connection is well made, or done by means of a letter requiring a diacritic.

- le resultat . J'ai 16 ans et demi bien -
j'ecris il neige. J'aime assez car lors-
il ya un risque à sortir, on prefere
t la télé. Ca me degoute. l'horloge sonne,
ruf de temps pour ecrire . Je comble en
vais je ne sais plus quoi dire . Euo
retrouverais dans cette etude .

141 **Boy, 16 and a half years - Lower 6th**
Despite the false connections (and the jerks and telescoping) of the words which dance on the line, the writing progresses in a lively and astute manner towards the right, notwithstanding the clumsiness.

JERKY
TELESCOPED

JERKY writing is one where the letters are connected to each other with a tense, badly-controlled and clashing movement.

The stroke, abruptly handled, advances in jerks. Angles, arising from clumsiness or stiffening, take precedence over curves and the dimensions, badly controlled on the whole, are particularly irregular in the connections between letters. Besides, it very often happens that the writer, in his attempts to control this unchecked movement, reduces his pulling towards the right, always in a clashing way. Letters or parts of them, which then suddenly get compressed into one another, are called TELESCOPED[13].

This is what children do, due to their graphomotor clumsiness. Those who write well, in relation to their age, have had no problems in integrating that cursive movement which, in linking letters to one another, helps the writing to progress towards the right. If one imitates this jerky movement, one can understand the influence of continuity on movement and, by extension, on the distribution of words in space; if one cannot control the spacing between letters, there will follow a reperscussion on the spacing between words.

By direct analogy, the interpretation of jerky writing points to bad harmonization of impulses and their realisation. The inner tension causing jerks results from great emotivity and the efforts made to control it, because it is probably felt as potential vulnerability. The writer feels everything intensely, is never indifferent, and easily becomes touchy. His reactions, however, are not always the same, as the amount and the level of control can vary greatly.

Generally speaking, adaptation is not very easy. Self-expression, rhythm of action, even judgements, are not well adapted to situations, if the writing is very jerky. Indeed, jerks can appear momentarily in people who are basically nervous, especially if they are tired, or if an event has been felt particularly strongly. One can also come across jerkiness in disease and old age.

---

13 Letters which are telescoped owing to bad control of progression, must not be confused with letters which mingle because of inhibition owing to lack of rightward expansion. The Italian authors of the Morettian school call the latter 'adossata' letters [25]. See writing no. 111.

Woman, 65 years - Spinster

This very taut, jerky, angular, thrown writing unevenly spaced, with strong pressure, is progressive even though it is badly controlled in its movement (propulsive with flying strokes). The initial and the final in the signature, which is close to the text, are particularly tense and abrupt.

142

Intelligent and lively, but with a difficult character, the writer was unable to remain in any of the various groups in which she worked. In spite of the lined paper, the lines have both rising and descending tiles.

Slightly jerky and telescopic writings are not uncommon in adolescence. This arises from a principle similar to that which causes alternate width and narrowness[14], affecting the distribution of space. In this age group, one also

14 See Chapter on Dimension.

sees mingling letters : they are of particular interest in the word "*je*"[15], which reflect inhibition in getting down to things, or in committing oneself.

SUSPENDED
UNFINISHED
LAPSES OF CONTINUITY

A SUSPENDED writing is one which leaves part of the letter in suspension either within words or at the end : the letter does not join the baseline, or remains incomplete. The movement, whether vertical or horizontal, stops in its progression, creating a sort of gap in the letter.

A retraction, an interruption occurs. Such things may be caused by mere shyness or by a stronger inhibition. They may be more or less intentional, and have an effect on actions, on exchanges, or on both. This, in particular, applies to *t*'s which do not reach the baseline, when found in a graphic context which is not very active or realistic; such *t*'s indicate that the writer finds it difficult to achieve and to commit himself consistently (the baseline, the line of reality, loses some of its density because of this). At the end of words, suspensions have more to do with exchanges. Writers who make lots of suspensions can be baffling; they stop and look as if they had taken back the trust they had given, suddenly keeping something quiet. Spontaneity is reduced.

If suspensions cannot be classified among regressive gestures, they cannot be classified among progressive ones either, and they are often associated with signs of restraint such as looping, t-bars at the back of the stem and straightenings-up.

A writing may occasionally have one or two suspensions, it may also have lots of them, and interpretations will range from delicacy or modesty, to inhibition. In some rather unspontaneous contexts, they will range from prudence to mental restriction, or dissimulation.

---

15 "I" in French (T.N.)

Negligence does not come into it : a brake simply holds back the writer whose writing is suspended.

When the writing is UNIFINSHED, the graphic line is incomplete and, here, neglect is more likely. Word endings, letters or parts thereof are missing, or are very badly formed, accents are very incomplete, or some t-bars are left out. The writing speed must be considered; rapidity can, up to a point, account for some omissions or skipped bits. A critical examination will have to be carried out, taking into account the writer, the nature of the document (work notes, rapid messages) and the addressee. On the other hand, some professions oblige one to write fast and frequently. An uncultivated writing needs to be well finished, or else it lacks rigour; so must children's writings, for the same reason.

Some professions specially require the capacity to be precise, careful, punctual and meticulous for the sake of a particular technique for instance, and writers with unfinished writings will not be suitable, whereas they could be satisfactory in some other professions.

One should note however that casualness, indecision, elusiveness, agitation and escapism often assume these graphic characteristics.

In writings with LAPSES OF CONTINUITY, the spacing between letters is badly controlled; gaps appear in a rather anarchic, unpredictable way. Such accidents can occur in a grouped writing, making the gaps between the breaks irregular, or unexpectedly separating a letter from the others. They can also happen in disconnected writings, thus reducing the wholeness and cohesion of words.

In all cases we are dealing with more or less anxious thinking which causes interruptions and dissipates concentration, for shorter or longer periods, according to the general control and the rhythm of the script. The handwritings of emotive people are more subject than others to these sudden interruptions. In a creative context this may provide a channel, for a flash of intuition.

See writing no. 135 and also writing no. 106 which is less spontaneous and more homogeneous.

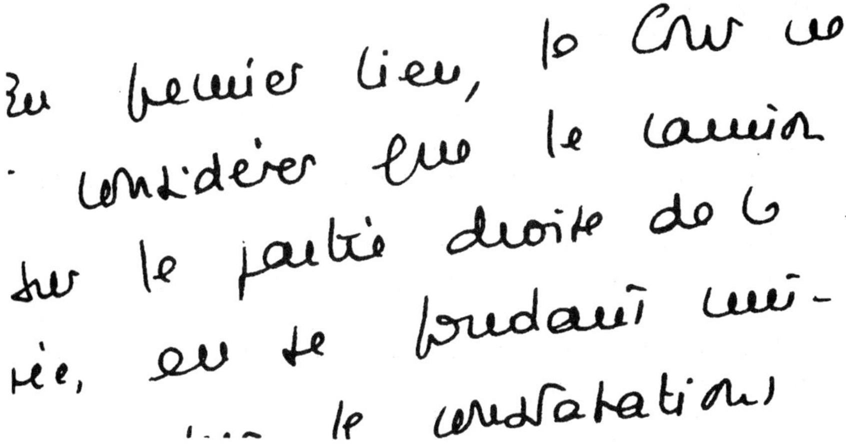

[handwritten French text]

Woman, 32 years
Numerous suspensions in the finals, the 'a' of the last word of the third line is unfinished (this is a work document about which we should be more tolerant).

Association of quite a lively basic movement with a large middle zone, a well-nourished stroke, slightly rising lines and some restrained movements (suspensions, loopings and straightenings-up) which cannot create harmonious spacing.

Professional life is managed with much greater freedom than emotional life. Control of emotions and feelings is uneven. The character is uncompromising, a little violent, with unexpected silences, refusal and implicit reproaches.

143

AMENDED
COVERING STROKES
SUPPORTED
SHARK' S TOOTH

In AMENDED writing, one alters what has just been written, stopping to rectify a letter, or part of a letter considered imperfect.

This breaks the course of a word or sentence and unnecessarily darkens the letter.

There is more to an amendment than just a break : there is regression towards the left. One does not find a free-flowing writing which is amended (we do not mean here corrections of spelling mistakes or even an odd addition to an extension which may be a bit narrow, for instance); amendments are signs of inhibition.

The degree of inhibition depends on the graphic context It ranges from an anxious professional conscience, scrupulous concern for precision, right up to excessive love of details at the expense of the essential, systematic fear of error, constant hesitation, obsession, or even repression.

---

144 **Man, 38 years** - *A very amended writing with very irregular spacing, as much between letters (juxtapositions, telescoping, lapses of continuity, a few groupings) as between words. Prolonged up, superelevated with a small, crushed, and plump, uneven middle zone. Inhibition.*

In amendments, the pen stops, sometimes causing those thick and heavy dots which indicate anxiety (of a much more paralysing than action-provoking kind). If, however, one stops only at the end of a sentence to add that sort of dot, the train of thought is less interrupted; getting down to things and expressing oneself are done with greater freedom than when the subject - as is the case with someone who amends lots of letters - keeps on going back on his own work, destroying it rather than improving it.

When the pen faithfully goes over what it has just written instead of letting the writing go towards the right, we no longer have amendments, but COVERING STROKES (see writing no.93).

145

This is a gesture of auto-surveillance, which slows the writing down by putting a brake on its progression. It can arise from strong control, from pronounced fear, from a weakness felt in one sphere or other and to which one does not want to give in, or even from a tendency to repress spontaneity, together with a tendency to ulterior motives (if other signs point in the same direction).

SUPPORTED writing is one in which connections go back along a stroke before going towards the right. It may be the remains of a Sacré-Coeur type of writing (rarer and rarer nowadays), or of German origin.

When it appears regularly in a script, its meanings are close to those of the covering stroke and reinforces them. This connection is based on angles and is thereby significant. It is significant also owing to the fact that it branches off in relation to its first direction.

Some graphologists detect a particular and rare form of support called SHARK'S TOOTH.

Its interpretation is negative. Pulver [24] sees in it the meaning of an avid and crafty character (the terms he uses are 'carnivorous' and 'cunning').

mes salutations distinguées.

h. Marguerite Cou.

146 Woman, 44 years
(Writing presented under no. 168 in Slow Writing)

Covering strokes, shark's tooth on the third downstroke of 'm' of "mes" and on 's' of "salutations". Double-joins, loops, stops.

6

FREE SIGNS

accents (diacritics), punctuation, t-bars
initials and final letters

The relative graphic freedom given to accents (diacritics), punctuation and t-bars, makes these signs interesting for graphologists to observe.

Free signs may indeed confirm the general meaning of a writing by reinforcing or balancing it, or perform various compensatory roles.

1. Accents and Punctuation

Although usually studied together, diacritics and punctuation differ in their aims. A diacritic makes a letter more specific, or completes it (the i-dot, or the j-dot, if the latter is taught), or it qualifies the letter (grave or acute accent). Punctuation, by adequately separating the different elements of a sentence, contributes to its meaning; it goes hand in hand with the progression of thought, and requires more reflection on the part of the writer than accents, which, especially among those who are accustomed to writing, almost become a reflex action. Punctuation cannot easily be left out; whereas a text with no diacritics can still be understood, the meaning of a text with no punctuation, or bad punctuation is either lost or distorted.

The zone for punctuation is the middle zone, that of accents has more scope : i-dots and accents are therefore freer.

Free signs will be studied under three aspects:
- respect for the rules of diacritics and the interference with continuity.
- the zones of the graphic space where these signs are placed.
- Crépieux-Jamin's major categories, of which they are a part.

Regarding punctuation, the first aspect is not relevant, as the rules of punctuation, have to do with the actual comprehension of the text above all; besides, one cannot determine at which point the signs have been written down. The second aspect is reduced to the right and left zones. It is the third aspect which is the most open to interpretation.

a) Respect for the rules of diacritics. Interference with continuity.

It is easy for a graphologist to see whether these rules have been adhered to or not, and the interpretation can take place straight away. Scripts in which accents are all present and accurate, show respect for rules and desire for order, rigour and precision. Yet the opposite is not invariably true : if it is true in the case of writers who completely neglect their diacritics, more nuanced interpretations are needed in the case of other writers. Indeed, experience has shown that some writers whose rigour and precision have been ascertained, do not always put in all their accents nor place them very accurately in relation to letters.

The text must remain clear, and the most important thing is the graphic context. A structured writing whose letters have a clear outline, is a good guarantee of rigour (even for jobs which are demanding in this respect). On the other hand, very precise diacritics bring elements of compensation to a writing with a medium degree of structure.

Undoubtedly, it is with writings which are still close to the school model, have been written with application, are not very rapid and have a dominance of form, that the graphologist will not be so tolerant.

Some omissions matter more than others : *i* for instance, needs a dot; without it, it can be confused with other letters and especially with parts of other letters. A *j* does not run the same risk, and some diacritics can be left out without causing serious confusion.

147

At first glance, both writings have points in common, but the generally condensed aspect of the top one (connections, proportions and the spaces close together) provides compensations which the connections (which almost have lapses of continuity), the large blank spaces and lack of weight on the baseline of the lower writing, cannot provide.
Much greater professional success in the case of the first writing.

When, however, pronounced signs of rigidity or inhibition are added to very orthodox accentuation, the interpretation will point towards perfectionism, to a writer who is anxiously scrupulous, finicky, even rather a fusspot.

Excessive punctuation should be noted. Some writers, for instance, overdo exclamation marks and others overdo dots : the first generally have a slightly quixotic temperament, the second may have difficulties in being definite, in making up their minds. An excess of quotation marks, of parentheses, comes from a desire to be precise and well understood, as well as from a slightly anxious mind.

Whereas, faced with a written text, one cannot know exactly when the punctuation was done, one can, for accents, make hypotheses by deductive guesses. Interference with continuity occurs.

Desire to perfect the letter one has just written, may dictate the degree or mode of connection (groupings, false connections). Also, a certain degree of connectedness may dominate, from which a particular way of adding the accents will derive : a very connected writing goes together with blocked accentuation, and logically, disconnected writing goes together with literal accentuation[1] .

In the case of grouped writing, one wonders which alternative has been chosen; even if one can assume grouped accentuation, when the break occurs just after a letter requiring a dot or an accent, one can be really sure of it, only if the free sign has been incorporated with the next grouping by means of a combination.

The interest of examining a chosen type of accentuation is real, since types of attention, rhythm of thought and action, or intellectual processes, differ from case to case. Literal accentuation facilitates analysis; it may also contribute to the reassurance of an anxious mind, if the graphic milieu confirms this. Blocked diacritics may come from someone who thinks more synthetically and concentrates more, and, if the retrograde gesture is made quickly, it provides an opportunity for efficient overall checking : the short time wasted by this regressive movement, is made up for by the fact that several signs have all been put down together.

There is a rationale in inserting diacritics, in relation to the length of words, just as there is in breaks within words. Good general adaptation is confirmed by variations in diacritics, as long as homogenerity is shown, and contributes to economical acceleration towards the right. These variations reveal supple logic, diversified approaches and methods.

A good number of combinations originate from free signs : if they are successful, original but sober, they indicate a capacity for inventiveness and for making associations. However, a certain monotony may set in, or on the contrary, a studied effect.

b) Zones of the graphic space where signs are placed.

The scope offered to diacritics is wide and one can see i-dots or accents placed sometimes at a distance three, four or five times the height of the letter to which they belong, and yet the writing remains within the norm. One often finds this in small sober and accurate writings; after a period of

---

1   Accentuation is called literal when a free sign is put down immediately after the letter has been written. It is called syllabic or grouped when it is put down after a group of letters, and blocked or global when it is distributed after the word has been written.

concentration, the writer probably relaxes through this expansion, thus offsetting the balance, neverthless without harming the desired legiblity and the accuracy.

If, however, slack writings are involved, then a lack of control is confirmed.

The zones in which free signs occur, take their meaning in accordance with the symbolism of space[2]. Dots, accents and apostrophes can emphasise the upper zone even more, in a writing which is already prolonged up, or give a low writing the dimension it was lacking, directing it towards dreams, ardour, aspirations, noble or delicate feelings, or dissatisfaction, according to the signs to which they are related.

If they are placed low, they bring moderation and realism; or, if they are heavy, they show a burden, an inhibition, or a tendency to depression. If they penetrate the middle zone, or are pointing downwards, they may indicate an inclination to self-disparagement.

The zone on the right confirms the progressiveness and the speed of a writing, dots and accents placed ahead of letters are sure signs of this, and sometimes even the only ones, in controlled writings.

The zone on the left indicates restraint, return to one's experiences, need to check, as well as difficulty in trusting, or in being open.

Punctuation also can be studied in relation to where it is placed, even in relation to its displacement towards the right or the left. It seldom goes beyond the height of the baseline; one meets, however, with commas and full stops which seem to obey an attraction from the lower zone, and can thereby confirm some pessimism.

Writings overloaded with dots[3], before or after words, or in the body of a word, indicate some hesitation or anxiety. They make the writing heavier and delay the rightward, cursive movement.

All sorts of interactions take place between writings and free signs, but also between free signs themselves : dots can be placed high and accents low or vice-versa (in which case one talks of reaction against pessimism). The

2   See Appendix 1.
3   Unnecessary dots: one of Crépieux-Jamin's signs (Continuity).

graphologist is sometimes surprised by the life of these graphic movements, detached from the middle zone and from the line of reality, less socially involved than the rest of the writing. The intensity of feelings turned inwards, the aggressiveness which education teaches people to repress, reveal themselves particularly clearly here, as well as, sometimes, anxiety and inhibition which can be masked by certain selected forms that are aesthetic and drawn with ease.

Diacritics and punctuation firmly distributed and precisely placed, but without stiffness, always enhance a writing.

Slight disorder may indicate variety of interests and reactions. If it is excessive, it shows lack of self-control, or even lack of emotional balance (in a graphic context permitting this interpretation).

c) Crépieux-Jamin's major categories, of which free signs are part.

With this aspect of accentuation and punctuation, most categories are involved. Free signs are indeed large or small, curved or straight, rapid or slow, heavy or light, sharp-pointed or clubbed, firm or weak, and all these may or may not be homogeneous with the writing.

Poised punctuation, by marking out the course of thought, can moderate excitability of character and of reaction, big vertical commas can act as landmarks which a hesitant writing may lack. Commas lend themselves to greater pressure and downward prolongation. Parentheses and apostrophes can also provide an opportunity to assert oneself vertically. Commas, starting from the baseline, can discharge bottled up tension or resentment; it is not unusual for commas to be sharp-pointed towards the left, and they sometimes are the only signs of aggressiveness in acquired writings among young people - girls in particular.

Full stops can be stretched to dashes, become gestures of rejection, of holding at arm's length, this blocked, extra space having some analogy with secondary width. Dashes are sometimes called "magistrate's dashes".

The i-dot also lends itself to being stretched towards one zone of the graphic field or another, and to its shape being based on angles or circles. Angles - bird-shaped accents - are seen as a sign of anxiety; they hesitate, in this upper zone, as to what directon to take, and are neither decisive like a precise dot, nor full like a circular dot.

The circular dot is related, in a child-like way, to fashionable writings and writings which are double-joined, regressive and designed. This dot may be a residue of a habit among professionals from the graphic arts.

2. T- Bars

The fact that *t* has two elements increases the possibilities of transformations of the school model, and gives rise to them. Children themselves quickly find their own formulas.

The crossing of these two elements is said to be symbolic of self-assertion and realisation, and while the analogy helps the interpretation, observation of the firmness of the writing as a whole should not be neglected. The different *t*'s, of which we give a few samples below, should be examined in relation to the stroke (texture, tension, pressure and edges), the form, the dimension, the way they reach the baseline and the zones where their bar occurs. They often derive from a sign with which they should be associated: sharp-pointed, clubbed, with extensive movements, or inhibited. They can also constitute one such as whips, and they sometimes look so striking that the sign can be interpreted as a typical gesture [52].

Whip writing consists of a movement which leans first to the left, then flies to the right in a movement of release, and t-bars lend themselves to this particularly well. It is a sign of impulsiveness, impatience and opposition, which can extend to anger or aggressiveness, rejection, indiscipline, repudiation in a very inharmonious graphic context.

Chart 1. - T- bars

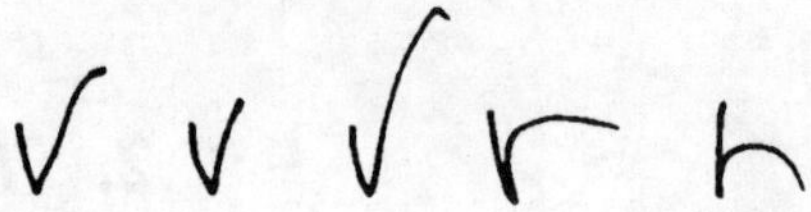

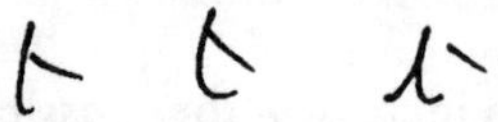

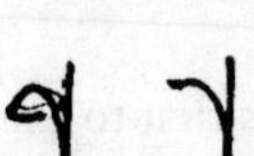

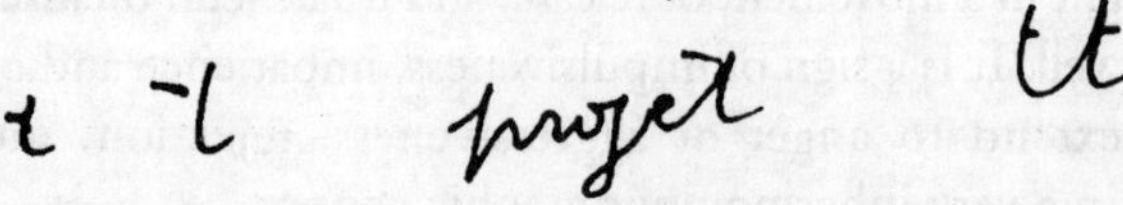

CHART 1 : t-bars

(a) The lasso-shaped *t* is made with a skilful, enveloping and regressive movement. According to its form, its firmness and its spontaneity, it can indicate captivation, tenacity or creativity.

(b) v-shaped *t* : rejection, dissatisfaction, bitterness, recriminating demands and revolt, if it is offensive; in a weak context, it shows that one lets oneself go or one gives up easily. Targets are different according to the direction in the space and the underlying force.

(c) When the t-bar falls : powerlessness, obstinacy or self-depreciation, according to the tension and the strength, the direction, and whether the sroke is sharp-pointed or not .

(d) A wavy bar indicates indecision or seduction.

(e) Placed above the extension the bar is associated with the symbolism of the upper zone; it may be a superelevation: independence, or domination. In a light context with little structure, it is said to be indecisive. If very long, it loses some of its force.

(f) Firmly crossed low or crossed twice, *t* comes from a tenacious, obstinate, imperious writer.

(g) Some t-bars return to the left with an aggressive gesture : lack of trust or lack of a spirit of cooperation.

(h) A *t* with a bar behind it or not crossing it attests to great prudence or inhibition (one can find accents placed ahead of letters together with t-bars placed behind them; more enthusiasm for a goal than actual realisation). Double *t*'s barred separately is a sign of scruple and also of inhibition.

As far as left-handers' t-bars are concerned, see Chapter 14 (part 4).

3. *Initial Strokes*
Finals

Starting strokes and finals should also be linked to the major signs to which they belong and, like *t*, can become a major sign or play the main part in it (suspended, diminishing, enlarging, ornate and complicated writings). They can also influence the general proportions, confirm or moderate a form which is angular, round or copybook (eg. the starting stroke of the school model)[4].

Due to their position in the word, initials are more linked to the writer's attitude regarding his past, to what his left margin represents for him. Likewise, finals relate to outside situations.

Below we give a few initials and finals, with no claim - just as with the *'t*'s - to being exhaustive. What is said of initial strokes is also true of capitals, taking into account that these magnify their meanings.

CHART 2: initial strokes (or starting strokes, or initials)

(a) Curved starting strokes, more or less pronounced, skilful or complicated, are calls for attention and for other people's feelings (they are often called affective requests); they show amiability - even obsequiousness, if the context points to that interpretation - or they can show cheerfulness, or a need to exteriorise, in an ample, animated writing.
     C lends itself to scrollings (spirals); when shell-shaped, it is said to be narcissism or coquetry; it is occasionally seen in small, sober writings, sometimes the only sign of regard for oneself.

(b) Commercial amiability;

(c) A lively sharp-pointed comma suggests the curve of the starting stroke.

---

4   French copybook style teaches several letters with a starting stroke. (T. N.).

(d) Contradiction between the starting stroke of the *c* (shell-shaped) and that of other letters (direct) suggests emphasis on the self (short finals).

(e) If the starting stroke is short, proportionate, firm and supple : reliance on experience.

(f) If the stroke is very long, it is reminiscent of the "umbilical cord".

(g) a stiff starting stroke confirms a spirit of contradiction, prejudices, and a tendency to quibble.

(h) In a very prudent and more or less inhibited writing : need for support, verification and, in a very conscientious writing : remains of the copy-book model.

(i) A direct and firm starting stroke (starting from the middle or the upper zone) is a simplification, a sign of speed, and it shows a decisive mind.

(j) A loop-shaped start : dream, fantasies (quite frequent in pre-adolescents) .

(k) Mirror start : one looks at oneself.

(l Starting strokes coming up from below the baseline : reflection, anchorage, calculated progression from known and safe bases; if exaggerated, they mean oddness.

Finals are parts of letters deserving graphologists' attention, as the writer's control slackens often more at the end of words than at the beginning. They play an important part, since they prepare the connections with the following words.

A script with firm finals, progressive in their movement, open towards the next word, aims at continuity in action and in relationships. It also bears witness to a sustained effort to reach objectives, and to a job properly completed. If sacrificing finals a little is in keeping with a very rapid, simplified writing, one should however, especially in certain contexts, think of haste, negligence, and a bit of contempt for other people. In writings still close to copybook, one is entitled to expect well-formed finals.

A final in the form of a supple and open curve speaks of receptivity and friendliness.

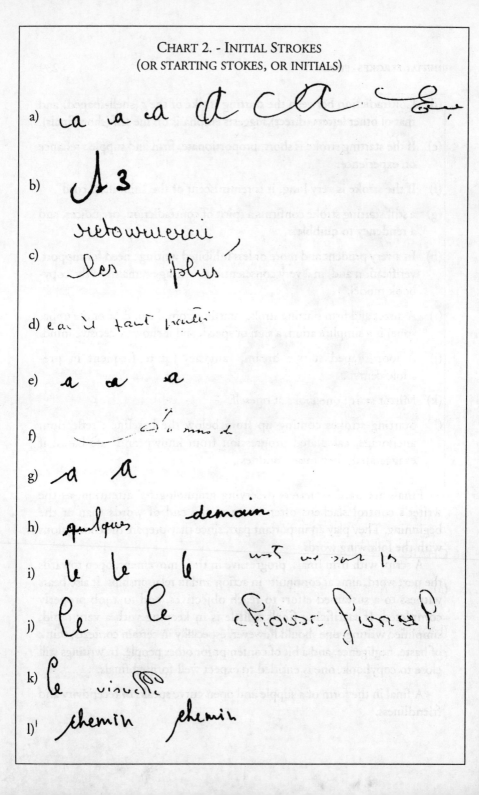

CHART 2. - INITIAL STROKES
(OR STARTING STOKES, OR INITIALS)

CHART 3. - FINALS

a)

b)

c)

d)

e)

f)

CHART 3: Finals

(a) If the final goes above the letter with the beginning of a left-tending gesture, one can think of distrust, or possessiveness.

(b) If it is rapid and directed to the right (centrifugal) : reactivity.

(c) The final can bend back towards the left from underneath (centripetal), in an angle or a curve in a more or less pronounced

manner : withdrawal, refusal, selfishness, a monopolising attitude; *m,*
n and *s* particularly lend themselves to this.

This type of final originates in a regressive movement.

If, however, the writing is spontaneous and progressive, one can
interpret a regressive final *s* as restraint, in a rather hasty flow (one talks
of the hooks of nervous people).

(d) Some finals emphasise their movement downwards. According to the
strength, the tension of the stroke, or lack of it, one will think of a
decisive mind, an assertiveness which could easily be peremptory, or
of defeatist attitudes and discouragement.

(e) Finals can also be prolonged, or stretch towards the right, thus
cancelling the space between letters: this is a kind of dash, and a
distance is maintained to keep others at bay (according to context), to
act in their place, to say "no" to them categorically, or to project on to
them what one cannot accept about oneself.

(f) It can, on the other hand, be short, stressing a general restraint, which
sometimes is only shown by this sign. Preference is given to the left
zone over the right-hand one, and with it, discretion, shyness,
prudence, or inhibition are expressed.

It can also be very short and suspended.

Finals can also be irregular in all these peculiarities, either in a nuanced,
manner, thus merely reflecting life, or else excessively so, revealing
changeable, even unpredictable attitudes.

All the variants of free signs, of *t*'s, starting strokes and finals, must be
constantly repeated in a writing in order to be justifiably interpreted.

*Ci - joint lett
amusante de Viol
trouve seulement;
escargère, car a*

Woman, 40 years
148
Large writing, angular, right-slanted, with strong pressure, thrown, sharp-pointed, precise, with double-joins, false connections, congestions, 't's in whips, large accents. Her drives are not easy to control. Strong and biased reactions can be foreseen.

*quelques commentaires,
e qui elle parcent l'intere
mens autant que lui et
mo urs autant de Tikres.*

149 **Man, 54 years**

It would, on the other hand be, a mistake to see an expression of aggressiveness in these 't'-bars, a typical gesture belonging to both whips and lassos : there is not enough tension in the writing and the texture of the stroke is not sufficiently dense. Here, it is some sort of rather utopian idealism, that of a sensitive and imaginative "youthful" and almost rather naive man who wishes to carry others along with his poetical and humanitarian ideas and whose character is changeable and reactive. The writing has round letters, open ones, inflated forms, and a not too well kept baseline. Finals are uneven, there are straightenings-up, angles, breaks and bird-shaped accents.

7

DIRECTION

The category of DIRECTION deals with:
- the slant of letters,
- the general direction of the graphic line.

The direction of lines appears in the chapter on Space : lines are studied according to their trajectory in the graphic field and the part they play in it.

The slant of letters is defined by the angle formed by the vertical axis of the writing with the baseline. This angle is measurable with a protractor, all the more easily and precisely if the writing shows fairly large prolongations up and down. In order to assess this angle more easily, one can prolong the vertical parts of the writing (the upright strokes) (53) over a section of a line.

A writing is called vertical when the angle formed thus is 90°, left-slanted when the angle is more than this and right-slanted when it is less.

VERTICAL, LEFT-SLANTED and RIGHT-SLANTED represent the three principal degrees of slant, which we shall study in succession; we shall then look at the irregularities of direction : IRREGULARLY and VERY IRREGULARLY-SLANTED writings. The latter sign gives rise to PULLED-ABOUT (also called VACILLATING) and VARIABLY-SLANTED WRITINGS.

One and the same writer can appreciably vary the slant of his script according to the nature of what he writes, his addressee, the time he devotes to it, and even, with a fairly long document, according to his endurance, his own self-discipline with regard to legibility, and his emotional reactions, which may change because of and in the course of that written communication.

This is why one should consult several documents before reaching important conclusions based on the degree of slant.

This is also why the degree of slant is a graphic characteristic that one can change easily, which leads the uninitiated to think that it is easy to disguise one's own script.

Letter slant does not constitute a major category, except if it is very pronounced, or very little in keeping with the rest of the writing. In most cases, it goes together with the writing, helping to confirm or still further reinforce the general meaning.

Fashions have changed and and continue to do so[1], although handwriting, nowadays, is losing some of the social connotations associated with aestheticism and rank. The proportions of right-slanted writings is much lower than in the past, and represents only 25%[2] of writings at the moment . Verticality dominates. When it is not very marked, this direction is the most neutral, the most natural, and seems related to the type of communication we have today.

One is entitled to think, in this connection, that it might be more suitable to talk of a way of being, rather than a way of writing, if one thinks of those writings with a predominant, large and round middle zone, which are commonly described as fashionable. Indeed, do they not reflect a need for personal and emotional fulfilment, a need which constitutes the psychological and social phenomenon in fashion?

Also, the teaching of slant varies; at the moment, a vertical slant is usually advocated, while a left slant never is. Children soon stretch the rules of the copybook model and their slant, if pronounced, will therefore be significant.

---

1   Klages [23] already gives explanations of these facts in relation to this time.
2   Statistics deposited with the authors.

1. The slant of letters

VERTICAL

VERTICAL writing is that which slants neither to the right nor to the left and forms a 90° angle with the baseline.

One seldom meets with a perfectly and consistently vertical writing, unless it is very controlled and thus close to being static and rigid.

Since this degree of slant is the most widespread today, one should reduce the importance of the classical meanings given to it and reserve its strong meaning for writings which are not only particularly vertical, but also strongly marked by a convergence of other signs pointing to the same interpretation.

The general meaning given to verticality is that of control, reserve, independence, attempt at non-commitment and a prevalence of reason over emotions, all of which elements favour objectivity, if the graphic context confirms it[3].

With regard to the symbolism of space, the writer whose writing is vertical adopts a restrained and slightly reserved position, both toward the zone of the right, which for one reason or another attracts the writer with a right slant, and towards the zone on the left, which the writer with a left slant chooses in avoiding the zone on the right.

When letters are written at an angle scarcely more or less than 10° from the 90° position, the slant is not very significant.

To assess correctly the meanings of independence, control or rigour in a vertical writing, one should see whether the writing is sufficiently supple and free and if its movement is not constrained. The proportions between the vertical and horizontal dimensions and between the three zones of the

---

3   Note that recent studies have, apparently, shown a significant correlation between a vertical slant, in association with other components, and high performance in a series of intelligence tests. C. Chardon - P. Gilbert: 4th Congrès de Psychologie du travail de Langue Française - Montréal 1986.

writing must be looked at. It is certain that the narrower the writing and the more the amplitude of its curves is reduced, both in the body of the words themselves and in the outer loops, the greater the constraint will be. A very precise stroke accentuates the effects of verticality; so does angularity (rigour may become intransigence), as well as lapses of continuity and very short finals.

Woman, 38 years - *Writing in blue ink with irregular pressure, fairly large in the middle zone. Some curved forms are fairly supple, others less so. The horizontal dimension is sometimes narrow, sometimes wider, the upper extensions are high. The writing is lively but not free, its movement is vibrant and a little restrained.*

Here verticality, which is medium, because of self-respect (superelevated 'j's and 's's) and because of vulnerability (irregular dimension and pressure), controls the expansion of emotions and the putting forward of the self.

150

The right margin is very wide and accentuates the effects of the verticality. The considerable and uneven spacing leads one to think that the writer has not found the integration needed by her rigorous, but sensitive nature, which is demanding at all levels.

Verticality can act as a defence, as a compensation in a writing which is too open, too wide. A slightly rigid verticality can, on the other hand, be tempered by openness, width, and suppleness of the baseline.

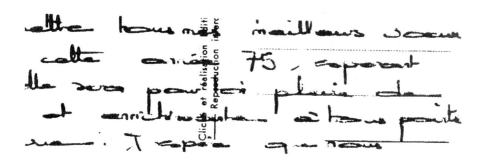

Female student, 19 years

151
A writing much more rigid in its verticality than the previous one, still, constrained, crushed, with such wide secondary and primary widths, particularly in the plump ovals, that they amount to emphasised narrowness. The stroke is straight and pasty, which for Hegar[4] is an inharmonious combination. Very strong unsatisfied, emotional demands.

LEFT-SLANTED
STRAIGHTENED-UP

LEFT-SLANTED writing is one which slants leftwards at an angle greater than 90° to the baseline.

As long as the left slant remains slight, near the vertical, it does not mean much; it is when the slant is markedly towards the left, in an apprehensive or reticent context, that defensiveness appears.

This apprehension and defensiveness remain to be measured. When they are slight and well controlled, channelling the progression and the movement of the writing without putting a brake on it, or only very slightly

---

4   See Chapter on The Stroke.

so, the control will be efficient and will not affect contacts. One often finds such restraint of slant in firm and dynamic writings among people who have important professional or social responsibilities. Thus they find a way not to be too influenced by personal and subjective aspects of their emotions, their convictions and their motivations, in order to divert the resulting tension towards their objectives. One also comes across this kind of restraint in small, sensitive and simple writings which, in this way, indicate reserve, even self-effacement.

Adolescents, a little fearful of their future and of the outside world, sometimes experience this type of defensive vigilance[5]. In children, it might be effort, or resistance to giving in to what is facile.

To be able to talk of difficulties with contacts, mistrust and opposition, the left slant must be pronounced and the graphic context must be manifestly reticent or inhibited. A writing which is too large - or very small - superelevated, angular, spaced out, very compact, or even very irregularly spaced, can indicate refusal, systematic opposition (remember that handwriting is never taught with a left slant). Pride, fear of havings one's worth questioned, may be obstacles. A left slant accentuates the closedness of narrow, looped and double-joined writings; in an overconnected writing, it shows obstinacy or lack of spontaneity if the forms are also complicated or ambiguous.

A distinctly left-slanted writing often goes together with reared movement, showing an attitude of resistance, or defiance if the writing is intense, and indicating antagonism between impulses and the barriers put up against them. It is seldom found with controlled movement, or rhythmic writing, unless we are dealing with a very personal rhythm which does not fit into classical harmonies, reflecting strong personalities, difficult to integrate in any case.

Quite often one finds a pronounced left slant combined with static disconnectedness and marked secondary width.

---

5   Research done on upper 6th formers gives a percentage of only 18% left-slanted or slightly left-slanted writings as against 52% vertical and 25% right-slanted ones [11].

One often comes across writings which tend to be vertical or slightly right-slanted, but which slant a little leftwards under certain circumstances or even in certain letters or certain words : the writing is then said to be STRAIGHTENED-UP. The writer wishes to correct himself and pull himself together when faced with a slightly difficult task, when flinching from effort, or when dealing with someone causing him fear or reticence, or with whom self-control seems the proper thing.

One can also meet with writings which straighten up in the course of a lifetime, or as a consequence of a particular event, and possibly go as far as reaching quite a marked leftward slant : a painful experience may be the cause.

Man, 40 years
Very left-slanted, large, angular, reared writing, with descending tiles, precise stroke and a little sharp-pointed; diacritics reinforcing the descending gesture, interrupted connections around the narrow 'o's.

152 *Obstinacy, struggle, a demanding and difficult character which, in spite of constantly renewed effort, does not very successfully control intense emotions. Great professional commitment and success in a small business which the writer was able to keep up and improve, in spite of very arduous circumstances.*

Dans un pays moderne, la notio
est très important. La consomm
ité d'un pays dépend de nou c

153

Girl, 15 1/2 years - Lower 6th, science section
*Straightenings-up in a vertical to slightly left-slanted writing; mixture of
script and cursive, disconnected with some groupings, considerable spacing,
reverse and sometimes suspended letters, vibrant movement: a typical graphic
syndrome of some adolescents, in a state of expectancy, wishing for independence in order to protect themselves. Selective communication,
interiorisation.*
*Good schoolwork. Independent thinking and intuition given by the light,
rapid and lively overall context where air circulates relatively freely.*

RIGHT-SLANTED
VERY RIGHT-SLANTED

A writing is right-slanted when its angle to the baseline is less than 90°.
It is said to be slightly right-slanted if the angle is between 85° and 75°,
RIGHT-SLANTED between 75° and 60°, very right-slanted between 60° and
45°, and exaggeratedly right-slanted below 45°.

A very slight rightward slant is no more significant than a very slight
leftward slant and both are said to be based around the vertical axis. If from
being very slight, this slant becomes slight, it may indicate, - if the stroke
and the forms do not contradict this - a participation a little easier than in
the case of vertical or left-slanted writings, an acceptance which is a little
more spontaneous because more instinctive. However, to associate a
rightward slant systematically with sociability does not seem correct. This
used to be more justified in the days when writing was taught with a

rightward slant; consequently vertical and left-slanted writing stood outeven more so, owing to their independence, or their insubordination.

Right-slanted writing gives more impression of movement and speed than do other degrees of slant. An organised and well-considered synthesis is needed however. Indeed, for a right-slanted writing to be really lively and rapid, its movement must truly carry it along, and some of the main signs recognised as indices of speed must activate its rightward progression, but if it is tense and unrelaxed, it can have the opposite effect; if one often comes across right-slanted writing in a dynamic context, it is because the high spirits, impulses and passion common to both, will produce graphic effects of the same order.

More than sociability, a VERY RIGHT-SLANTED writing indicates a need for others, due to two very different motives: on the one hand, the need to express oneself, to act for or against someone or something and, on the other hand, dependency. The tension, firmness and resoluteness of the overall context, or their opposites, will distinguish those who find a motive for action in an emotion, a feeling, or an ideology, from those who merely follow an impression, who wait for the support and approval of others. The former are active, the latter passive. The former look to others in a spirit of cooperation, or confrontation and find here an opportunity to prove to themselves their own power, or their ability to delegate, the latter look for comfort. In both cases the writing lacks straightening-up, showing, in the first case an overpassionate attitude, impulsiveness and possible aggressiveness, and in the second, surrender and dependency.

In children and adolescents, one sometimes finds writings of the second type, a little weak, with no tension, with either too light or too heavy a stroke; they indicate lack of motivation, a tendency to give up and rely on others (on parents more often than not), to resign themselves, and a tendency to sullenness. Writers with a large right-slanted middle zone demand attention and affection which are tangibly shown, but if they are too passive, their demands remain unknown to those who could respond. Large capitals more right-slanted than the rest of the script, must be taken into consideration: they express an appeal of a rather child-like nature.

Depression sometimes takes on this heavy, right-slanted aspect.

J'espère que tu vas bien, regrette que tu ne sois pas venu e end; remarque nous n'avons pas grand chose: nous ne pourrions pas

Boy, 16 1/2 years - End of 4th year, difficulties with schoolwork

154 *Rightward slant of dependency here here supported by the lack of strength and ardour of a light, blue, very uneven, amended stroke, the rather weak and distended forms with fragmented letters, the lower extensions pulling leftwards (see the "J"). Yet the clear writing, with a few vertical strokes which have strong pressure, the good layout, the well-placed signature which could not be reproduced here, enable one to be hopeful regarding this adolescent's evolution.*

Heureusement que le nipluro me fau oublier avec la mer le soleil qui eme ville peut être aum ommer..... A Bientôt

Éditions Normandes LE - 10, rue du 11 Novembre - CAE

Man, 25 years - *The large middle zone sometimes slants to the right quite*

155 *a lot, and sometimes withdraws, with straightenings-up, telescoping, narrowness of some letters ('m' in particular). The stroke, a little heavy, does not flow readily; the cursive movement is a little cramped.*

*A lot of human feeling, possibilities for empathy but, on the other hand,
affective dependency, difficulties in making choices. Disappointment and
discouragement are latent, with moments of depression.*

See writing no. 148, or Coco Chanel's writing, no. 66, which is angular.
The regular right-slant, the connections, the overall firmness of the writing,
all express strength and passion geared towards action. The writing is
dynamic and resolute, the rhythm strong.

Man, 50 years - *Right-slanted writing. Yet participation is very selective
owing to the narrowness and the large spaces between words, the precise stroke,
the finals irregular, but short more often than not, the very large right -hand
margin (this writing will be found again in Chart 5).
Sensitivity. Discerning judgement. Intuition.*

156

IRREGLARITY OF DIRECTION
PULLED-ABOUT (VACILLATING)
VARIABLY- SLANTED

Rhythm goes well with with slight irregularities of direction, with these
small alternations around an axis, whether it be slightly right-slanted,
slanted, but not excessively, or rather vertical.

They indicate emotional and intellectual sensitivity, life, and adaptability to whatever occurs; people, things or events. A writing with a fixed direction lacks life, freedom and self- expression[6].

It is when the irregularities are too pronounced that they indicate hesitation. If the stroke is too light and the letters insufficiently well-shaped, too uneven in both the vertical and the horizontal dimensions, choices, initiatives and commitment are difficult. If the stroke is stronger, but tense, with an overall context which appears more structured, the writer feels he has to act in spite of everything, and runs the risk of taking more or less sudden decisions and of being clumsy; his general behaviour, as a result, can be puzzling for those around him.

This is not surprising in adolescence, nor at the beginning of a professional life, which opens up a whole new set of questions, but it is desirable that the irregularities are not too pronounced and decrease quite early on.

If such is not the case, adaptation may cause problems, and taking on responsibilities, whether in a personal or professional framework, will not be easily accomplished.

A further degree of irregularity of slant produces a writing which the graphologist Jean-Charles Gille-Maisani calls PULLED-ABOUT (VACIL-LATING [54]. Here the slant is very irregular - even discordant - and the changes of slant occur very close to one another within the same word - sometimes even within the same letter[7]. There is then an internal conflict which the rest of the writing heps to confirm through its forms of expression, and its basis, which is to say discomfort and dissatisfaction strongly felt, with energy probably badly managed and organisation of thought and action likely to be illogical.

Another sign involving important changes of direction, is VARIABLY-SLANTED writing. The irregularities affect groups of words, sentences, sometimes pages.

---

6   One can call it Rigid if the baseline is also very straight, and if there is practically no sign showing a little suppleness (in dimensions, pressure or forms).

7   With these strong irregularities which pervade the writing as a whole, one could al-most talk of a pulled-about (vacillating) movement.

The reader's eye, looking at writing with changes of direction, notices the different slants, but in fact, one often finds other irregularities[8] also, and noticeable variations occur in the general handling of the graphic line. One should then wonder how reliable, how consistent and logical the writer is in his behaviour.

When the variations affect the slant only, the diagnosis is less severe. This is often seen in the writings of people who are not very used to writing and in adolescents whose plans are a little unstable. Homogeneity is not generally disturbed.

Two peculiarities should be mentioned regarding changes of direction; some methodical writers who wish to be clearly understood, are keen to make certain words stand out, and with this object in mind, give them a slant different from that of the rest of the text (or a different dimension). This emphasis can also be made without the writer being aware of it (usually in a less pronounced way); in this way, he singles out a word which is important to him, an emotive word, probably interesting to the graphologist.

Man, 50 years - *The small irregularities of direction associated with the fine and simple forms tell of the intellectual mobility and the general reactivity of this firm, homogeneous, progressive and dynamic writing.*

157

Very condensed signature, a little more left-slanted, a lot narrower, with a little extra pressure, which confirms reflection, tenacity in projects and the realistic and effective demands of the wtriter.

---

8   See part 4 - "homogeneity" in Chapter on Form.

The other peculiarity consists in either slanting rightwards, or straightening up the first letter of a word, or its first syllable, which may mean that an initial trust, in the first case, may be withdrawn, and, in the second, an initial mistrust may soften. The letter, or group of letters at the end of a word may also straighten up, showing hesitation, or a change of mind when the writer is about to take action.

Je suis actuellement à PARIS (car j'y effec
service militaire. Je vais avoir 19 ans
et demi. J'ai suivi des études de banque
ans. Il y a un an et demi que j'ai quitté
et cela va faire cinq mois que je suis

Boy, 19 years - *One can discern several aspects here if one tries to "live the life of the writing" [55].*

158 *We are dealing with variably-slanted writing, for the directions, and especially also the tension and general control differ, which affects the homogeneity a little. Some words have a very clear outline, some do not. A very hesitant boy, both supple and reticent, a little aggressive if one goes against his wishes, seeking independence and also dependent.*

2. General direction of the stroke

The general direction taken by a stroke in its progression towards the right, can be placed under the signs of right-tending or left-tending. The importance of this characteristic is greater than that of the slant of the letters, because it has more bearing on the writer's state of mind and on the subject about which he is writing.

Indeed, here we have two fundamental tendencies which are opposed to each other regarding the arrangement of a script and the respect for the copybook model. Our model favours a rightward tendency.

A rightward tendency in a writing is a process which increases its urge towards the right. A left tendency is the reverse process.

The general direction of the graphic line will deal with RIGHT-TENDING, and LEFT-TENDING writings, and then with SOARING writing, a very minor sign, before going on to a more analytical study of direction with REVERSE and TWISTED writings.

RIGHT-TENDING

RIGHT-TENDING writing, which is given 'progressive' as a synonym[9], is writing produced by a set of movements which openly favour its direction towards the right. What could hold it back towards the left is reduced, whereas what drives it towards the right is amplified; so, one finds width, simplifcations, openness, and combinations which shorten the route in order to lead the script towards the end of the line in the most direct way.

When the right-tendedness is successful, that is to say when it is not detrimental to legibility and is driven by a positive tension (the writing is then progressive), one can understand that it is a sign of intelligence, as well as of activity and openness to life and to other people.

To produce a successful right-tending writing, one needs graphic freedom helped by constant practice in writing[10], backed up by intellectual

9 All right-tending writings are not progressive. See 'Progressive' in chapter on Form.
10 See Chapter on Organisation.

and psychic freedom. It is not so much the writer watching himself act, as being driven towards goals which seem achievable and which do not involve only the present time; he can see the essential factors of problems at the same time as effective, inventive and prospective solutions for them.

Françoise Giroud's writing

159 *A very rapid trajectory, very simplified through reduction to essentials. Linear script, a little geometrical, but not stiff, made up of horizontal and vertical strokes. The right tendencies would be excessive if they were not held back by the very sober left tendencies given by the vertical sticks : these form a firm restriction in relation to the right-hand zone, by taking the place of loops and curves (the upper and lower extensions, the 's's); the finals too are shortened in the same way. The final hook of the signature which comes back towards the left, confirms these overall tendencies of the writing. See again Georges Pompidou's writing no.78, in the Chapter on Form, last part.*

Two main obstacles may, however, endanger a right-tending script : on the one hand, a slightly elusive haste, bringing slackness, and on the other, too rash a haste, close to impulsiveness. Right tendencies can indeed weaken the structure of a writing, owing to simplifications close to imprecisions, or unfinished letters, and the openings thus facilitated, opening of ovals and pincer, or bowl-shaped[11] lower extensions, by means of width. They may exaggeratedly increase tension towards the goals, stiffening the writing as a whole, with thrown movements, jerks, or a stroke which is stretched out and loses its elasticity.

Some left-tendedness is necessary.

LEFT-TENDING

LEFT-TENDING or 'regressive' writing is based on movements going back to the left (when the copybook model is not very conducive to this), or clearly amplifying some part of the letters towards the left.

With regard to the positive meaning of this sign, looping[12] or double-joins may be involved which, if they are neither very numerous nor very pronounced, restrain the writing, strengthen it and moderate its progression to the right.

On the other hand, generally regressive movements may be involved, affecting and pervading the whole script, which then appears to progress only reluctantly.

These returns to the left may take various forms : twisting, archings, too wide ovals, lassos, finals curved backwards, free signs to the rear of the letters, shells or scrollings.

Lower extensions, of *g*'s, and of *j*'s in particular (anything concerning the *j* is significant, this letter being related to the ego), and of *f*'s also, are found sometimes hanging down, or excessively open towards the left[13], in

---

11 See Chapter on Form and writing 138.
12 See Chapter on Form (Chapter 2).
13 See Chapter on Organisation (part 2).

a curve (see writing no.126), or in an angle (writing no.113). Lower extensions may also appear pulled to the left (writing nos. 141 or 160), indicating dependency on the family environment. When the angle is emphasised, it suggests assertive demands for one's rights, resentment. The angle may be open or closed.

If numerous regressive signs mark the script, or if some of these are present en masse, oneshould consider of a generally possessive, secretive, even dissimulating or monopolising tendency.

One may also be dealing with people whose very complex, or very inhibited psychic lives take these forms of self-defence.

Man, 20 years

A writing whose overall movement is weak and regressive, pulled to the left. No letter seems capable of going forwards to the right. The 'd' and 'u' are arched leftwards, the 'e's are reduced to a stroke as if to avoid incorporating the white towards the right, the second lower extension of "quelques" hangs down leftwards, and the 'b' of "table" is decidedly misshapen.

160

The overall writing is very inhibited.

Man, 40 years

Here the writing borders on the bizarre, many letters are reversed and regressive as well as twisted and angular. See the 'j's in particular, which form something resembling a 3 and almost seem like mirror-writing. The 'P' of "Pourquoi" also is angular, doubly regressive and reversed, the 'd' also is angular and reversed.

161

One can look at writing no. 65 again, in part 2 of the Chapter on Form. The writing is regressive owing to its forms which go back broadly to the left, but its general movement is considerably more ample, more active and therefore more efficient than that of the two writings above.

SOARING

In SOARING writing, some letters, or parts of letters rise towards the upper zone, as if moved upwards by some sort of surge.

It is quite a different matter from upward prolongations or super-elevations.

With prolongations and superelevations, all the proportions of the word are changed. In soaring writing, there is an impulse.

Certain letters lend themselves to this lively movement towards the upper zone : letters with upper extensions, 'r's, 'v's, finals, also some signature paraphs and some capitals.

It is the upper zone which is selected in this upward movement, and one has the impression that the letters are sucked upwards.

Is it merely an emotive discharge towards that zone which leads to extension?

Is it, as some people say, mysticism? If so, it is not because the upper zone is necessarily - or solely - the spiritual zone (many writers whose religious sense is acknowleged, have writings which are low, reduced through concentration and sobriety, or even prolonged down); it is more due to the sort of excitement which underlies this excessive movement, to the sort of imagination expressed by the expansion and freedom taken in this way. The elation and imagination can occur in multifarious areas and in different ways. The rest of the writing will help the graphologist to make a judgement.

It is not unusual to find a writing which is prolonged up as well as superelevated and soaring; the soaring might thus confirm the need to surpass oneself, to search for something different from what one is at the time (see writing no. 97 in the Chapter on Dimension).

REVERSE
TWISTED (or with twists)

With REVERSE and TWISTED writings, we are dealing with the direction of the strokes of the letters. In order to study them, one must retrace the movements which inscribe them and make them progress, the bases of handwriting.

Some writers break away from the direction taught to form the letters: these letters are reverse letters. A writing is called REVERSE[14] when a certain number of letters drawn this way appear in it.

Numerous letters of the alphabet lend themselsves to these infringements which, through their reversal of the norm, bring certain more or less important changes in the form.

It is therefore not just an unimportant graphic detail, particularly when one notices several letters changed in this way; this is a modification of form loaded with meaning (and more particularly so in the case of affective letters, for instance); there is a modification of the movement of projection and of the symbolic zone, which is thus covered or uncovered.

CHART 4 : the main reverse letters

(a) The modifications of this form may be minimal in their visible result, as in the case with the 'o's which are used to connect two letters when the oval encloses a more or less reduced area of white, and the graphic path is radically reversed .

(b) The drawing of the reverse *v* is close to that of this type of *o*; the reversing is the same; the regressivity of the gesture may be more or less considerable, more or less skilful.

(c) Reverse *a* is generally reminiscent of the Greek alpha, and can be produced in several ways which are more or less aesthetic, infringing the norm to a greater or lesser degree.

---

14 For J.Ch. Maisani, a writing is in reverse when it systematically does the opposite of the normal copybook model, whether it is a matter of slant, continuity, speed, form, direction, even its diemension, or pressure. He considers reverse writings as a major sign in graphology [54].

CHART 4. - REVERSE LETTERS

a)  ‎ sont à rebours

b)  ‎

c)  a a a

d) 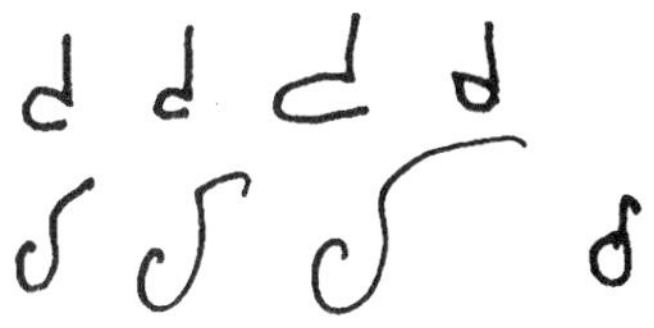 d d d d

ʃ ʃ ʃ ʃ

e)  b b b

f) P P P P P

g) r r r

h) a d a

i) f g g f

j) 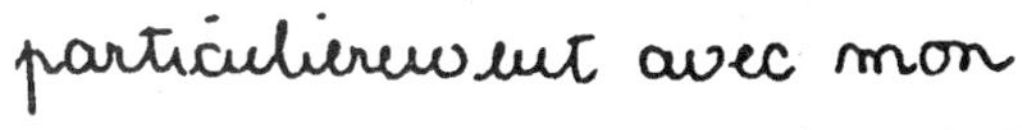 particulierement avec mon

(d) The oval of *d* or its upper extension, or both elements, can be changed. The *d* called 'pipe-shaped' has mostly a flattened oval, and because of its swelling, is akin to plump writing. The upper extension flying rightwards can be more or less supple, more or less strong or sharp-pointed; the prolongation may be more or less controlled and long (diminishing its strength incidentally, if it is too long). The *d* can also be delta-shaped.

(e) In reversed *b*, the form really changes; it creates an unexpected arcade[15].

(f) The letter *p*, because of its movement of assertiveness, is loaded symbolically with an image of authority. This letter can easily be reversed in many ways : either the arcade[16] can be emphasised instead of opening towards the next letter, or it can be drawn on the left of the lower extension, or the *p* can even be drawn from bottom to top.
The *t* also can be made in reverse. Some kinds can be seen in Chapter 6, along with the free signs, which also can be drawn in a direction opposite to the norm, and with finals, some of which very definitely curve leftwards.

(g) A reverse *r* is often found in disconnected writings, in certain typographic scripts, or in combination with other letters; it is usually simplified, and directs towards the right that part of the letter, which in the copybook model *r*[17], goes down towards the next letter. It lends itself well to a gesture of attack or defence.

(h) Starting the ovals from the bottom is never taught; those who proceed in this way may reveal some uneasiness, some vulnerability, or, in a context confirming it, may not wish to show themselves up, and to act in an underhand manner rather than in the open[18].

(i) Lower extensions, looped or not, are sometimes produced in reverse.

---

15 French copybook model 'b' is *b* (T.N.)

16 French copybook model 'p' is *p* (T.N.)

17 French copybook model 'r' is *r* (T.N.)

18 Pulver [34] is very severe regarding letters open from the bottom and reverse writing, and sees there signs of insincerity, but he denounces only those reverse letters which accumulate : letters opening towards the bottom, substitution of form, arcades and breaks within the letters.

They may be more or less regressive, complicated or angular.

Reverse letters are quite often found at the beginning of adolescence, or during that period and may be only a passing phenomenon. Some graphic forms induce them.

(j)   The *b* is often met with, so is the *f*. Some garlands, which look more like upside-down arcades than real garlands, could be put in the same category as reverse letters.

The interpretations of reverse writing tend towards the general meanings of independence and individualism. The signs to which they are related, (personal, stylised, confused writings, closed, typographic forms, for instance), lead one to think of either originality, complications of the mind, independent, non-conformist personalities, or of opposition, restiveness, or a spirit of contradiction.

Reared, left-slanted and regressive writings reinforce the meaning of opposition conveyed by reverse writing. On the other hand, a simple, clear and rather progressive script can include a few reverse letters without this being detrimental; they indicate autonomy (see writing no.153).

In TWISTED writing (or writing with twists), some letters show deviations - twistings - in their vertical trajectory. Their direction is thereby modified.

Upper or lower extensions may be involved, but some middle-zone letters also.

Children make twisted letters, especially in their looped upper extensions[19].

Those who write really badly can produce this "arching" of *'m*'s, *'n*'s, *'i*'s and *'u*'s, one of the items in the the scale of dysgraphia [8].

Adolescents and adults also produce twists in their letters. They are a sign of anxiety and inhibition and affect writings more when they occur in the middle-zone than in the upper and lower extensions.

---

19 J. Peugeot (*La Connaissance de l'Enfant par l'Écriture* [44]) gives them as signs of vulnerability, sensitivity, suffering and anxiety, if the rest of the writing confirms this, and if they persist beyond the age of 11; excessive attachment to the mother, if they are very emphasised towards the left.

They must be particularly noted if they affect the capital or small *j* or *m*: here the assertion of the self, the 'ego' are in question.

Concerning these, it is often said that they are physiological signs : no validating research has been done on this subject.

162 **Girl, 10 years**
Very childish writing, search for security.

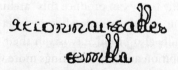

163 **Boy, 15 years**
Dented, shaky, amended writing. Inhibition, vulnerability, worry.

164 **Girl, 18 years**
Anxious writing, sophisticated.

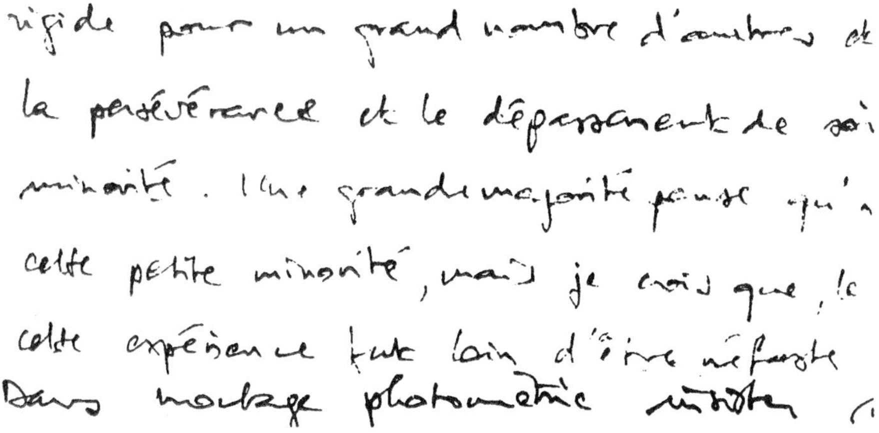

[handwritten French text]

Man, 29 years

165

Tormented writing, very much in reverse and very combined, slightly twisted, very personal, with irregular spacing, rather compact, wavy on the baseline. The level of intelligence is not in doubt, but a normal level of communication would be looked for in vain.

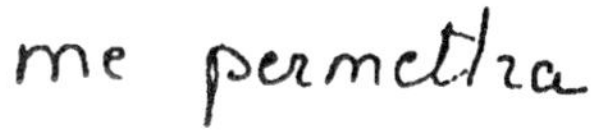

me permettra

Woman, 36 years - Scientist

166

Slightly twisted overall context, on a hesitant and fine background, where clear, slightly stiff form dominates. The direction of the baseline is irregular and a little descending, so is the slant of letters. Reverse 'p', with a covering stroke.

actuellement au chômage.

Man, 40 years

167

Black, congested and twisted writing, with regressive 'l's in the middle of a word. A not very progressive writing, telescoped in the word "en".

8

SPEED

The category of Speed concerns the rapidity with which handwriting progresses.

This category can be measured technically and exactly while watching the person who is writing : the speed can be measured according to the number of letters per minute.

On the other hand, speed can no longer be assessed once a script has been produced, except by hypotheses and deductions, recognising the signs which are logically likely to increase the speed of a writing.

Crépieux-Jamin, not having devised a category for movement, had in fact, in his category of speed, established two sorts of signs without distinguishing between the two:

- the first sort, which can form a real scale of speed in a strict sense, that is to say which can if necessary be confirmed by measurement. Only these will be studied in this chapter : slow, slowed down, poised, accelerated, rapid and precipitated writings.

- the second sort, which do indicate motion, but are first and foremost a type of movement, have been studied in the corresponding chapter. They are : carried-away, thrown (flying strokes), restrained, constrained, resolute, animated and dynamic.

A speed of execution specific to each of them, certainly does underlie these modes of movement, but it cannot be measured and is not what is most important.

Speed is very much connected with inner freedom and harmony, as well as with quick thinking, but above all, it is connected with graphic fluency.

As long as one is slowed down by learning difficulties and as long as practice has not made the act of writing fluent, one cannot write fast. Speed of writing increases with age and with the socio-cultural level. Graphologists must always take these two factors into consideration when they assess the rapidity or slowness of a writing.

Speed is a physical dimension : it can be measured. It is and has been the subject of very serious reflection and experiment, as well as of the enumeration of classical graphological elements correlated with the speed of writing. Various methods and suitable machines have been used. Robert Saudek [57] is one of the people to whom graphology is the most indebted on the subject. Jeanne Dubouchet [5] and François Michel [59] have studied this question a lot; a 'script-chronograph' has even been invented [60]. The use of speed tests is a simple matter.

Note, however, that tests measure only what is being examined, and in particular, that tests carried out on a specified, familiar sentence, eliminate two important factors concerning handwriting as an object for study:

- *spelling*, for it has been statistically checked that good spelling, causing no hesitation, is a factor of speed.

- *comprehension*, or the elaboration of a text which is not repetitive, dictated or being thought out.

This is very important, for one can again see the reason for the classical interpretations of speed as a sign of rapid thinking, comprehension and intelligence (and even abstraction, according to Klages). Writing indeed remains the sphere of the brain, of cerebral activity and of the domination of language.

Speed tests on a specified sentence are therefore only one element for assessing possible graphomotor rapidity. In particular, a child who manages to write 130 letters in a standard[1] test at accelerated speed, does not necessarily write as fast as that in his schoolwork.

It is quite obvious that speed is an important factor in success at school (note-taking, success in competitive examinations), but this is tautological,

---

1   Gobineau's test [8], for instance, taken up and standardised by Ajuriaguerra, which consists of writing "je respire le doux parfum des fleurs" (30 letters) as many times as possible in one minute, at normal speed, then at accelerated speed.

for young people capable of being successful at school necessarily write quickly[2]. By the end of secondary education, the usual score is 180 words a minute[3], which corresponds to Crépieux-Jamin's rapid writing.

In the great majority of cases the graphologist is faced with a text which has already been written and is therefore going to have to assess the speed at which the writing took place.

The various studies and observations, the correlations established between experimentally measured speeds and graphic elements present or absent in writers with rapid writings, have made it possible to list, on the one hand the signs of rapidity and, on the other, those of slowness.

The latter are numerous[4].

Among the main signs of rapidity one can mention :

- simplifications, small irregularities, suppleness, combinations,
- accents thrown ahead of letters,
- an increasing left margin when the writing is dynamic,
- finals directed towards the beginning of the next word,
- everything that facilitates right tendencies and fluency.

A writing with a dominance of movement, if under control, is conducive both to speed and an alternation of up- and downstrokes, also to firm, conscious backward and forward movements, controlled by cerebral processes, and to movements that are dynamic and flowing.

Among the main signs of slowness or of slowing down, one can mention:

- still movement, static writing,
- complications, excessive left tendencies,
- penlifts, if they are numerous and badly calculated[5],

---

2   With the exception of a few dysgraphic writers.

3   With present day instruments, speeds are decidedly greater than those resulting from the pen-written tests given by H. de Gobineau [19]. Recent statistics, compiled in Liège, give 150 letters a minute at accelerated speed for a ch ild aged 13 [61].

4   Pulver, using Saudek's work, makes a list of them in *The Symbolism of Handwriting* [24].

5   A very large number of statistics demonstrate that cursive writing is always more rapid than typographic writing [62].

- very deliberate diacritics, written with strong pressure, amendments,
- pressure that is too strong, too heavy, deviated, very pasty, or too light,
- insufficient or excessive tension causing slackness, or precipitation owing to badly controlled gestures[6],
- all that which slows down a writing, even in simplified and right-tending writings; acquired forms, narrowness, too great regularity;
- it should be noticed that angles do not seem to be a significant factor of slowness.

One can also see writings which are slowed down by the anticipation of the effect produced by Klages's *Leitbild*[7].

Some writers have a rapid stroke[8] but stop, start again, hesitate; others write quickly owing to a constant, or rapid movement, but are slowed down by stiff or complicated letters.

Each writer has his variations of speed, depending on the sentence or word, and even, according to Pulver who refers back to Saudek on the subject, depending on the zone of the word.

The type of slowing down is itself significant : even with the same score for speed, the writer slowed down by spacing is not the same as the one who, for instance, is slowed down by complications.

In François Michel's experience, a writer can accelerate his writing by enlarging it, for in this way, he can throw his movement more easily[9]. All the same, this does not mean that a large writing is more rapid than a small one : strictly speaking, a reduced length of graphic line causes a saving of time. The statistical study of pre-adolescents done in Liège shows that people with a small writing write faster than the others. A small writing, incidentally, is a component of autonomy[19] and rapidity goes together with a good graphic level. It also corresponds to the cerebral aspect.

All of us have our own speed and we can accelerate or slow down our writing only up to a point, or else we run the risk of reducing its efficiency or its spontaneity.

---

6   It is seen in dysgraphic children, or adolescents with whom a seemingly important movement (animated), or slackness, may give an illusory appearance of rapidity.
7   See note in the chapter on the relationship between Form and Movement.
8   Hegar associates rapidity of the stroke with capacity for abstraction [7].
9   Hegar [7] also notes that long strokes are more rapid than short ones.

Good facility for adaptation allows controlled variations, which very strong emotivity, or lack of psychic energy do not allow. A writing which progresses freely in accordance with the writer's tempo is a sign of homogeneity and assists graphic fluency and rhythm.

Movement and speed can be combined in the graphologist's observation, as these factors are interrelated; one must, however, be able to correct a visual impression in which direction also plays a part. A writing that is projected forward looks more rapid than a controlled and vertical one.

SLOW
SLOWED DOWN

A well adapted child acquires speed as he gradually learns to master with suppleness those very precise and connected forms of writing which constitute a word. Practice is essential; those who have not had enough of it cannot write very quickly without spoiling the legibility. On the other hand, as soon as handwriting has become a fluent movement, writing quickly is normal.

By reliving the movement which produces SLOW writing (less than 100 letters a minute), one should be able to come close to the reasons for the control a writer applies to his outward manifestations, and to understand better the kind of inertia which imbues his writing.

Pulver thinks that slowness is never exempt from factors related to the shaping of a letter [24].

The shaping of letters may be the object of care and attention for all sorts of reasons.

One of these reasons may be of a moral, ethical or social kind, and range from discipline to a desire for perfectionism, or to formalism, and may incorporate prudence, or the desire to be in full control of oneself and of one's emotions.

The care and satisfaction put into the prevalence of the shaping of letters, or the choice of such shaping may also arise from self-satisfaction.

One may also wish not to hurry in order to enjoy a word or an idea for aesthetic reasons, or in order to give time for inspiration, [63] or for reflection.

Each writer has his own tempo, and so has each epoch.

But a slow writing may simply be due to rather slow thinking (feeble-minded people have great difficulty in learning how to write, and in particular, never manage to write fast), or to generally reduced activity, or some laziness or passivity. In the last case, the overall context is weak, forms are slack and the movement is not very dynamic.

Strong inner conflicts, inhibition, also slow down a writing. It is known that inhibition takes all sorts of graphic forms and affects all the categories.

Finally, the control which guides a slow writing may be that of a calculating mind. This expression is laden with psychological implications, and the signs must be flagrant and numerous, to be given such an interpretation. Pulver, however, has classified under the sign of slowness, a whole list of graphic signs of insincerity, [24] which in themselves do not have such a meaning, even if each one of them is the result of a slowing down of the gesture, and which can have other meanings in rapid writings.

Rapidity does not account for everything, however, and one can find signs of insincerity in rapid writings.

For Crépieux-Jamin, a writing which is always SLOWED DOWN is simply slow [14].

So, this sign means a writing which occasionally slows down. This can apply to the script as a whole, or to some of its parts.

The slowing down can occur when, for instance, the writer is in a state of physical discomfort (great tiredness, cold, unusual conditions which make writing difficult), or in a particular psychic condition.

This last aspect is of interest in terms of its practical application to professional graphology. Indeed, it frequently happens that a candidate applying for a post produces a letter of application with a writing slightly different from that of his curriculum vitae, a little less free, a little more careful or impressive perhaps, and often a little slowed down. Emotive, anxious people, some beginners and those who regard their position as applicant with special anxiety (particularly if they know, or feel, their letter is going to be submitted to a graphologist), will be more likely than others to show their apprehension with an increased watchfulness which will slow their writing down.

This slowing down can be revealed in many ways : general inhibition, smaller or larger dimensions, pressure, tension (showing the fear of adopting a position), breaks, interruptions ... It will therefore be necessary to take both documents into account, as well as the degree of emotivity of the writer.

In a slightly different way, the writer having a position in mind and knowing that his letter will be read, may slow down the course of the script, wishing to make it clearer, more neutral, or more aesthetic.

With adolescents' writings, the comparison between schoolwork, "official" letters (one written for a graphologist, for instance), and more intimate pieces of writing, or rough work, is also generally very fruitful, especially for the assessment of speed. One knows, with regard to this, that speed is very difficult to assess in the writing of children, when one has not actually seen them write [44].

Where slowing down occurs more regularly, for one to talk of a slowed down writing, one should see words, letters or parts of them, written with a decidedly less rapid movement than the context as a whole. Indeed, the speed of a writing is never perfectly constant.

The following may be involved: emotive words, capitals, (the social aspect, how one appears), beginnings or ends of words (difficulty in undertaking, deciding, or committing oneself), the zone of the letters (refer to Appendix 1 on the Symbolism of Space), letters or parts thereof which have a particularly direct correspondence with the movement (verticals, upper extensions and t-bars, curves...).

Woman, 44 years - Who has not had much education

168 *The movement aims at rapidity, but is slowed down by the mixture of weakness, stiffness and complications, by supporting strokes, congestions and starting strokes before the letters. It is not so much because of a relative lack of writing practice that this writing is not very rapid, but rather because of* *a lack of spontaneity in the writing as a whole. Due to the hesitations between each word, the spacing is irregular and the baseline not very well sustained.*

pouviez me rendre ce service ;
et si vous pouviez garder cela
confidentiel.
Veuillez agréer ~~madame~~

Avec ma très fidèle affect

Marcel Pagnol

169 *Here the pen seems to take pleasure in choosing a design which takes its time to shape the letters in the three dimensions of the graphic space.*

Boy, 19 years - Who has failed his baccalauréat for the second time
The draft (the first document) is definitely more rapid than the letter. The writing is much more connected, has more condensed dimensions, is not very firm, but more active than the writing of the letter, which is very inhibited, with its disconnections, its fragmentations, its heavy and irregular pressure, its stroke thin as well as pasty, its small angles and narrow letters, its stick-shaped prolongations, all of which are signs that do not accelerate the script and show anxiety.

170

The general tension itself is different : the one in the draft, not yet channelled but fairly positive, enables the graphologist to speak about his potential to this sensitive and intelligent boy, who feels dissatisfied and disappointed with himself and others, and stays apart, dreaming of success and frightened of failure.

POISED

POISED writing (about 130 letters a minute) mostly corresponds to controlled movement, being equally efficient when the movement is firm. In a monotonous graphic context, it shows indifference.

à 15 millions. Drôle d'ef
jongle avec les millions comm
alles. Ce n'est pas très en
Y ais nos week ends sont lour

171

Man, 25 years - Civil engineer from the Mines de Paris, a grande école. *Poised to accelerated, aerated writing, which flows firmly and relatively freely. It gains time and efficiency in the relief (see the clear upper extensions) and the simple forms. But it wastes some of this in certain penlifts (called for by the accents), in the looping of the 'k' and the 's's which are important, and in some round forms which the writer seems to want to retain, and which can be related to the overall context which is still close to a very clear copybook model, wide, and with left and right margins almost missing. The top margin is large and may help to account for the fact that, as a reaction against strong* *authority, the writer has chosen a life of freedom, close to nature, and does not particularly bother about a professionally competitive career, to which his education would entitle him.*

In a firm context, it indicates good use of one's energy and control over one's emotions. Projects may be more modest than those of writers who have a more rapid or animated writing, but a certain quality of life and of relationships is preserved. The writer is not so impressed by competitiveness, by one-upmanship or by professional exploits, for instance. There may be less stimulating anxiety than in very rapid writings, less tension directed towards one's objectives, but also less negative tension, less stress.

In assessing the implications of poised writing on an intellectual level, the graphologist will often find reflection and common sense. A poised writing can be freer, better adapted, and indicate more security than a rapid writing. It is a factor of homogeneity and proportion.

In averagely evolved writings, it is the most positive of the signs of speed.

ACCELERATED
RAPID
PRECIPITATED

A writing classified as ACCELERATED produces about 150 words a minute, and a RAPID writing, 180.

It is difficult to distinguish between these degrees of rapidity. In both cases one should list a certain number of signs showing speed. They will be found associated with a few signs of slowing down, which is normal in a lively writing.

Generally speaking, the speed of a writing indicates the writer's activity. Nuanced meanings will be established, as to the quantity and the quality of this general activity, by judging the degree of speed and relating it to the graphic context.

In a progressive and firm context, speed will show spontaneous participation, prompt reactions, an enterprising mind, dynamism and a rapid passage of ideas into action.

In a slacker, less orderly context, speed reveals superficiality, evasions, constant searching for future goals while neglecting the present; conceiving ideas may be easy, but the reasoning is in danger of not dealing thoroughly with the consequences.

All the classical authors see in the rapidity of a writing, one of the expressive factors of intelligence and of abstraction (which is the highest level of human intellectual capacity), because rapid writing, translating a thought, demands rapid formation and coordination of ideas.

Graphologists, on the subject of speed as a mark of intelligence, acknowledge none the less, the possibility of rapidity due to a graphic skill which some writers do have. This makes the diagnosis less reliable and graphologists should therefore look for other positive graphic signs. Rapidity in a writing must always go with efficiency. For example, a rapid, small, simplified, clear, orderly writing, with a good layout, will be a surer sign of intelligence than another writing which is equally fast and equally small, but has narrow spacing between lines, stumbles against the right margin, and is very irregular, with slightly slack forms and flying strokes : the latter would reveal more uncontrolled and reactive emotivity, which finds release in quick actions and reactions.

From a moral point of view, while it is true that imprecisions, omissions, medium clarity are much more understandable in a rapid graphic context than in a slow one, one should, nevertheless, grade interpretations with subtlety, rather than succumb to a facile and dangerously black and white explanation of one sort or another.

Woman, 55 - Unmarried, interior decorator

The signs of rapidity are numerous and very homogeneous : progressive but controlled movement, right-tending writing, simplified, wide (a little crushed and filiform, with ovals forfeited), rather diminishing, connections grouped around the accentuation, with a few combinations.

172
The general control (movement, space, direction), lends strength to this personal script which shows a refusal of dependency through the slowing down effect of the small angles, the dashes, the slight left slant, the spaces and the finals sometimes pulled to the right.

A varied, open and realistic intelligence (open, right-tending, but structured forms, small irregularities) used with suppleness, but also with firmness (well kept baseline). The writing is rhythmic.

In PRECIPITATED writing, the speed exceeds 200 words a minute; it contains a maximum number of signs of rapidity and a minimum number of signs of slowness, but a minimum insufficient to hold back an impassioned and impulsive side, hasty thought and organisation. The thought, most often, is mobile, a little unstable. The writing is ebullient, its movement is either carried away or else effervescent (when it seems to remain in one place in spite of its constant activity), and its forms deteriorate. The intellectual level is not as obvious as all that; 'brio' is more frequent than depth.

Finally, one should note that a person may be intelligent and want to write fast, but have personal difficulties and write slowly, so great is the involvement of emotions with the functioning of intelligence.

Woman, 60 years - Dressmaker

173

Another rapid writing, in a lively context, but a lot less orderly and controlled (in keeping with the cultural level and the personality). Considerable irregularity dominated by the affective letters and the thrown movements. The right margin is very small, the lines are close together (tangled lines). The writer partly holds back her haste and her elan through the numerous loopings, the suspensions and the returns to the left. Comprehension is rapid, realisation a little messy. Time and energy are a lot less well managed than in writing no.172.

racteristique   de   mon   ecriture   ¨ ma

les pages qui suivront ne seront -pa

de rédaction soigneuse de ma part

Man, 22 years

174

The stroke is rapid, more so in the middle zone than in the verticals, more rapid than the writing as a whole, which is slowed down by tensions, by stops in the cursive movement (separated and fragmented letters), and consequently by rigid white spaces. The form is simple, not simplified, irregularly wide. The stroke is precise, almost a little trenchant. The spaces are large, the right margin is wide (some 't's are suspended).

Contacts are distant, thinking a little theoretical; there is overall mistrust with slightly clumsy self-assertion sometimes (mixture of filiformity, narrowness, small triangular lower extensions).

9

SPACE

Handwriting is achieved by means of a writing instrument and a supporting surface on which the written line is produced.

This surface constitutes the graphic space (stone, wall, papyrus, sheet of paper, etc). It is delimited by margins and structured as much by the arrangement of the lines on the page as by the alternation of the words and the intervals which separate them. These spaces between the lines and words are laid down by the copybook model, by the social and sociological rules, and by the personality of the writer.

Spacing between words is, in our present-day style[1], inherent in the progression of the graphic gesture inscribing a language made of words which are separate entities. It is taught at the same time as handwriting, yet without much strict supervision on the part of teachers. Initially, it is an elementary, given principle which soon becomes personal, but which demands evolved gestures in order to be mastered freely.

Spacing between lines is acquired at a later stage, since spacing is indicated for children - and even for adolescents - by means of lined or squared paper[2].

The same is true of margins, the right -hand margin remaining, however, the freer one. Margins, moreover, are bound up with national and cultural habits.

The general distribution of the graphic groups arises from these three important factors and forms the layout in its broad sense. Spaces between

---

1   It seems that spacing between words has historically appeared later than spacing between lines which is automatic.
2   In France, children are taught to write on squared paper. (T.N.)

words could have been studied with continuity[3] as they are , in fact, part of the cursive movement, but we include them with Space because they participate actively in its structure and because, in the present chapter, we are studying handwriting from the point of view of a global overall result. It must be understood that all the categories have contributed to this result, but less directly so than these three factors.

French writers usually deal with inter-word and inter-linear spacing together. We shall study them separately for teaching purposes, although they are connected by relationships, where homogeneity or lack of it, provides the graphologist with very interesting information, and we shall then have:

1. **Spacing between words in the following writings : compact, very compact, spaced out, very spaced out, with inter-word gaps, aerated, and irregularly spaced.**

2. **Layout :**
    - trajectory of lines,
    - spacing between lines,
    - margins,
    - new paragraphs,
    - the arrangement as a whole.

The analogy between the graphic space and the outside word is obvious and is immediately and, very logically, applicable to every act of writing[4] and to all graphological systems.

The child who starts to write, enters a world different from that of of his early childhood; he submits to new social and moral rules and his graphic space is the framework in which these signs will be inscribed, signs which he wants to become handwriting, but which he masters intellectually only little by little. One must be able to anticipate, so that the graphic act be-

---

3   Crépieux-Jamin classified spacing between words under Dimension, thus generalising movement in a concept of width and narrowness. Indeed, if it is logical for a graphic gesture to expand or condense both the area of a word and the intervals between words, it is also true that all combinations can be found.

4   See the Foreword: Scribbles

comes free in the sequence of words and consequently, of spaces. Those who are not used to writing often have rigid and irregular intervals, whereas their layout is correct[5.]

Handwriting forms a whole, in which space (the white) is inseparable from what is written (the black), from the moment the graphic gesture takes place. Once the graphic line has been produced, one can distinguish the form (what has been written, the black) from the background (what has not been written, the white space), and some French graphologists, in trying to discriminate between the significance of each of these elements, consider - this is specific to them - that space may possibly be representative of the unconscious, becoming secondarily a space exterior to the inner conscious world[6].

The background must be the framework for the form, it must allow a word to stand out from the text, it must enhance it. It must not drown what is written and itself become a meaningful form, reversing its function. Nor must it disappear as in handwriting which is too compact.

Space facilitates clarity and legibility, hence the primary interpretation of good intellectual organisation and adaptation, when the writing shows a good relationship between white and black.

Lack of self control, (whether due to impulsiveness, or slackness), lack of discrimination, of judgement, or control over one's thinking, difficulty in adapting to the outside world, all are recorded in those writings where space is perturbed (bad rhythm of distribution[7]) and does not fulfil its primary function.

A good rhythm of distribution is an essentially positive factor in any type of writing, both on its own account and because it is a compensatory element, where there is a more or less well controlled movement, for instance, or where forms are more or less well structured.

---

5   See Chapter on Organisation of handwriting.
6   Bernard Bernson and Elisabeth Koechlin Saint Morand originated this view.
7   Here we are using German terminology which seems to us very well adapted to space.

1. Spacing between words

The continuity prescribed by the copybook is that there should be a small interval between letters and that each letter should be connected to the next. Whilst rhythm of space, given through good distribution of the graphic groups, can be acquired only rather late, children, however, soon personalise their spacing when their writing has become evolved.

The three writings of children shown on the next page, come from girls of very similar ages, ending their C.P.[8], with the same teacher. All three of them wrote with a biro.

The mastery of spacing between words, assuming a well integrated cursive movement that has generated fluent continuity, is an important qualitative factor to be related to the graphic context.

This element is also very difficult to change, unless the writer slows his writing down in order to fake it. In any case, it escapes visual control more than spacing between lines or the arrangement on the page. Being mainly under the control of reflection, or of certain norms, the spacing between lines and the layout are less closely tied up with the graphic movement than spacing between words, which has more to do with our dealings with others and with our daily activities.

---

grenouille   grenouille   grenouille

feuille   feuille   feuille   feuille   feuille

une   grenouille   sur   une   feuille.

175/1

---

8   Cours Préparatoire : in the French school system, this is the first year of primary school, when children are 6 and learn to write. (T.N.)

2

3

175 The compactness of writing no. 3 comes from accumulated efforts and from a very anxious character; this child puts a lot into her endeavours (more than no. 2 does) and is less self-effacing than no.1, whose writing is very small, amended, with false connections, and slightly atrophied lower extensions, wide, irregular spaces as compared with the smallness of the writing, letters coming closer and closer together at the end of words. Writing no. 2 is the freest in its cursive movement and in its width; it is the one which masters its spacing best.

COMPACT
VERY COMPACT
squeezed (for Crépieux-Jamin)

In COMPACT writing, the spaces between words are definitely smaller than the width of two average letters of the writer's handwriting. In VERY COMPACT writing, they are smaller still.

A child who sticks to a fairly compact writing does not wish to stray from established rules, and gives him a feeling of security. His application and concentration will be facilitated in his schoolwork. If too pronounced, then compactness, being evidence of an obliteration of space, becomes fear of the outside world.

Adolescents, in general, write with spaces between words more than with compactness [11].

If the density of COMPACT writing is not detrimental to the general distribution of the text, and if control emanates from this, together with freedom of movement and open forms, compactness has positive meanings on several levels. Such subjects get involved in their actions and relationships, they are concerned, stable, they can be, and wish to be, supportive, to take part incommunity projects; they often have presence. On the intellectual level, they concentrate well, are efficient, can assimilate well; their judgement remains close to reality. In some graphic contexts, they can be creative[9].

But narrow spaces between words can be accompanied by a lack of control of movement; drives and impulses then override reflection and logic, activity becomes activism, especially if the layout does not obey the principles of order and moderation.

If on the other hand, constraint and tension appear, if the writing is too closed, double-joined, or stiff in its forms of connection, compactness then

---

9 In *Essai d'une orientation psychologique par l'écriture aérée et l'écriture compacte* [64], Maurice Delamain distinguishes the "ink lovers, intellectuals and ideologists who put things on record, and reason abundantly and creatively in writing" from the "ink fearers who do not think far ahead, grasp things by means of mental flashes, are poets, scientists, or men of action who take decisions".

becomes a defence against the outside world; openness, the capacity to listen, being at the disposal of others, can then all be subject to doubt.

In the case of VERY COMPACT writing, the signs of tension are very frequent and relationships with others are constrained, or cannot take place owing to the writer's preoccupations, and the fact that he retires within himself. Thinking tends to stick to systems and judgement becomes biased.

The meanings of compactness should be magnified or minimised according to the spacing between lines, which is concerned more with professional or social relationships, and on the intellectual level, distance and thoughtfulness; spacing between words is concerned more with closer relationships. Thus, for instance, someone whose writing has very big spaces between lines and normal ones between words, will have better intimate contacts than social ones.

---

qui me viennent à l'esprit, peut-être en ... je j'aurais souhaité, c'est aimer connaî- rapport aux orientations, aux points forts,

Man, 21 years - Student

176

Very compact writing, large with narrow 'm's and 'n's, and no margins, with no skill in the connections which are made of a few groupings, some juxtapositions and false connections. The writing is almost without apparent movement (the letters look as if placed one beside the other), the lines are close to one another. The gesture is tight, a little rigid and hesitant, not very fast, the forms are clear, simple, but look childish with their copybook style, the ovals are big, the writing is right-slanted. The writer would like support and contacts, but in this context, compactness reveals the fear of giving himself away if he takes a definite position, or stops being somehow exemplary

From the too perfect overall context, which does not have a very warm stroke and has sharp-pointed free signs, one can deduce underlying, slightly aggressive dissatisfaction and disapproval.

Woman, 43 years - Sales representative
Writing with a compact tendency and with irregularities.
The movement is not well controlled, the proportions not very good. The sufficient right-hand margin, the connectedness, the fairly dense texture of the stroke, made with a felt pen, the few angles, the closed 't's, the finals either short or turned leftwards, bring a control and a structure to this writing, which has a wavy baseline and is very irregular in all categories. Not a very harmonious script, but lively and supple.

177
While it is true that the ethical and social behaviour of this writer will be a little unpredictable, she can, however, apply the brakes. She is warm, very lively, active, intelligent, has a lot of tenacity and is very successful in her profession, which puts her in contact with very different groups.
The word 'nouvelles' in the last line, with its lapse of continuity and jerks, is telescoped and dances on the line; this word shows the positive role which connectedness and a reduction of the spacing can have; the compact tendency here is positive.

SPACED-OUT
VERY SPACED-OUT
WITH INTER-WORD GAPS

In SPACED-OUT writing, spaces between words are larger than the width of two letters; they are decidedly still more so in VERY SPACED-OUT writing. In writing WITH INTER-WORD GAPS, words are isolated in the space.

Since the background (the space) takes greater importance than in compact writing, it is necessary for words in SPACED-OUT writing to represent a group which is sufficiently strong in dimension, form and pressure. Then, spaced-out writing can be interpreted as a need for clarity, reflection and independence : the subject stands back in relation to himself, he observes, he assesses. If the writing is receptive and supple, he is open towards others, makes himself available to them, does not try to put pressure on them, and lets them have the independence that he likes for himself. If the writing is animated, or inventive, he can be open to ideas, to sources of imagination[10].

The bigger the spaces between words, the more necessary it is for the graphic gesture to remain well mastered. Indeed, tensely written words induce stiff spacing, indicating that the writer becomes selective, distrustful, and the gaps caused by slackly written words do not structure the space sufficiently.

If the writing is VERY SPACED-OUT, the quality of the script should increase even more, if it is to testify to the writer's good adaptation and efficiency. In a context which is generally narrow, uneasy, still or reared, with a bad quality stroke for instance, apprehension gets the better of reflection and of search for objectivity, and solitude gets the better of reserve and selectivity.

If the movement becomes floating and the articulation of words is no longer assured by good continuity, then fancifulness, inactivity and ill-controlled emotions dominate.

Extra spacing does not increase clarity and freedom.

One should see whether the continuity of the graphic thread is retained, whether it keeps some elasticity : it is practically broken in all writings WITH INTER-WORD GAPS; words are lost in the graphic field and communication no longer takes place.

---

10 Creativity, which is difficult to assess in handwriting, can be found in various types of spacing and scripts.

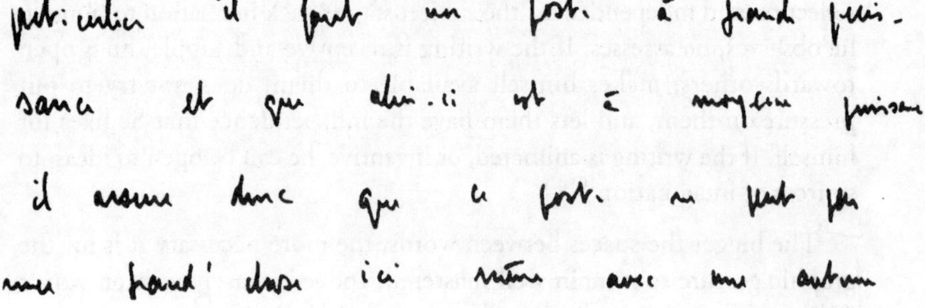

[handwritten text]

Man, 45 years

The writing is spaced out, but the spaces are not rigid: the writing, although very restrained, retains some suppleness. The script is efficient because of the well-nourished, firm and sufficiently elastic stroke, the connectedness, with a few groupings dictated by firm and precise accentuation, and the proportions which bring the elements of the writing together satisfactorily .

The spaces reveal the reflection of a concentrated, concrete and subtle mind (well-nourished, simple and simplified writing, small and diminishing), independent in its thinking and judgement. Emotions are interiorised, contacts are selective and loyal, as well as socially and professionally well adapted (simple but narrow forms, with openings, spaces proportionally bigger between the words than between the lines). The writer appreciates self-control and reserve, knows also how to appreciate solitude, but, without being expansive, he can be warm (the stroke is not dry).

He has been professionally very successful at the head of an important industrial concern, where he has spent his whole career; his qualities as a realistic mediator have been acknowledged in several circumstances.

178

179 Woman, 40 years - Married, two children

Very spaced out writing. In spite of the width, the words, though more ample[11], are less full [12] than in writing no.178. The space is less well

---

11 In the sense of Müller and Enskat [88].
12 In the sense of Klages [23].

179

structured by what is written. This is no longer distance, or reflection. The writing is crushed in order to muster strength and go forward, the stroke is not very firm, nor very firmly handled, the lines are a little floating, or a little convex, and two of them mingle. The form is both acquired and not very structured : the personality needs a protective outer façade, and uses charm to express itself.

Woman, 36 years - Arts degree, 3 children

180
The photo here reproduces faithfully the bottom margin : non-existent. The right-hand margin is very small. Writing with inter-word gaps.

AERATED WRITING

With AERATED writing[13], a good balance is achieved between the
graphic groups; they are well distributed, and words stand out "successfully", due to the spacing"[14].

Aerated writing constitutes both a medium degree of spacing between
words, and a more global sign since, as its name implies, air circulates easily.
Sufficiently well spaced lines, paragraphing and margins, contribute to the
clarity of the whole, and to really giving the word its body.

Nous pourrons en parler, ainsi bien sûr
que de votre vie, si vos pas vous mènent
à Toulon où nous serons heureux de
vous recevoir.

souhaiterions avoir votre opinion
importante de sa personnalité
et de nous assurer qu'il peut
manager au sens complet

181

---

13 A non-Jaminian term introduced by Maurice Delamain and used again by Gille-
Maisani.
14 We are indebted to Hélène de Gobineau for this formula, who makes this one of the
components auf Autonomy and of Personality in her scales.

181

> *The potential for efficiency of the authors of these two aerated writings, both of whom have a high degree of education and equivalent responsibilities, is very different. Flowing and firm movement, a slightly pasty stroke, but with defended edges, in the case of the first writer; dynamic writing with a slightly propulsive, but controlled movement, in the case of the second (right margin, finals, diminishing), whose stroke is precise.*
> *If both scripts were compact, the first writer would perhaps not detach himself from his rich, personal emotions and impressions; the second would increase his impulsiveness and dynamism, which may drive him a little too much, but are well socialised both through and in his profession (the spacing between the lines is sufficient).*

This is a positive sign which leads to graphic and psychic freedom and balanced rhythm. It enhances the quality of all types of writing, indicating that the writer's potential is well used, compensating for a lack of suppleness, or fragility, owing to the capacity to adapt and to interact which it assumes.

It is necessary to appreciate this, but it must not be overestimated : the strength and originality of the personality are given by the writing as a whole, in its homogeneity (or possibly, in its conflicting tendencies, if these are constructive). Aerated writing enables the other signs to interact harmoniously.

On the intellectual level, aerated writing reveals clear, communicable thought, measured judgement, the ability to discriminate between rigour and tolerance, since, whatever the level of the writing, thinking intervenes to enable the subject to distance himself, nevertheless without affective or human values being denied.

Constraints, inhibition, impulsiveness are not expressed by these types of spacing, which convey the feeling of genuine identity, and therefore of maturity

When the writing is too aerated, it approaches spaced out writing, which is often met with in adolescents [11].

j' ai l' honneur de solliciter un emploi
en qualité de Chauffeur Poids Lourds.
Je vous prie de bien vouloir trouver ci- j
intée vous donnant tous les renseignements néessa
j' espère que ma demande sera prise en Co

Long distance lorry driver, respected for his professional qualities.

182 *Very well controlled script, small, connected, well-nourished, clear, with aerated tendency. However, neither the slightly tense cursive movement, nor the rhythm, present in the two other scripts, permit free alternation between words and spaces.*

IRREGULAR SPACING

Irregular spacing is found in many adolescents related to irregularity in other categories, This shows lack of graphic control and, more generally, a hesitation in keeping with that time of life.

Whilst small irregularities are part of any lively writing, when they are not caused by a justified lack of graphic control[15], they do indicate some unease, some difficulty in adaptation, since they break the rhythm.

One must, however, note certain particularities which can in some precise cases, modify the spacing. For instance:

---

15 See Chapter on Organisation.

- the simple fact of having little paper and a lot to say (postcard), or intensified concentration on one piece of work, decreases it;

- hesitation about choice of a word or spelling, or emphasis on an emotional word (the meaning will have to be borne in mind), the reaction to sudden inspiration, increases spacing.

A specific irregularity consists in creating 'CHIMNEYS', a sort of vertical corridor produced by spaces repeated over several successive lines. These strike the graphologist, and could evoke the image of an irruption of an ill-controlled force, originating, perhaps, from the unconscious.

Woman, 20 years

183 *Acquired writing, structured in its basically angular form, automatic, large. Presence of chimneys.*

2. Layout

The bottom part of the middle zone letters forms the baseline. It is called the zone of reality.

It is the words that follow one another from left to right, in our writing styles, which constitute the trajectory of the lines.

The position of the first word of each line determines both the dimension and the regularity of the spaces between the lines at their start, a regularity which requires graphic mastery[16].

The starting and finishing points of the lines are what forms the margin.

1. The trajectory of lines - A line well mastered in its trajectory also requires graphic fluency : frequent stoppages of the movement, or hesitations, facilitate neither the horizontality of the base of words nor the regularity of alignment. In order to stabilise the words on the line[17] and make them progress towards the right, sufficient, well-controlled pressure, a certain speed and an initial movement are necessary. One needs to know what one wants to write, and one must have become used to anticipating by means of thinking.

a) *Horizontal lines* follow a straight, firm trajectory without rigidity. They denote a goal, stability in one's objectives, continuity in one's reasoning and control of one's moods. They are in keeping with a well-mastered writing.

b) *Rigid lines* are formed without suppleness. They can be more or less heavy, more or less tense. Duty or conventionality put a constraint on the

---

16 See Chapter on Organisation.

17 The items concerning the lines are numerous in the Children's and Dysgraphy scales [8] embodying well the difficulties children have in controlling both the words and their progression on the page. Irregular spaces at the beginning of the lines (F 13), soon disappear (73% at the age of 6, 14% at 11). Dancing words (M 28) are signs of greater clumsiness than FLuctuating lines (M 26) and come from the difficulty in stabilising words on the line, and it is significant that between the ages of 10 and 11, dancing words drop more noticeably, from 68% down to 49%, a percentage which until then had not changed much.

writer, and are synonymous with strictness and intransigence if other signs of stiffness are numerous (angles, reared or very constrained movement, rigid letter slant) and dominate the signs of adaptation.

Rigid lines are not frequent in children and adolescents and are never a positive sign.

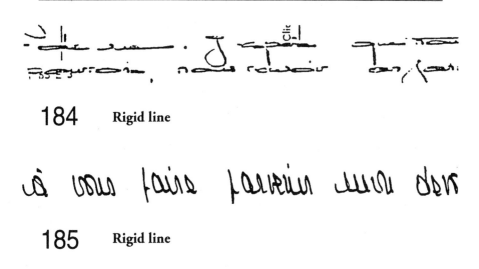

184   **Rigid line**

185   **Rigid line**

c) *Wavy lines* have an undulating trajectory[18]. Several kinds can occur in adults whose graphomotricity is evolved :

The script as a whole is floating, not very structured : the waviness of the baseline confirms the lack of firmness of the personality, unsure of its identity and not very stable in its projects, or else led by strong emotivity[19] (writing no.186).

---

18 Crépieux-Jamin makes no distinction between wavy and fluctuating lines, a consequence of item M 26 still present in 76% of children aged 11, still persisting for a long time in adolescence, and often found in writings which are socio-culturally not very evolved. The graphologist must allow for the difficulties of learning how to write.

19 M.T. Prenat [65] made many studies on the waviness of lines using T. Lewinson and J. Salce's graphometric method.

accueillir dans le nouveau cœur du " Verger "

186   Wavy line

The writing as a whole is skilful, not very spontaneous : the general attitude tends towards opportunism, the writing being capable of suppleness, just as much as of firmness, or even slight rigidity (writing no.187).

par la suite vous pourriez trou-

187   Wavy line

The writing as a whole is clear, sufficiently structured and spontaneous: the slightly wavy lines are signs of adaptation.

It also happens that, as in the writing below, sustained intellectual work focuses the writer's attention, to the detriment of the horizontality of the baseline: a condensation of the movement - even a tension - appears in the connections, the dimension; the spaces between lines remain controlled and sizeable (writing no.188).

Pardon pour ces taches que vous

188   Wavy line

d) *Concave and convex lines* present a curve, open respectively towards the upper or the lower zone.

In the case of the concave line, the writer pulls himself together after an initial lack of ardour and self-confidence, and his energy or interest intensify in the course of action.

nous mêmes dix jours à Calvet et ailleux. Mais de puis que nous som

189 Concave line

In the case of convex lines, the initial drive, being a little excessive to start with, is not sustained, either because of an impatient temperament geared towards a goal (first of the two writings below), or because of lack of constancy. Convex writing can also indicate struggle against discouragement, disappointment and disenchantment (second writing).

J'ai trouvé des écrits de.

190 Convex line

excuse pour cet après-midi, mais nous somme

191 Convex line

e) *Rising and descending lines* take an upward or downward direction in their trajectory to the right, independently of the course of the line, which can be straight, wavy, concave, convex, or in tiles.

A momentary impulse can provoke an ascending direction, but so can a more constant state arising from enthusiasm, emotional stimulation or a tendency to elation, illusion, even utopia, if the letters do not sufficiently rest on the baseline.

The ascending direction can also come from some tension, which either is directed towards a goal and indicates, by means of forcing, some élan, combativeness or ambition, or may be an attempt to compensate for some deeply felt difficulty, for a state of fatigue, or one of discouragement.

Rising lines

192 *The above writer, who is very emotional, struggles against some latent discouragement and has, at the same time, a tendency to get excited about things : the writing is tense and a little floating, inflated, straightened-up, with secondary widths.*

A descending line reveals temporary, or more permanent discouragement, pessimism, or low spirits. The script then seems to lack direction towards a goal and its pressure is generally heavy.

However, when the writing as a whole is stiffened, it reveals opposition[20], obstinacy, even emotional blocking.

---

193 Descending writing

---

20 These two interpretations are also found in children's handwritings [66].

[handwriting sample]

194 Descending writing

A peculiarity of the descending line is *the diving line* at the end of a line: the last words of the line fall because the line goes too far on the page, either owing to lack of restraint, or of anticipation (see writing no.173), or owing to refusal to leave a space, which could indicate mistrust.

If the line itself descends in a context of discouragement, or depression, the downward drop of the last words will increase its meaning.

Depression can be indicated just as much by descending lines as by tense rising lines, but also by heavy writings on a monotonous and rigid baseline (writing no.151) or lines which are weak.

f) In writings with *ascending* or *descending tiles*[21], each word rises or descends independently of the line. In both cases there is a constantly renewed effort, and therefore a difficulty felt. The writer who uses ascending tiles, wants to recover his courage, his ardour (he can also wish to control his impulses). The one with descending tiles struggles against discouragement or defeatism.

[handwriting sample]

195 Writing with ascending tiles

[handwriting sample]

196 Writing with descending tiles

---

21 Also called *galloping up* or *galloping down* in Renna Nezos's book *Graphology* (T.N.)

Lines are very sensitive to changes of mood, taken in its broad sense. The same writer can, according to circumstances, give his lines different trajectories or even adopt several directions in the course of one piece of writing, particularly if he is sensitive or emotive.

Too big irregularities are detrimental to the homogeneity and to the general distribution, and can lead to bad rhythm.

The best adapted people are those whose baseline remains horizontal and supple. Suppleness of line can moderate a few signs of rigidity. Rigid lines must throw doubt on apparent suppleness.

2. Spacing between lines - Good spacing between lines contributes to a good overall distribution of black and white.

Reflection, control of emotions and feelings by means of thought, are revealed by relatively large spacing between the lines. The more these come close to one another, the less the subject stands back, and the more subjective he is. Well spaced lines, attesting, in a good graphic context, to the capacity to synthesise and be objective, will therefore be essential in the writings of candidates applying for positions requiring the ability to take decisions and assume responsibilities.

Lines too spaced out draw the attention of the graphologist to a risk of lack of awareness of reality, or of insufficient commitment, especially if the signature is placed far from the text.

When the lower extensions of one line and the upper extensions of the next lines intermingle, the writing is said to have TANGLED LINES.

This kind of writing results from too little spacing between the lines, as much as from excessive up and down prolongations.

Tangling lines almost always indicate a lack of capacity to stand back, bad judgement, poor sense of relative values, and also, interference. In the better graphic contexts, one can talk of activity, of involvement of self - even if these qualities are far more instinctive than thought out and organised - or, in very evolved writings, of inspiration drawn from deep down in the psyche[22].

---

22 Blaise Pascal's writing has tangled lines of this kind.

In less good graphic contexts, those where writing becomes confused, the drawbacks of tangled line writing are added to those of too prolonged writing.

Too large, too small, or too irregular spaces between lines, because of their lack of proportion, are detrimental to the overall distribution and destroy its rhythm.

3. **Margins** - Margins are strongly expressive as far as the symbolism of space[23] is concerned and are studied mainly from that angle.

Everyone soon manages the norms proposed for margins (it is known however that children acquire that notion only later [44]), and margins remain very significantly constant, in different samples of someone's writing and even in his messages and envelopes[25].

a) *The top margin* - It is related to authority and consequently to autonomy. If the top margin is too large, and especially if the writing is crushed, authority has been felt too strongly. If it is too small, the writer finds security in complying with that authority (one often finds this in children). In either case, the writer has not found satisfactory and autonomous links with others, and this is reflected in relationships and particularly in professional life, in ways which the graphic context will specify.

b) *The bottom margin* - It is normal to leave a blank space at the bottom of the page : this balances the distribution of the text and corresponds to a certain demand for order and aesthetics. When no margin is left at the bottom, one may either not know when to stop one's actions, or be seeking security.

---

23 See Appendix 1, *The Symbolism of Space.*

24 Beside the placing of addresses on envelopes, well-known to be constant in relation to the 4 symbolic zones of the graphic field, the wording of an envelope, very social in its destination, can be compared with the text, as capitals can be compared with small letters, or the text with the signature (allowing for the fact that the signature does not contain only the social self - see Chapter on The Signature). The authenticity, the simplicity, or their opposite, can be confirmed by it. Besides, figures, being present on any envelope, give information by their precision and their dimension.

c) *The right-hand margin* - It is related to the future, the outside world.

On the intellectual level, the notion of organisation of time leads one to manage a sufficient, supple margin on the right.

A big right-hand margin can be a compensation for a very thrown, or very right-slanted writing.

Regarding contacts, the selectivity of a narrow, and spaced-out script is reinforced by a large right-hand margin, whereas a tendency to be invasive, or importunate, can be shown by a margin that is too narrow. In some graphic contexts, a big right-hand margin sometimes indicates mental reservations, a "mental restriction" [67].

The right-hand margin can be either even or uneven. Irregularity, if considerable, suggests behaviour which is variable in actions, in contacts with others, and in the trust given to the outside world. One should, however, see whether the writer would have had the room to write one more word on the line, as some writers prefer not to subdivide the words.

d) *The left-hand margin* - A socio-cultural acquisition which appears fairly early in all writers, the left-hand margin is, moreover, symbolically heavily loaded : it is perhaps the most significant of the margins.

The left-hand margin is related to the past, to incidents that occurred in childhood, to the family and its norms. If it is very narrow, the attachment to these values restricts independence at all levels. If it is within the norm (approximately 1/5 of the line), a satisfactory independence has been reached. If it is very wide, the past has made a strong impression and continues to influence the writer in one way or another. In adolescents, one often meets a fluctuating left margin, which shows the alternation between their dependence and their search for autonomy.

In writings which are not very structured or spontaneous, the unevenness of this margin shows a not very demanding moral conscience.

If the left margin is rigid, principles, on the contrary, are strict.

The left margin can be progressive (increasing). When it remains supple, this denotes activity, ardour, spontaneous participation. When it is rigid, it shows more an escape into activism. If the script is slack, the graphologist will suspect a lack of continuity in actions and planning.

The left margin can be regressive (decreasing as the text reaches the bottom of the page); this indicates some holding back, retraction, contradiction, or inhibition of one sort or other.

Small left and top margins are often found in children who do not allow their nature full scope.

In all cases, both right and left margins will be studied jointly: for instance, it is logical for a fairly big left margin to coexist with a small right margin.

e) *Absence of margins*[25] - This is a left-over from childhood which, if the graphic context confirms it, indicates a state of mind close to that of earlier times, and is shown either by dependence, or by a lack of awareness of one's relative importance, or else by a desire for omnipotence and omnipresence.

Absence of margins can also come from absence of conventions.

Observation of the writing as a whole is particularly important as far as this peculiarity is concerned, as the absence of margins can arise just as much from constraint, or lack of adaptation, as it can, more rarely, from real independence, or from non-conformity.

f) *Typographic margins reproducing printing margins* - Culture, aestheticism, can lead to choosing this style of layout, but also a search for individualism, a showy side to one's nature, or also, in other contexts, the need for a framework with rules which give a sense of security.

A typographic layout can isolate a condensed text; this thereby increases the meaning of reduced openness to the outside world, the writer may, or may not, be able, or unable, to direct his interests elsewhere; some literary people proceed in this way[26].

A few more peculiarities can be mentioned : convex or concave margins and funnel-shaped ones.

Convex or concave margins, whose curves are open respectively towards the left or towards the right on the page, show in both cases a difficulty in breaking away from the left zone.

---

25 A writing that has margins neither on the left, nor the right, or has very few margins, is also considered a writing without margins.
26 See writing no. 100 again.

Funnel-shaped margins progressively increase both on the right and on the left as the text progresses on the page, they indicate either some increasing pessimism or some difficulty in maintaining activity or relationships.

4) New paragraphs - A classical arrangement, in our present-day writing style, dictates new paragraphs to separate the text into sections, according to the main ideas. Americans, for instance, usually indicate their paragraphs simply with a larger space between the lines. Some writers follow this fashion.

Well delineated paragraphs lighten up and clarify a text and testify to a comprehensive outlook, which is either clear or seeks clarity, and also respect for other people. The more its distribution is condensed, the more a text suffers from the absence of new paragraphs; this indicates difficulties in discriminating between what is important and what is not, also in making balanced judgements.

CHART 5

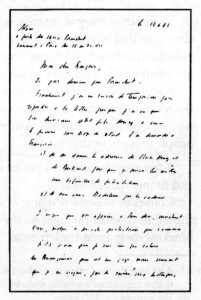

a   b

CHART 5 *cont'd*

c

d

Large spaces between paragraphs show a desire to be clearly understood, and in certain contexts, the desire to assert oneself and to prove one's worth. Exaggerated spaces between paragraphs are a sign of obsequiousness.

a) Very large left margin, slightly increasing. The text seems a little lost in the page and shifted to the right and towards the top. Good distribution of the words which are brought out clearly by the spacing. Supple baseline.

b) Large right-hand margin, a small one a little uneven on the left, slightly descending lines. Small top margin. Spaced-out lines and words. Administrative paragraphs (the writing can be seen at no.156).

c) The very large top margin, the extremely small and regressive left one, reveal a constraint which the writing confirms.

d) Large middle zone with very little apparent movement (the writing can be seen at no.106, practically no margin, very uneven spacing between words.

5. Overall arrangement - Each writer arranges his text on the page in a personal manner, so closely linked to his personality that the graphologist, going beyond mere examination of the layout, finds what has led the writer to this projection of his graphic movement in space. A certain style of using the space - which is a global approach to an initial perception of a writing[27] - can then be defined.

Setting out a page by distributing the written elements (text, signature, date and heading) and the non-written parts, in accordance with what Pulver [24] calls an individual principle of movement and layout, is always very positive.

The structure given to the page in this way, is directly related to the whole psychic and intellectual structure of the writer.

This type of layout is not the way of a child, nor that of someone who is little used to writing. Children do not, of their own accord, have the notion of layout, and it is only after the age of 12, if they are evolved, that they begin to position their texts on the page well [44]. With children, and even with adolescents, it is necessary to recognise a successful layout. And if most people of lesser socio-cultural level have a layout which keeps to the rules for margins and placing of the signature[28], rarer are those who produce that well-mastered, lively distribution in which interlinear spaces and word distribution play a part. This kind of distribution requires having total mastery of the graphic act

This needs, in addition and above all, homogeneity and maturity : the subject dominates the situation and is at ease with his projects in relation to the outside world.

It is from this well-mastered, lively distribution that rhythm of space distribution arises; the more evolved the rhythm, the more the writer is capable of autonomous and innovatory action.

---

27 See Chapter on Methodology.
28 These norms are more and more taught, or recommended, and some publications designed for job applicants deal with this subject.

Tél domicile
bureau

Chère Madame,

Comme nous en sommes convenus, je vous prie de bien vouloir trouver ci-joint le dossier constitué par ma fille Florence conformément au schéma que vous m'avez indiqué -

Vous y trouverez une lettre de présentation personnelle de Florence, deux cartes et une lettre rédigées pendant les vacances, quelques devoirs dont l'un rédigé en 3e et l'un en 6e et enfin des notes de cours prises en juin 1984 -

Je ne crois pas inutile que vous disposiez aussi d'un exemplaire de ma propre écriture, au travers du présent courrier. Vous trouverez également dans le dossier quelques notes de mon épouse rédigées récemment -

Je vous prie de croire, chère Madame à l'assurance de mes sentiments les meilleurs,

Man 50, writing reduced by one third

197 *Well-controlled organisation of the page, balanced layout, lively and personal rhythm of distribution, given by the proportions of the elements of organisation of the layout, the graphic groups and the spaces.*

10

The SIGNATURE

With his signature, a writer takes responsibility for what he has just written, or what is written, in the case of a document, or a dictated letter.

Its importance is therefore considerable as a statement of identity and as authentication of a text. It is well known that a signature is often scrutinised for forgeries, especially in the case of wills and cheques.

Its effect on graphology is such that a serious graphologist will refrain from carrying out graphological analyses of documents where the signature is lacking.

In the business world, where letters are typed, where computer techniques are developing and where people write less and less, the signature remains an individual, irreplaceable element, one which will not disappear, even if it is dangerous to interpret it by itself, away from the whole which comprises both the normal handwriting and the signature.

The signature is both expressive of the ego, with which it identifies itself deeply, and representative of the social ego, of the image of himself which the writer, more or less consciously, wants to give to others.

This two-fold aspect of the signature can make a graphologist hesitate as far as its interpretation is concerned, but in fact, it is usually revealing at both these levels : a spontaneous signature, related to his intimate self, means that the writer makes no difference between what he is and what he wishes to appear to be; but the writer who fashions his signature in order to play a social role, also reveals his motivation through the choice of his script.

The signature gives a synthesis of these two aspects of the ego, all the richer symbolically, as it leaves greater freedom to the graphic gesture than the writing itself.

Being less subjected to the constraint of the school model, and due to its paraphs and gestures which bring it closer to drawing - even abstract drawing - the signature makes it possible to project unconscious images rich in meaning, provided, however, that the beginner in graphology does not project his own fantasies into his interpretations, without realising it.

Very personal signatures, a sign of individualism and independence, are frequently met with in France where they are not obliged to be legible. One does not meet them as often in Germanic[1] or Anglo-Saxon countries.

It is essential for a graphologist analysing the handwriting of a foreigner, to know the graphic customs of that writer's country, if there are any. For instance, in the U.S.A., it is fairly usual to recommend that the signature should be placed at the bottom and to the left of a text, the margin of which is very small. If he did not know this, the graphologist could select a mistaken interpretation.

Statistical studies[2], made on homogeneous groups of French people of different socio-cultural levels, show that the signature nearly always stands out from the text with an emphasis, in particular, on capitals, dimensions, rising direction, and underlinings. In a few cases, the differentiation can be minute, or negative: reduced dimension and lack of firmness, for instance.

The signature is a microcosm in itself which requires, each time, profound consideration; this is often difficult, because of the importance of the consequences of the judgements it involves, particularly regarding professional recruitment, where it influences the final decision, if the latter is uncertain [69].

The graphologist pays special attention to the following: the position of the signature on the page in relation to the text, the basic elements (name, surname), comparison with the writing of the text (how close to it, or how

---

1   In a comparative study of French and German signatures, Béatrice von Cossel stresses the fact that German signatures seldom have paraphs, seldom rise, are generally homogeneous with the text, and well placed on the page in relation to the text. She sees here a national characteristic of unity between the individual and his behaviour in relation to society [68].

2   Held by the authors.

it differs from it), and the graphic entity it constitutes with the addition of its paraphs, free strokes, transformation of the letters, etc.

1. The position on the page and its relation to the text

In France, it is accepted that the proper position of the signature is on the right, but not too much so, a little more than one interlinear space away from the text (about one and a half times the space between two lines).

Children and adolescents, more often than not, sign in the centre : they do not yet participate in working life.

Adults who sign in the middle have not always made their choices, but if their signature is larger than the text, this can express a need to be at the centre of a world of feelings, or a world of work, according to the context and the dynamism of the writing (affective avidity, or professional ambition, need to be in the limelight).

Someone who signs to the left, apart from the case mentioned previously in the U.S.A., expresses the fear of committing himself, too great an attachment to his past. Someone who signs too much to the right, on the contrary, shows an excess of zeal, a lack of moderation in activity, too much hurry in wanting to go too far or too quickly.

The distance of the signature in relation to the text, vertically, has to do with the involvement of the writer in relation to his actions and his judgement : if the signature is too far, the writer keeps his distance to too great an extent; he may be estranged from what he does, and not participate much. If it is too close, the writer does not stand back enough, may be lacking in judgement and act impulsively. If the signature goes into the text, he may be capable of thoughtless actions.

2. The formal elements of language
(surname and name, when they exist,
in their possible relationship)

The emphasis on capitals, which is frequent in signatures, corresponds to the fact that capitals easily lend themselves to the expression of the social self.

Most often, the first name is reduced to an initial, in a grouping joined or separated, sometimes by a full-stop, before the name, apart from cases of initials after the name, a survival from a different social practice.

The reciprocal importance of both elements, which appears mostly with the capital, gives information on the way in which the writer experiences his identity, the value he allots to his family name, what this represents for him, or to his first name, which may be smaller, as if crushed by the family environment, or on the contrary larger, expressing the need for and the fact of assuming a personal role (frequent in self-made people), or for attracting attention; sometimes vanity, narcissism, or lack of acceptance of family roots, when the surname is left out. In some cases, the writer unwittingly gives biographical information.

One may also notice the signature reduced to initials, a habit which may be kept for friends, but is nevertheless a bit casual, with regard both to others and to one's own identity.

When the signature is left out, even only temporarily, the omission speaks eloquently regarding one's self-doubts, even one's own existence.

3.   Signature similar to the text

It is the signature of young children, who have as yet no notion of what the signature represents and write their name simply, but often differentiating it from the text by underlining it, frequently with a lasso.

In adults, a signature similar to the text is considered by the graphologist as a sign of the writer's naturalness, spontaneity and genuineness; he does not try to appear different from what he is, but does not reveal anything else either. It is found at all socio-cultural levels, from the simplest to the most advanced ones.

One should not overestimate a signature similar to the text; the interpretation is the more positive, the more the writing already expresses moral and intellectual qualities.

It is spontaneous to the same degree as the writing itself. Most writers with acquired writings have signatures similar to the text, which is the best way of revealing only the acquired aspect of their personality; but in this way, they also demonstrate that this construction, through force of habit, has become second nature.

Quite a considerable number of signatures similar to the text are underlined, bringing thereby an element of self-assertion, of will, of a search for a basis of support, or of a desire to appear self-assertive, according to the context. This underlining, often adopted by children as we have seen above, may be abandoned in the course of time, the writer who used to underline no longer feeling the need to do so, being more sure of his authority, or less desirous of so much.

A signature can also have a paraph above it, indicating a need for protection, for shelter or, on the contrary, a desire to dominate. Placed between two parallel lines, it means that the writer puts himself on, or between rails, with the interpretation which can be inferred from this, according to the context.

Sometimes a signature is crossed through, usually by means of a paraph which goes through it instead of underlining it.

Illogical, a subsequent negation of the written identity, the crossed through signature is a bad sign as far as self-confidence is concerned. It is often found in children and adolescents, thus expressing their doubts, their difficulties in asserting themselves at a particular period; this peculiarity often disappears with time, and when self-assurance has been restored. One should take more notice of it in adults, in which case one must look in the text for signs of possible fragility, for it could simply be a remnant of a former signature which has not evolved, for instance among writers who have not had much education.

One must not confuse crossed-through signatures with those where the name is written astride a line drawn beforehand and which serves as a kind of hand-rail, or a support. To a graphologist who does not carefully look with a magnifying glass, the signature could seem crossed through afterwards, and give rise to mistaken interpretation.

A signature with a similar appearance to the text, can differ from it in one category. We shall deal with the main points, as the multifarious possibilities do not permit us to be exhaustive.

a) *Dimension* : a signature larger than the text, statistically very frequent, is in keeping with the signatures's role of social assertion, and the awareness - whether justified or not - that the writer has of his own worth and of his role in society. If the disproportion is too great, it shows exaggerated ambition, an excessive feeling of self, and in the case of a small, unsure writing, an overcompensated feeling of inferiority. If the signature is smaller, it expresses self-doubt, fear of responsibilities, an interpretation which is reinforced if the stroke is lighter, of bad quality, and if the movement is weaker. In some cases, the height can be considerably reduced after a trauma, or a failure.

b) *Direction of lines* : in France signatures frequently rise whilst the text does not, and the classical interpretation of ardour must be moderated, in view of the statistical frequency of this characteristic.

This can express a desire to give the impression of being more active, more self-assured, than one really is, if the rest of the text is not particularly dynamic, or if it reveals psychological difficulties.

A descending signature indicates resignation, discouragement, or sometimes aggressiveness, if the stroke is sharp-pointed. If it dives at a 90° angle, it is a sign of despair which should alert the graphologist : Hitler's signature [70] before his suicide, and that of Napoleon in St. Helena, had this particularity.

c) *Direction of letters* : a change of letter direction, less statistically frequent, is more significant.

A left-slanted signature in a context which is not left-slanted, indicates fear of contacts, difficulties in communication and fear when facing a commitment. If it is right-slanted when the text is not, it means that the writer is trying to make contacts, or that he wishes to give the impression that he is trying to make them.

When the text and the signature have a very different slant, we are dealing with a writer drawn apart by different aspirations, lacking in homogeneity of character, and pulled about by contradictory desires or choices.

Signatures can end with a full-stop : the writer puts a punctuation mark, rather like ending a sentence, which does not leave open a dialogue with others, and indicates mistrust.

This sign is seldom found in children and adolescents, who do not usually put a full stop after their names at the top of the sheets of paper on which they do their schoolwork[3].

d) *The stroke and the movement* : still looking the same as the text, a signature can present differences in the quality of the stroke, the pressure, firmer or less firm, the movement, dynamic or weak. Some signatures are more constrained and tense than the text, and there are others, on the other hand, in which the graphic movement is liberated.

Through these differences, the graphologist gathers very precise indications as to the writer's powers of resistance, his capacity to struggle, or on the contrary, the risk he runs of no longer being able to face up to things, despite an activity which had stood fast until now.

As with the direction of letters, these differences are statistically less frequent; therefore they depart from the norm and are indicative of a possible lack of homogeneity in the personality of the writer.

All we have just said about underlinings, punctuation, and the differences of dimension, direction and pressure in signatures similar to the text, is even more applicable to signatures which differ greatly from it in several categories at once; these depart radically from the text owing to a complex

---

3 At secondary school stage, children in France do their school- or homework to be marked on loose paper, not in exercise books. (T.N.)

of gestures in which even the writing of the name is transformed, skipped, or annihilated, often in favour of complications made out of paraphs, or the fabrication of ciphers.

4. *Signature very different from the text*

The signature is generally illegible, resulting from a graphic construction based on very simplified, unfinished writings. Graphologists tended to judge them as expressive of a lack of frankness, and a desire to present a secretive self-image, more calculated than spontaneous.

In fact, nowadays, many signatures are in this style and often come from dynamic and creative writers whose genuineness can only rarely be doubted.

Indeed, in professional life, one finds many signatures transformed into ciphers, from writers who have important functions and sign frequently; firm, rapid, animated by a structured movement, the signature, like a seal, then represents an objective identification of the professional function and can be misleading. The meaning is generally positive, and the graphologist can try to retrace the gesture from which this cipher arose, the cipher itself revealing a few indications through the movement that creates it, in keeping with the writer's basic movement.

This seal must be clearly distinguished from a signature which also is abstract, but which has a weak movement, is sometimes too slow, has a poor structure, and thereby indicates a weak ego, which is afraid of responsibilities, dares not assert itself, wonders about its identity, or conceals itself. In some cases difficulties of identification can be compensated for in daily work, if the writing of the text is livelier and firmer.

In other cases, one finds more or less complicated signatures which may be either illegible or may preserve the legibility of the name despite the additions. In fact, the exaggerated paraphs, very much in use on the 19th century, which highlighted the social role of a person, among the few who could write in those days, had been replaced by simpler signatures which made complicated ones look like anachronisms and did not inspire confidence with regard to quality. The reappearance of complicated signatures nowadays has given rise to a sociological hypothesis [71]. Allegedly, this type of signature corresponds to a defence, is a response to the anxiety created at present by the uncertainties of professional life : one inflates, complicates, asserts one's identity with a whole system of gestures, the imbroglio of which the graphologist will have to sort out and which do not necessarily arise from insincerity. One frequently finds them in an average socio-cultural context[4].

These signatures, dissimilar to the text and, as we have already stressed, closer to drawing than to handwriting, also help the projection of unconscious images related to the writer's ideals, his aspirations, his projects, and sometimes to a close identification with a profession. Some biographical elements can also be symbolically evoked in them.

The symbolism of space, form and movement will help the graphologist decipher these signatures, which is often difficult : captivating lassos, big paraphs which start a long way to the left, i.e. the past, or those which are attracted to the right, the future, those which grasp, protect, enclose or attack; those belonging to overactive temperaments which love contact and express themselves with volutes and whirls; those which belong to determined temperaments, expressing themselves with cross-shaped gestures, or appear claw-like, sometimes occurring with a sober, condensed text.

One can understand that a writer may feel like making his mark with a signature which has some panache or some originality, offering a different aspect, for his identification, from that of his writing, the language which transmits thought. But it can also happen that some writers, due to administrative necessity, retain a complicated signature, fabricated in adolescence, imitating a signature by chance and without its corresponding to any real identification[5].

---

4 Observations retained by the authors.
5 According to Florence Lièvre, the signature is an essential symbol of one's personal identification, and is therefore subject to evolution. The writer should ask himself about the suitability of this graphic symbol with regard to his identification, and not hesitate to develop new signatures, if need be, and to do so in spite of the administrative bother this can involve [72].

It should be noted that, in the case of writer's cramp, when the subject can no longer write, he can still preserve his signature intact, freer from the restraints of the copybook.

It is up to the graphologist to make use of all the synthetic interpretations regarding the form, the movement, the life of the script, and the stroke, before arbitrarily making a derogatory judgement which might be unsuitable.

Finally, graphologists who have the handwritings and the signatures of the members of one family, or of writers working together, can, by paying special attention to the signatures, deduce very important information on how the members will react on, or influence one another, and how they will, or will not, get on.

Below, we give first a few samples of men's signatures, then of women's.

We shall put an asterisk each time we have had to delete the ending of a too legible signature, for discretion's sake.

5. *A few men's signatures*

198

Boy, 12 years
* *Signature in the centre, written simply like his usual writing; underlined with a slightly curved, rising rapid and firm stroke. Need to assert himself.*

POUR Fête de NOëL

199

Boy, 14 years
Signature to the right, but smaller than the text, and ending with a paraph which goes round the Christian name, protects it, but also partly crosses it through, by putting a spike through it. When this child signs with his family name, he makes the same paraph, which partly crosses out what he has just written. The signature is always a little smaller than the text, whether the text is in typographic, or cursive writing.

This boy, overprotected by his mother, has doubts about himself, and has not yet reached the autonomy to which he nonetheless aspires.

200

Boy, 10 years
Signature on the left, with a very large, disproportionate capital on the first name, no capital on the surname, and at the end, a very large lasso-shaped paraph - a form frequently found in children - underlines the signature.

This boy has an exaggerated need to draw attention to himself, to be highly regarded, in order to compensate for a deeply-felt fear of being abandoned.

Je vous prie de croire, Madame, a pension de mes sentiments distingués

Hid

201

Boy, 20 years
* *Signature similar to the text, slightly to the right. The initial of the name is connected to the surname. The signature rises whilst the text is horizontal, the accent is very low. Genuineness, but also need to appear more self-assured than he is in fact (which is also confirmed in the text by reduced 'j's).*

Ava full man amitié

Dominique Isa

202

Man, 50 years
* *Signature on the right, underlined, similar to the text in all categories.*
Homogeneity between the intimate and the social character, identical behaviour in both cases.
Only the underlining, light, like the writing, shows up the fact that this really is a signature.

203

Man, 25 years
Signature in the centre, legible, a little larger than the text but nearly the same, complicated, double-joined like the writing, and more connected.
The writer does not deceive people about what he is, but one does not feel like trusting him entirely, owing to his complexity and his need to seduce.

prie , Madame , d'accepter mes
respectueux

(signature) 203

respectueux et distingué

(signature)

204

Man, 55 years

* Signature a lot larger than the text, on the right, at twice the distance between the lines from the text, very legible (partly deleted for discretion), but different, owing to a supple, round and liberated movement, whereas the writing, also very connected and rapid, is jerky and lacking in a little freedom in the cursive progression.

Justifiably conscious of his worth, the writer is capable of assuming his role in human relationships with 'savoir faire', presence and skill, as well as controlling an underlying nervousness and impatience.

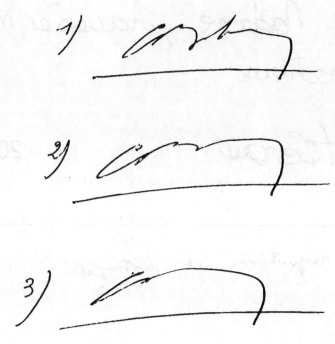

205

Man, 49 years

Transformation into a cipher of the signature of a man with high responsibilities, especially reproduced for us by the writer himself.

The signature starts with the name connected with the surname, finishing with a plunging final, and is underlined with a stroke crossing through the final.

The signature as a whole rises like the text.

The name, already very simplified at the start, becomes a script, keeping the initial of the first name and the general curve.

The cipher reveals a rapid and productive gesture; constructive due to the arcade, combative due to the straight line and the cross, expressive, from the start, of the writer's personality in his professional role, which he owes to his own merit.

206

In this signature to the right of the text, the cipher is more ambiguous, for it is slower, and ending with a full stop of mistrust and closedness. This double tent, a simplification of the initial of the name and surname, linked by a small bridge, retains something enigmatic, like its author who has quite a difficult character.

Man, 40 years

Je vous prie de croire, Monsieur, en l'assurance de mes sentiments très distingués.

207

Man, 28 years

* *Signature to the right of the text, rising, underlined, with very large capitals, whilst the text is small, a little clumsy, and horizontal.*
Overcompensated feeling of inferiority, in this young engineer who is not unlikely to have difficulties in a team.

208

Man, 65 years

Signature to the right, the drawing of which evokes, to adepts of symbolism, a sword held forward, to the right, ready for attack.
Underlined with a firm and rapid stroke.
Notice the use of a broad felt pen for a very assertive gesture, with a splendid spatial distribution of the text.
A man of great worth. Has been successful, thanks to his own battles.
Warm presence of a generous man who enjoys being popular.

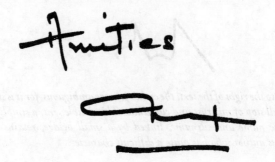

208

209

Man, 40 years
This writer is very proud because he imagines he has several signatures.
In actual fact, one can still find the same brisk basic gesture, a mixture of inflated loops
and paraphs, forming an overall, complicated signature, closed with a full stop.
A voluble talker, need to please, but the inner personality remains secretive, with a very
different, not very rapid, copybook writing.
Need also to compensate for his socio-cultural background.

210

Man , 44 years, holder of a C.A.P.[6]
Signature to the right, rising sharply.
The name, written like the text, is surrounded several times over by a lasso-shaped paraph, starting from the very large and inflated capital C. The gesture is brisk, rapid, full of life, despite being complicated.
Skilfulness, some showing-off perhaps, but the signature is in keeping with the socio-cultural level.

6. Remarks

We have separated the few examples of women's signatures from the men's, because when we selected them for this book, we noticed that there was a very large number of women's signatures similar to the text, or differing from it only in the classic manner with an underlining, a rising direction, a slightly larger dimension or an emphasis on the capitals[7].

It would therefore seem, and this can be statistically checked, that women project themselves more rarely than men in signatures either very different from the text, or stylised, or personalised with originality.

Several hypotheses can be put forward for this sexualisation of the signature, as is the case also for the sexualisation of handwriting.

---

6 C.A.P. : Certificat d' Aptitude Professionnelle, a low-level qualification (T.N.)
7 See Appendix no. 2.

Women, through their signatures, may perhaps confirm their attachment to conventions and their conservativism, because their role through
the ages has been to ensure the continuity of the species, and this despite
the transformation of their social status. It seems that women do not dare
to assert themselves regarding the outside world as men do, that they are
attached to an identification which give them a sense of security, their social
or professional life, more often than not, remaining closely interwoven with
their private, emotional life.

The present-day changes through which women share new responsibilities in professions similar to men's, will probably have an influence on
women's writings and signatures. But the fundamental differentiation
between man and woman will nevertheless remain the same, since women
are also attached to deeply-ingrained values which are not necessarily the
same as men's.

One can also put forward the hypothesis that women, being more
applied, concrete and conscientious by nature, and less abstractly creative,
are happier with a legible signature.

Professional women [73] exercising their professions, do so with their
own qualities and do not necessarily have signatures similar to men's.

Nevertheless, a point needs to be made regarding the signatures of
women doctors: they are freer and more like those of men practising a
profession. This seems to us, in France, the consequence of a profession[8]
which enhances the self-image given to their people through the importance of their rôle.

---

8   In France, the title of Doctor, which goes with the name, is reserved solely for doctors
     of medicine. The medical doctor has become *the doctor*.

7. *A few women's signatures*

adresser les voeux très sincères que je forme pour vous et tous ceux qui vous sont chers, pour 1986.

M. V. Boller

211

Woman, 43 years
Clear writing. Signature to the right, underlined, similar to the text. Genuineness.

l'expression de mes sentiments les plus respectueux.

212

Girl, 18 years
Signature like the text, with capitals, initials of the first name and of the surname joined up with personalisation, rising a little, underlined with the final paraph, but placed to left of centre of the paper and even more left-slanted than the text, very inhibited as a whole.
This girl is not without projects, but she is circumspect, and is afraid of involving herself. She easily goes on the defensive, although very affective.

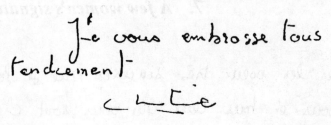

213

Girl, 19 years

Very shapeless signature, with a very filiform middle zone, but ending with a very pronounced 'e' (the first name is Christine), underlined with a short, light descending stroke, placed near the text, in which inhibitions, childish forms and a superelevated 'J' can be noted.

The writer is very sensitive, fragile, not very realistic, not very mature; she is dissatisfied, capable of stubbornness and of acting on impulses.

Ran away from home once.

214

Woman, 60 years, doctor

Signature in keeping with the text, connected, rapid, assertive. Originality of the initials of both the first and the surname, written with a parallel movement.

Assertive and warm contacts of this woman conscious of the importance of her role.

doiwut être
ō a Texte Trop

J·J

215

Woman, 60 years - Head of a medico-psychological centre for children
Semi- cipher whose two capitals are 'j's, the first sword-shaped, the second with a looped, amiable curve.
Gesture of assertiveness in the verticality and also in the horizontality, due to a very heavy t-bar. The assertion in these two axes is in keeping with the writing, the signature is a reinforced image of this. The writer, a strong, original personality, fulfils her rôle with a mixture, at times, of sharp authority, and charm.

PART 2

Guiding Syntheses

Methodology

Handwriting of Left-handers using the left hand

11

EVOLUTION OF HANDWRITING and ORGANISATION

Age, socio-cultural level
and level of education, intelligence.
Disorganisation due to old age. Dysgraphia.

Longitudinal studies have shown a constant, intricate relationship between a human being and his handwriting.

Closely linked to education, of which it is an essential tool, handwriting goes hand in hand with motor, intellectual and affective development of children and adolescents. It will then continue to record the history of adults: their periods of euphoria, discouragement, illnesses (without precise details of diagnosis), and the wear and tear resulting from to old age[1].

If one observes the modifications of the personality, the questioning which appears quite specifically at the time of adolescence, for a considerable percentage of writings, one notes aspects which change (sometimes with a temporary adoption of typographic writing), hesitations in direction

---

1 One must nevertheless admit the fact that the relationship between the writer and his writing varies from person to person; and if, in most cases, the relationship is very close, there exist neutral scripts in which it is more remote and in the face of which graphologists have to admit their limits. There are also writings, fortunately rather rare, which are commonly called "trap writings", as they seem to arise, for what reasons one does not know , from graphomotor activity which has little to do with the writer's personality.

which can even extend to variable slants, expressive of difficulties of inner choice. Nevertheless, in the case of these writers, when they reach the age of 20 or so, one often finds that their writing is somewhat reminiscent of their writing at the age of seven[2], the beginning of a period of latency, expressing thereby a return to inner calm, a relaunch of balance.

Other writers show greater homogeneity in their evolution, which enables them perhaps to adapt more quickly and to enter adult life more easily, but only provided the homogeneity of their writings is not due to rigidity or constraint, a strait-jacket which a child would not dare to leave. A profound identity of handwriting throughout time is not incompatible with a few irregularities in adolescence; they are, actually, even desirable.

---

216 **Boy, 11 years 10 months, ahead with his schooling**
Well-nourished, connected writing, rapid for his age, a little compact, thrown t-bars; the capitals are becoming personalised.

217

---

2   An observation made by many graphologists, R. Olivaux, in particular [74].

The same writer at 30 years : strong identity

One can recognise the pressure, the appearance, with very strong similarities (look at he capital 'I' in particular), the very connected writing, very rapid, with a little excess (the flying t-bars), in this document based on notes.

217   *The personalisation, incipient in the writing at 12, has evolved in the same direction: right-tending, wide, very small writing. The compactness has been replaced with fairly small, but rhythmic spaces.*

After leaving a "grande école"[3], the writer later entered an active professional life with no problems in adapting.

In other ways, a recent statistical study [11] on considerable numbers of adolescents following normal schooling, has shown that adolescents' writings retain a significant percentage of characteristics of children's writings, and, it seems, longer and more strongly than in the past.

From this observation, one can adduce the hypothesis that, at present, adolescence is overextended; there is a desire to maintain a state of dependency, a form of childhood security, when faced with the uncertainties of adulthood, long studies, uncertain prospects, or even studies which are too long, imposed and sometimes of no interest in socio-cultural milieus where aspirations are different.

These sociological conclusions may change in the future along with different conditions of life; it is therefore relevant to review graphological studies of groups as time goes on.

In this chapter, we shall not present longitudinal studies of handwritings, which belong to a particular area. We shall keep to transversal studiess of homogeneous groups, which belong to the general domain, which have been statistically verified, and the results of which are an indispensable help to graphologists.

Leaving aside pathology, which is mentioned only very casually in this book, and the influence on handwriting of some mental diseases, drugs, or alcohol [75], whose effect on the quality and the behaviour of the stroke has been very specifically studied, the evolution of the handwriting of an organically normal human being depends on:

---

3   See footnote 10, Chapter 2. (T.N.)

- age (which coexists with the maturing of his motor functions),
- intellectual level,
- emotional maturity,
- regular practice of graphomotor activity, kept up by education and by some professions, to which one can add, for some writers, a graphic skill [23] more developed than average.

Remember that an adequate intellectual level is necessary in order to learn to write normally[4]; proof of this is given by the inability of feeble-minded people to achieve the organised writing of adults. Slightly feeble-minded people can at best manage a slow writing, more or less reproducing copybook writing, if they are well adapted; the others, if they can write at all, produce very clumsy and unorganised writings in Crépieux-Jamin's terminology.

Boy, 20 years - I.Q.[5] of 50 in the Wechsler-Bellevue test
Unorganised writing.
Very sad attitude of the personality, with profound discouragement. This is the only writing of a feeble-minded person in this manual.

218

4   See chapter on Speed.
5   Intelligence quotient: relationship assessed by appropriate tests, between the mental age and the actual age, the average being 100.

1. Age as a factor of evolution. Children's handwriting and intelligence.

The growth of children's handwritings has been studied and books and articles, often quoted in the bibliography of this book, have been written on the subject. We shall not mention it again in great detail in this book mainly devoted to adults, but let us recall a few important notions and results[6].

It is Hélène de Gobineau who was the first person in France to have had the idea of making a statistical study of the growth of the writings of children aged between 6 and 14, using a scale of 37 items[7], all of them graphic characteristics recognised as being specific to children's writings.

Later a team of psychologists, led by Professor Ajuriaguerra, refined the scale and made it very rigorous, by limiting it exclusively to the components of developmental motor difficulties (30 items), i.e. decreasing statistically with age, for boys and for girls separately, then adding them up.

The scale stops at 11, by which time children normally have mastered the school model, enter a post-copybook stage and personalise their writings.

Alongside age, the statistical decrease of the items has also been studied in relation to the school year, from the CP up to the CM2[8].

This scale enables one to calculate the graphomotor age of a child, in relation to his/her real age and to his/her school year[9].

The fact that the scale stops earlier than Gobineau's, does not preclude its use for children whose graphomotor abilities are backward, or for those

6 This chapter refers to graphometric scales which the interested reader can find collected in a "Que sais-je" (What do I know?) on graphomotricity [33].

7 The word 'item' has been chosen on account of its neutrality, which was in keeping with the attitude of the researchers. We often replace it with 'components' or 'characteristics' [19].

8 See footnote 7, p. 290 for CP. CM2 (Cours Moyen deuxième année) is the last year of primary schooling, when children are 11 years old. (T.N.)

9 The scale is divided into 14 items F of childish forms and arrangements, and 16 items M to do with malformations due to graphomotor difficulties. The statistical decrease is studied item per item; one adds up the 14 items F, then the 16 items M, and the total of both lots gives a total E which represents the graphomotor age.

who, usually for emotional reasons and/or because of difficulties[10], retain too many infantile items which ought, statistically to have disappeared.

This scale has confirmed the fact, already observed[11] by other authors, that children whose writing corresponds to their age, their school year, and especially those, who are ahead of their graphomotor age, are both intellectually gifted and well adapted to their schooling, and are proceeding satisfactorily with their emotional development.

Since the growth of handwriting reaches a stage of copybook reproduction between the ages of 8-9 and 11-12[12] , intelligent and well adapted children will have small, clear and simple writings, with good respect for form well, and not very original, apart from a few attempts at simplifying letters, or at personalising some capitals.

On the other hand, the opposite is not applicable, inasmuch as in the case of a child who is backward in his graphomotor ability, say even a dysgraphic child, the graphologist can infer nothing regarding the intellectual level of the child, who will have to be tested using a different approach.

For children, there exist well perfected tests to study this question very closely. It is obvious, starting with a minimum level of schooling, that the I.Q. is normal, that there is no question of mental deficiency, but the actual level of the I.Q., for children of normal intelligence, may vary greatly.

Boy, 7 years 4 months, CE. 2[13]

219
Writing on the way to organisation : pre-copybook stage.
Small, careful writing, with strong pressure, good legibility, fairly clumsy.
Notice the arrhythmic white spaces (irregular word spacing), the small jerks,

---

Footnotes on opposite page ☞

*the twists, the irregularities of direction and dimension, normal graphomotor
difficulties at that age; the shortened lower extensions in relation to the
extended upper extensions, a sign of effort and fear of not succeeding, is found
fairly often at this age.*

Boy, 9 years 6 months, CM. 2

220

*Writing which reproduces the copybook model perfectly.
The very regular verticality, the very controlled movement, the slightly large
and narrow writing, the hanging onto the left margin, and the almost too
perfect appearance, indicate a perfectionist character, which is not without
some dangers. Top of his form, he will eventually be a prize-winner at the
"concours général"[14] in French at 16.
Will do brilliantly in his studies, in spite of constant questioning regarding
himself.*

---

10 Laterality, or dyslexia, for instance.

11 A very strong statistical correlation between "good handwriting" and "good pupil".

12 All the authors interested in children's writings have stressed this, Crépieux-Jamin
included.
Even if the time devoted to learning to write was much longer in the past, the
demands of most teachers more exacting and the graphic instruments different, it is
nevertheless true that graphomotor difficulties are the same, whatever the period, since
they are related to the general maturity of the child, which is also assures the
permanence of the main results of the Children's scale.

13 In France, CE 2 is the third year of primary schooling (CE=Cours Elémentaire)
(T.N.).

14 In the French elitist system, this is a nation-wide competition, in which the best pupils
from French lycées can take part, in individual academic subjects, in the last two years
of their secondary schooling, i.e the 2 years before university or higher education in
general. (T.N.)

Tous les membres de notre société sont conte

221

Boy, 11 years 6 months, 2nd year of secondary school
A very intelligent child, but anxious, and overprotected by his mother.
Small, clumsy writing, amended, irregular in dimension and spacing; a poor quality stroke.
The writing, which ought to have reached and gone beyond the copybook stage in accordance with the norm, expresses the child's psychomotor difficulties and does not reveal his very high intellectual level, in spite of the relative success of the word "tous".

Here a remark is needed : many graphologists, among the great ones of the past, put forward the idea that for a good graphological analysis, an organised writing was necessary.

They therefore thought that a graphologist could not interpret children's handwritings, because the graphomotor difficulties inherent in these writings prevented their expressiveness [76][15].

This position is now quite outdated, as much in France as abroad. Indeed, helped by the precise knowledge of the normal learning difficulties at a given age, a limited, nuanced and prudent graphology of children's writings is quite accepted and is a great help, especially when considering the difficulties peculiar to childhood [44, 77].

If the growth of handwriting through the disappearance of the graphomotor learning difficulties with age, can be very objectively studied, and has been, the question of the study of the evolution of handwriting now arises, once these difficulties are over, i.e. when it is organised.

Crépieux-Jamin uses the term "organised" to describe a writing produced fluently and correctly. This is the case, he specifies, with a large number of children when they leave school after the age of 13. He adds

---

15 "At the beginning, one forces oneself to think of the act of writing, but later, one only thinks of what one writes. The attention focussed on the writing diminishes spontaneity and puts a brake on the instinctive motor impulses in which, alone, the writer's individuality can be expressed in all its originality"

"those who go on studying, improve their writing, arrange it with more skill and simplify it, while retaining its precious character of legibility". With this comment, he shows himself a precursor of the studies made on the correlation of certain writing characteristics with the level of education.

From the time when motor learning difficulties have more or less disappeared (towards 14), the studies of the correlation with the level of education can indeed replace the correlation with age.

It is certain that the social milieu plays a part, and so does the type of profession; researchers have taken this into account in the groups of reference which were used in making their Scales.

2. Relationship of handwriting to educational and socio-cultural levels

1. Introduction : the scales of Autonomy.

The question of unorganised writing of adults is no longer a problem nowadays, schooling in France having been made compulsory up to the age of 16 since the Ordonnance of the 7th January 1959.

In principle therefore, one finds unorganised writings only in children[16], but in this case, "writing on the way to being organised" seems to us a more appropriate term.

Nevertheless, the presence in France of a population of non-French-speaking immigrants who have had almost no education, may bring back the question of badly organised writings among adults, who may well have a good intellectual level, but who have not mastered the written language.

Graphologists must be very discreet in this area.

---

16 We exclude the writings of the mentally handicapped, which are not the object of this book, as we have made clear in the case of writing no.218.

Woman, 35 years

222

A badly organised writing of an intelligent Spanish woman who hardly knows the French language, and is not very well educated.
The irregular slant in particular is related to the motor difficulties of this woman who has a perfectly stable character.
The skill of the 'd's and the general appearance are not reminiscent of a child's writing, in spite of the clumsiness.

This important point having been made, it is quite obvious that handwriting, beyond the usual amount of minimum schooling, continues to evolve along with one's education (even if only for reasons of speed).

It was in fact in the hope of using handwriting to test intelligence that Gobineau had had the idea of creating graphomotor scales[17].

Indeed, alongside her scale of items belonging to the childish looking aspect, she had constructed a second scale of Autonomy, describing 31 items belonging to adults' writings, freed from difficulties connected with childhood, and representative of the handling of handwriting in relation to homogeneous groups, differentiated by their educational level: + or - CEP[18], higher Education.

Through the interplay of these two scales, she was hoping to encompass intelligence, to the extent that higher education generally underlies a high

---

17 See works already quoted for the handling of the scales. We mention only that, in a writing , "discreetly"present items are given a value of 0.5, and "strongly" present items are given a value of 1.

18 Certificat d'Études Primaires (T.N.: an old school leaving examination, taken at the age of 14). It still exists, but is optional.

level of intelligence, and lack of maturity (or autonomy), to the extent that the persistence of childish components in adults, especially if they go on studying, or write frequently, is a graphic anomaly expressive of personal difficulties.

The interplay of these two scales has not been retained in the case of children, as the scale of Autonomy is not sufficiently sensitive before the age of 15; but we have seen in the previous chapter that one can get positive information (never negative) on a child's intelligence through his graphomotor age.

On the other hand, the idea of a scale of Autonomy for adults has again been taken up by Roger Perron and Marguerite Flamand.

To construct the scale and select the useful items from a provisional scale of 63 items, they used two groups of reference comprising :

- 100 adult men, with an average age of 22, having either the CEP alone, or completed with a CAP, or a BEPC[19,] or a baccalauréat, whose results in Bonnardel's BV8 intelligence test are known;

- 75 adults of a cultural level at least equal to a degree, university people, engineers, professional people (doctors, psychologists) and administrators.

These two groups of reference have made it possible to refine scale A by devising two sub-scales. The usual graphomotor assessment has been kept, but without a coefficient of weighting of the items, unlike Ajuriaguerra's Children's Scale.

- *Sub-scale A1* differentiates between the lower levels, CEP + or -.

20 items: the graphic line gets rid of the graphomotor difficulties specific to childhood (statistical assessment of the disappearance of the components of the E scale), movement becomes firmer, the page gains in clarity and organisation (layout, spacing, signature).

---

19 C.A.P.: Certificat d'Aptitude Professionnelle.
  B.E.P.C.: Brevet d'Etudes du Premier Cycle (T.N.: a possible school leaving examination, taken at the end of the 4th year of secondary schooling), replaced by the Brevet des Collèges (T.N. a "collège", in France, is a secondary school, not a higher education establishment).

- *Sub-scale A2* differentiates between the higher levels; higher education followed by professional activity.

44 items: development of right-tending forms in order to facilitate a rapid, rightward progression of the graphic movement : personal, simplified and original forms of connection, for small and very connected writing, with possible breaks, and observing a considerable left-hand margin.

(Note that with some items, we are quite close to Crépieux-Jamin's "combined" writing. For him, this sign represented the highest degree of organisation and an important sign of intelligence.)

Any writing should necessarily be studied in the light of both sub-scales. The total obtained indicates the overall level of the writer, which can be compared with two kinds of standardised gradings : general gradings divided into nine degrees, ranging from bad to very good, standardised around a central degree of medium graphic level; and gradings corresponding to the three following cultural levels : primary, BEPC or Baccalauréat, and higher culture.

The partial levels obtained in the A1 and A2 scales can also be compared with the average levels of the reference groups.

Scale A2 has been accused of being too representative of university academics and professional people, and not enough of senior executives and business managers.

It is true that it takes little note of the accurate writing, with a good relationship between form and movement, of many engineers (not to mention the clear, but sometimes very simple and not very combined writings of some scientists).

Nor does it take much into account the firm and structured writings of some executives with whom left tendencies are often as present, if not more so, as right tendencies.

The quality of the stroke does not appear much in the items.

The writing of people in new professions where communication and information are specially important, often freer in their organisation on the page, are not represented either [78], nor are women who hold an increasingly important place in professional life.

One tends nevertheless to forget, in this criticism of Scale A2, that the level of a writing results from the sum of the items seen in both scales. Also the necessary presence of items from Scale A1 counterbalances the possible overrating to the rightward tendencies of Scale A2 which, deprived of items A1, may give rather illegible, precipitated writings or writings lacking in firmness. The presence of A1 items, in writings of a high A2 level, denoting an evolution far beyond the copybook model - due to freedom and with no skipping - is a guarantee of equilibrium and efficiency on the part of the writer.

Having said this, a scale done on more modern and varied groups, could usefully complete Perron-Flamand's work, most of whose data can still be used, especially those of Scale A1; Scale A2 needs rather more critical judgment, as it does not cover all the groups of high intellectual and professional level.

2. Comparison of handwriting with the educational level.

A knowledge of these scales, of their statistical results, even if the graphologist does not use them in their precise graphometric application, makes an important contribution, constantly verified in graphology, as it helps in avoiding errors and directs the judgment regarding the efficiency of a candidate.

Indeed, in professional selection, letters of application are always accompanied by a curriculum vitae. The graphologist therefore knows the level of education which can then be compared with the level of the writing, according to the scales of Autonomy[20] (and sometimes of Children, if there are remnants of a considerable number of items E) which place the writer in relation to verified norms.

It is quite obvious that the graphologist must not adopt the same graphic criteria to judge a writer who has not had much education, as those for a writer who has had higher education.

---

20 Bear in mind that the standardized assessment is done at three levels.

For somebody whose writing corresponds to an educational level higher than his own, the interpretation is very positive, whereas it will be the opposite for someone whose writing does not come up to his own educational level.

We shall specify a few principles regarding this immediate data given to the graphologist, which are the first data to be studied, as Crépieux-Jamin used to do when he started by looking at what he called the organisation of the writing.

a) *Handwritings of modest level and of average level:* According to scale A1, the most important thing in these writings is to find mastery of the graphic movement, a good organisation on the page, clarity, firmness and a signature which stands out clearly.

The survival of copybook forms in writings of level A1 ('*m*'s, '*n*'s, '*p*'s and '*t*'s in particular) is frequent and normal; it can indicate positive conformism, respect for hierarchy or, very often, simply that it has not been necessary or possible, owing to a lack of graphomotor skill, to transform these basic school forms for the sake of speed.

Some narrow letters, which compensate for a medium mastery of the graphic movement (a component of effort), can be a sign of application and seriousness. The same can be said of a slight left slant, quite frequent nowadays. Left-tending movements are often a sign of tenacity.

These writings may be a little inharmonious, without this being pejorative: a few ornaments (more discreet these days than in the past), some superelevations (capitals and the letter *p* in particular), stressed initial letters, can be a compensation for the socio-cultural level.

Signatures, often enlarged with complicated paraphs, do not necessarily have a derogatory meaning because of this: they may simply arise from a need for self-assertion, from a desire to be well thought of, or from dynamism, better expressed through this movement than through a writing which has not freed itself from graphomotor constraints. On the other hand, the position of the signature in the page is independent of the socio-cultural level and is to be interpreted accordingly [79].

School-like capitals are frequent. It should be noted, regarding this, that they may remain, like '*d*'s for instance, the only graphic copybook remnant in self-educated people whose handwritings are very evolved in other ways.

Some schools (for draughtsmen or accountants) can give rise to particular graphic habits such as typographic writing, or a particular aspect of a letter.

Some styles may accompany certain professions : large capitals and amicable lassos in shopkeepers, for instance.

The very frequent occurrence of open, or emphasised lower extensions, for which one can give several hypothetical graphomotor explanations, makes it difficult to believe the classical interpretations based on immaturity in handwritings of modest level [79].

It is obvious that anything which advances beyond the copybook model towards simplified forms, and the presence of items A2, will suggest the hypothesis of a higher intellectual level than that required for the level of education described in the curriculum vitae, and will be a sign that the writer is capable of further advancement, but there must be no slackness in the movement.

Man, 40 years, modest level
This gardener of C.E.P. level of education, has a small writing superior to his educational level, fairly rapid, with simplifications (v, t, x), neat and precise figures. He is serious and efficient.

223 *Notice the spaced-out writing, indicating a concern for clarity, but with irregular and not very rhythmic spaces, showing imperfect mastery of the graphic gesture. See also the irregular dimensions and angular 'm's and 'n's, close to those of children who find it difficult to make arcades. Notice also the 'p' in two parts and slightly superelevated. These characteristics are frequent and normal in handwritings of this level.*

Indeed, graphic freedom statistically increases with the socio-cultural level and is not dependent on the writer's manual skill. As a result "graphology is not competent to assess the manual capacities and the level of psychomotor skill of an individual" [80].

Man, 25 years - Holder of a C.A.P. as a metal worker

224

Good general layout and spacing between lines for this school-like, rather clumsy, very legible, careful, slightly angular and narrow writing.

Signature to the right, strongly rising, reproducing the name and ending with an underlining paraph, rapid, going towards the right, reminiscent of the sharp-pointed t-bars of the text.

The writer is serious and motivated, but his contacts with people are not always easy.

This writing is well related to the its author's educational level.

Man, 25 years - Holder of a C.A.P. as a central-heating engineer

225

The general layout is reasonable. The writing, which respects the forms of the school model, is clear and legible. Rather clumsy, it has more rigidity than firmness.

The difficulty of graphomotor mastery is particularly noticeable in the way the baseline is kept.

Note the attempt at personalisation of the capitals, the prolongated upper extensions, the open lower extensions, in keeping with what has been said before.

*En vous remerciant de l'intérêt
porter à ma demande, Je vous
Monsieur le Chef du Personnel
sentiments distingués*

The signature, not reproduced here, is similar to the writing, enclosed between two big paraphs, placed in the middle and at some distance from the text. It reveals some uncertainty and some defensiveness regarding the future.

---

*De mon côté je me ti
disposition du cabinet
entretien éventuel*

*En vous remerciant p.
bienveillance avec laquelle vou.
me recevoir à*

Man, 44 years

226

Not much education to start with (C.A.P. as a turner), he later completed his education with the CNAM[21], a management institute and English courses.

This writing, very well organised and orderly on the page, with good proportions and cylindrical, indicates a capacity for sustained effort in a man who, justifiably, is applying for a post as a manager of a small, provincial factory (he is competent, serious and hard-working). In spite of having been

---

21 CNAM : Conservatoire National des Arts et Métiers, a higher education establishment which mostly trains engineers, but not through university channels.

educated at a later stage, his writing often still retains traces of his former educational level : the very copybook 'm's, 'n's and 'p's, the 'p' being a little superelevated and in two bits, the 'd's and 'a's also in two bits, in this writing connected by means of stuck-on (added) connections, with not very skilful and frequently copybook capitals. The signature which, we are not reproducing, is firm, to the right and underlined.

---

allons faire du Camping. à suivre en liberté. Dès qu place nous trous étudier de sport que cette sille

Woman, 30 years - Wages clerk

Large writing, slightly narrow, orderly (with a left-hand margin and a social margin), well organised in spite of the prolongations, which reduce the interlinear spacing, with very supple and skilful connections, even though one notices superelevations (p, v). The writing is more evolved than would normally be expected from her educational level.

227

She is a stimulating and thoughtful young woman, capable of well-sustained, attentive application. She has a quick temper, but knows how to control herself through an awareness of her responsibilities, persevering energy, realistic "savoir-faire" and a need for precision.

The characteristics of her personality, revealed by her writing, place her above her position at work; she would be capable of improving her technical and general skills through day-release courses for people at work.

J'ai suivi de loin ce que vous entrepris au cours de l'Année. Les magnifi‑ succès que vous avez eus dans le Monde ‑ et ne peux attendre jeudi pour vous dire dès à combien je suis ravi que vos mérites soient off.

Man, 50 years

Small and very connected writing, with a few good breaks[22], a connectedness both fluent (facilitated by small lassos) and firm, careful, very clear and legible (respect for form), simple, with simplifications, personalised capitals, a very good layout, adapted to the small size of a postcard.

228

Well-nourished, precise stroke. High and accurate diacritics.

This writing, of a good graphic level, is superior to the writing corresponding to the socio-cultural level of the writer.

Manager of a business which he created himself, the writer has been brilliantly successful.

Man, 40 years

This writing, like the one before, is of a graphic level very superior to the statistical norms corresponding to the educational level of the writer (Brevet)[23]. Small writing, connected with right-tending downstrokes and a few breaks, simplified, legible, very orderly despite the slightly reduced spacing between the lines. Garlands facilitating a movement both rapid (flying t-bars) and controlled

229

Well-nourished, pasty stroke. Firmly kept baseline. Accurate diacritics.

Signature to the right, clearly standing out from the text, ending with a full strop, and original: half a cipher, the surname of which is underlined, and the initial of the first name executed with a broad movement.

---

22 We are using the term adopted in the scales to describe the breaks in the continuity. Scale A2 : item 22 : few breaks; item 24 : good breaks, i.e. in keeping with the logic of movement (breaks to put an accent, a t-bar, before 'a's, 'd's, etc).

23 Same examination as BEPC (see footnote 19, p. 347).

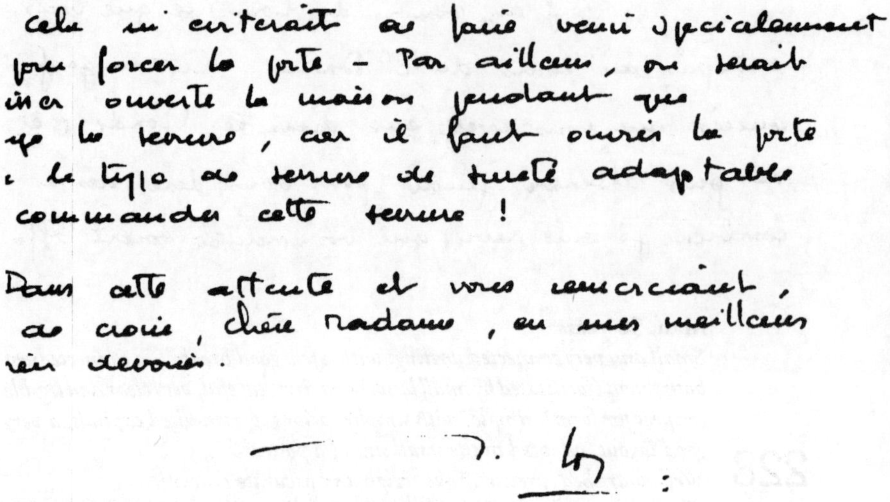
cela m'éviterait de faire venir spécialement
pour forcer la porte - Par ailleurs, on serait
ouverte la maison pendant que
la serrure, car il faut ouvrir la porte
le type de serrure de adaptable
commander cette serrure !

Dans cette attente et vous remerciant,
de croire, chère Madame, en mes meilleurs
dévoués.

229 *The writer, who started his career as a foreman on a building site, afterwards became the responsible assistant to the architect, for important building sites. He is very successful, has proved his efficiency and his authority is acknowledged and respected.*

b) *Handwritings of high educational and socio-cultural level :*

When the factors which facilitate speed of writing are matched with firmness, the corresponding writings are expressive of intellectual qualities coupled with a solid character. They often are writings of high calibre executives and business managers.

When rapidity, right-tendedness and sobriety are at the expense of structure, legibility and firmness, but are at the same time compensated for by a very good organisation of the page, especially in the relationship between black and white, we are often dealing with the writings of intellectuals, in the usual meaning of the term.

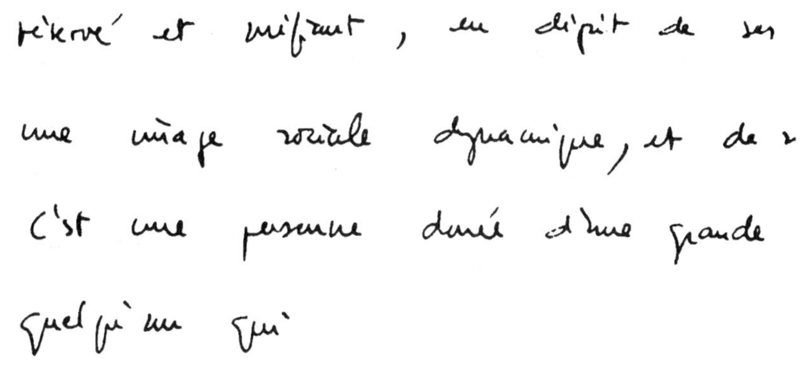

[handwritten sample]

230

Man, 25 years. Former student of "l"Ecole Polytechnique" and of "les Ponts et Chaussées"[24]
Writing of very good A1 and A2 level : small, connected with good breaks, simplified, combined, right-tending, fairly clear, aerated, with large interlinear spacing in particular. Well-nourished and firm stroke. Rapid gesture.
Quite a harmonious writing in Crépieux-Jamin's terminology.
Also noticeable are the liveliness of the vibrant movement and the reverse letters, very expressive of the writer's character, quite apart from the fact that the writing corresponds fully to his level of education.

Whenever there is a big discrepancy between the educational level and the writing, the graphologist is entitled to wonder what is masking the expressiveness of that educational level in the writing.

More often than not in such cases, components of autonomy as well as remaining childish components coexist, showing difficulties of adaptation, weakness of character and lack of maturity, which can affect the writer's efficiency negatively, despite his level of education.

The higher that level, the greater the discrepancy will be, as well as the possibility of serious difficulties.

Below, we give a few examples of surviving components of the Children's scale in the writings of some adults.

---

24 These are very selective, elitist higher educational establishments where engineers are trained in France.

c) *Components (items) of the Children's scale remaining in the writing of adults :* this must be considered only if there is a group of items : if one or two survive, they are meaningless (*d* frequently in two parts, for instance, if there are no other signs, has no significance).

The survival of components of form, close to a slightly clumsy copybook model, is normal and frequent among writers of modest level, as we have seen before.

Nevertheless, too many components of form, allied to lack of firmness, i.e. to surface writing[25], may be a sign of emotional retardation, whatever the level [19].

A fairly frequent group of components, expressive of dependence, lack of maturity and often narcissism, are united with a lack of firmness and inflated forms : surface writing, also plump, badly differentiated zones, a layout without margins, '*a*'s, '*d*'s, '*g*'s and '*q*'s in two parts (*d* especially), fluctuating lines.

In adolescence, this syndrome may be temporary and is sometimes replaced by a stylisation of the same forms, particularly in girls, in a deliberately conventional attitude.

As far as the absence of margins is concerned, it is nearly always significant, and even more so if it is associated with a high graphic level; indeed, the notion of organisation of the space by means of the margins is already decidedly present in handwritings of modest level.

False connections (solderings), associated with components of mal-formations caused by poor motor ability[26], a bad quality stroke, amendments in particular, often show an anxiety which, in some cases, can be motivating, but beyond a certain limit, can also be annihilating.

Jerks and telescoped letters, irregular direction, which indicate bad control of the graphic movement, can be be found in the script of writers of high level, who do not control well a nervousness typical of some people described as "cerebral".

With the emphasis on the smeary aspect of the stroke, the effect of which is often produced by a graphic instrument deliberately chosen for it,

---

25   F1 in the Children's scale [8].
26   Items M in Ajuriaguerra's Children's scale [8].

a writer may keep, in his character, traces of "potty training" [27], in his childhood : miserliness, uncleanliness, or aggressiveness of character, for instance.

Woman, 50 years

231

Good educational level, shown by a good distribution of black and white, some clarity, simplifications, an attempt at rapidity, but the "surface" writing, of slightly irregular dimension and direction, with mingling letters, school-like 'p's, 'a's and 'd's in two bits, open lower extensions, slightly descending and fluctuating lines, express the fragility and the dependence.

Man, 55 years

232

Level A2 for this small, connected, personalised and right-tending writing, with a good distribution of black and white, but in which one can also note

---

27 What Freud called the anal stage.

clumsiness (jerks, irregular dimension), lack of legibility, a strongly descending direction[28], usual in this writer.
In other ways, the writing is small, simplified and personalised.

Man, 23 years

233   *An Economics student, high socio-cultural level, but the association of the false connections, the numerous amendments, the bad quality stroke (smeary), the congested letters which are choking, express annihilating anxiety in this young man, talented in other ways. He suffers from a serious failure complex. The writing is otherwise, small simplified, personalised.*

---

234   **Man (age unknown)**
        Is preparing a Ph.D.

---

28   Descending writing is a childish component: M27 in the Children's scale.

The schoolboy-like writing (note in particular the capitals, the 'p's, the double 't's crossed separately), the clumsiness of the false connections (very numerous), the amendments, the compactness and the badly kept left-hand margin, do not correspond to the level of studies he has undertaken, perhaps rather late, unless these items reveal personal difficulties.

Man, 19 years
We shall end with a case [81] of spectacular graphic regression, which has caused the sudden appearance, in the writing of an intelligent student, of a vast number of childish components.

235 *Writing a): wide, connected, with a filiform tendency, a little inflated, small to crushed except for the first three words which are bigger due to an attempt to structure the form. Accurate and heavy diacritics; 'a's and 'd's open towards the left.*

Writing b) : produced after an attempt at suicide, it has regressed to the childish forms specific to the motor difficulties of very young children : surface writing, plump, dented, jerky, fluctuating lines, fragmented 'a's and 'd's. Notice also the irregularity of the left margin, the very left-slanted 'j's. the 'n's and 'm's with three and four downstrokes, the complicated signature placed to the left (the name has been removed for discretion). A not very encouraging prognosis for a boy who has already made several suicide attempts.

To sum up this chapter, it is up to the graphologist to perceive the interplay of the different constituents and their possible compensations. It is difficult to know how far an intelligent person can go, in order to overcome his personal difficulties.

And to what extent can one see intelligence in handwriting?

3. *Intelligence and handwriting*

All through the chapters of this book, readers will have noticed that the graphological interpretations had more to do with personality, character and behaviour, than with precise descriptions of intelligence and particularly of intellectual level.

Indeed, handwriting certainly does restore this complex unity, the human being, whose intelligence can only arbitrarily be extracted.

Let us also recall that intelligence is a difficult notion to define, and difficult to perceive with precision in a specific human being.

The IQ can be assessed quite adequately in children by means of suitable tests. But when it comes to evaluating the intellectual level of adults, one comes up against the poverty of means, and difficulty of devising really meaningful tests, with the exception of those designed to measure sequential intelligence, which is relatively easy.

"Intelligence is what my tests measure", Alfred Binet once said pithily, summarising the difficulty of defining intelligence and the approach to it.

In the same spirit as Alfred Binet's laboratory experiments, Hélène de Gobineau, as we have said before, had hoped to solve the problem by making handwriting an intelligence test, thinking that intellectual level could be directly grasped through normal graphomotor activity, inseparable from the cultural level.

Hélène de Gobineau came up against several difficulties : first, in order to find the components (items) expressive of intelligence, she had to take the writings of adults of high educational level, or whose profession represented that level.

Therefore, it is the educational and socio-cultural levels that are shown, and not intelligence as such. Intelligent individuals who have not had a higher education cannot then be detected; besides, the correlation between intelligence and educational level, although accepted in theory, is not absolutely infallible.

Also, from Gobineau's viewpoint, the components expressive of intelligence, called components of Autonomy, needed to be completed for the purpose of comprehensive graphological study, together with components of Personality[29], as certain graphic characteristics are unlikely to have any connection with intelligence.

Unfortunately for Gobineau, the opposite is not true as far as the components of Autonomy are concerned, which have also been found to be components of Personality: for instance, a small writing, of 2 mm or less, which is a component of Autonomy, is also an important component for the expressiveness of character (see the sign, "Small" in the Chapter on Dimension, page 130).

What counts in assessing the level from the writing is the sum of the items; but with the same total, the items can be very different, and this lack of similarity expresses the differences in the writers' characters more than in their intelligence[30].

---

29 Note that the breaking down into very analytical items of adults' writing into very analytical items, which have, by definition, been mastered, is often questionable; for example, breaking down the assessment of "suppleness", a global sign, into 10 items.

30 It is the same for the graphomotor age of children : similar totals do not mean similar writings. Even if the clumsiness is normal due to the learning difficulties, the unconscious choice of a particular sort of clumsiness is expressive of the character.

The ambiguity of the components of Autonomy, in fact accounts for the difficulty in separating intelligence from character and perhaps points to the wisdom of not doing so; what matters for graphologists is what an individual achieves with his intelligence, and handwriting does restore this totality[31] well for us. To grasp an intellectual level in the abstract is difficult, and, in the end, of limited interest.

The study of the development of intelligence shows that emotions and intelligence cannot be dissociated[32].

Emotions in children are factors of acceleration or retardation, and, in adults, of inhibition or stimulation, and this is true even for those who accept that children's cognitive structures, and later, the intellectual level in adults, are independent elements in themselves[33].

In fact, if intelligence without character is not very significant, as popular common sense would maintain, and if it is better to have a solid character allied to common sense than a brilliant intelligence without character, graphologists must remember, above all, that a human being has the intelligence needed by his character, and often a certain type of intelligence, things which are all faithfully represented in handwriting : the kind of intelligence needed for research in reflection and solitude, or that needed for active discovery in a team, and sometimes in adventures, or the synthetic kind of intelligence of those who see quickly and far, or the concrete intelligence of those who conceive tangible organisations, etc.

Gobineau, it is true, had attempted to counter these objections which she had partly anticipated.

But it seems to us that, in keeping with times still close to scientism, she probably overestimated the function of the intellect itself. The term,

---

31 With a purpose opposite to Gobineau's in mind, some researchers see, in the practice of handwriting, the education and the socio-cultural level, which are detrimental variables that blur the expressiveness of a writing and ought to be eliminated in order to grasp the character [82]. This attitude ignores, on the one hand, that the personality is a complex unity, where all the factors play a part and, on the other, that each graphic sign is expressive on several levels.

32 One can quote Piaget's works in particular.

33 The hypothesis according to which emotions may also affect the formation of cognitive structures directly, is beyond the aim of this book.

Autonomy, given to the components reflecting intelligence, even though referring theoretically to graphic autonomy, reminds us of the basic data of moral intellectualism : if one judges correctly, one acts correctly, and if one is very intelligent, one is autonomous.

Also, the great many observations on handwritings do show that writing is first and foremost expressive of the writer's character and that it certainly is the best global approach one can have to character, with the added advantage that it is not influenced by the conditions of a test, or an interview.

When the difficulties of character and of socio-emotional adaptation are strong, their very forceful manifestation can interfere with the expression of intelligence[34]: childish components will coexist with the components of Autonomy, which, in some cases, may even disappear.

From all these considerations, it remains that graphology does not deal so much with intelligence as with character, in a wide sense, but that we must also pay tribute to Gobineau for her researches and keep in mind the following idea, stated in the previous pages, and which remains fundamental : that a writing must be immediately related to the general norms corresponding to the writer's educational and socio-cultural level, given in his curriculum vitae, and the correct conclusions must be drawn both ways in case of distortions, between the writing and those norms.

4. Disorganisation of handwriting through old age

Here we envisage only the deterioration of handwriting through the wear and tear connected with ageing in a strict sense, excluding any serious organic or mental disorder.

---

34 We saw this at the beginning of this Chapter, in the case of children.

The motor difficulties, very specific ones, progressively appearing in elderly people's writings, have always been noticed by graphologists.

Those writings have this peculiarity: what has been acquired in handwriting through the socio-cultural level and the personality, remains more or less intact, contrary to Jackson's law, according to which what is supposed to be affected first is what has been acquired last, as is the case for disorders affecting memory, for instance.

An old person's writing keeps its features and the possible originality of its form : it does not look like the badly organised writing of a child, although some of the graphomotor difficulties affecting it are similar to the difficulties of learning.

The difficulty of mastering the fine motor movements of the hand is mainly revealed by :
- the quality of the stroke, which becomes thin, brittle;
- the handling of the stroke with jerks, telescoping, dents, small trembling gestures;
- finals noticeable because they are thrown, or because they leave behind very fine, hair-like, small strokes
- atrophied letters.

The intervention of the will of the writer, who makes efforts to compensate for and hide his difficulties, causes not only slowness, but reinforced pressure, amended or fragmented letters, concealed penlifts (stuck-on connections), etc.

A badly kept baseline, irregular spacing, may also be seen, but real disruption of the layout, some missing or partly missing words, appear only when old age causes greater havoc.

It is quite obvious that a writing which begins to deteriorate through old age, has only a few of these signs.

A scale of deterioration through old age has been attempted [33], but its application has come up against the fact that, nowadays, old age starts later and that, even though human beings are still old at 80, they are in much better physical condition than they used to be and many of them are still in full possession of their intellectual and physical faculties and have an unimpaired writing.

Graphology can detect this phenomenon clearly thanks to progress in medicine and health care in the last few decades.

Woman, 90 years

The thin, dented and slightly trembling stroke, the small hair-like lines (underlined in the reproduction), the jerky handling of the stroke slowed down by the effort to control it, and the irregular dimension, are typical of the graphomotor difficulties caused by the very advanced age of the writer.

236

Note that the direction, layout, clarity (legibility), the form (see the capitals in particular) are well preserved in this woman whose intellectual capacities are intact.

237

237

Man, 70 years
The clear copybook writing, the effort to keep a good baseline, the regularity, the connections, all reveal the discipline of life and the density of work in this mechanic who left school when still very young and whose writing starts to show traces of aging : thin, dented, slightly trembling stroke; small jerks, pen stops, small finals either thrown or trailing, with very light pressure.
Notice the amendments of the three upper extensions of the word "insuffler", expressive of scruples and perfectionism, the skill and the tenacity of the connections with small lassos of the 's's, especially in the word "paraissaient".

See also writing no. 27 (Chapter on the Stroke, sign "Thin").

This is the writing of a woman of 90 where motor difficulties due to age coexist very significantly with right-tending transformations caused by what her socio-cultural level and her personality have given her : notice in particular the bars of the two *t*'s of "petites" done in one stroke, the reverse *d*'s, the tong-shaped *p*'s the very connected writing.

5. Dysgraphia

It seems that it was Ajuriaguerra [83] who first used this term to designate a disorder in the organisation of handwriting, mainly affecting children between 8 and 12, for no organic or intellectual reason.

Dysgraphic children do not manage normal control of their movements, and have very clumsy writings in comparison with the statistical norm of children of the same age, and more often than not, one cannot account for the reason with certainty. Usually there is more than one cause : etiological research has shown a good many predisposing causes : specific difficulties, such as laterality and dyslexia, difficulties of adaptation, varied emotional disorders, etc.

These children, for the most part, go through a normal schooling, although handicapped by their handwritings. Many of them eventually manage to sort out their writing, improving it with age, often helped by various forms of therapy, or making do with some compromise.

It happens, nevertheless, that a percentage of these dysgraphic children still suffer very strongly from this disorder as adults.

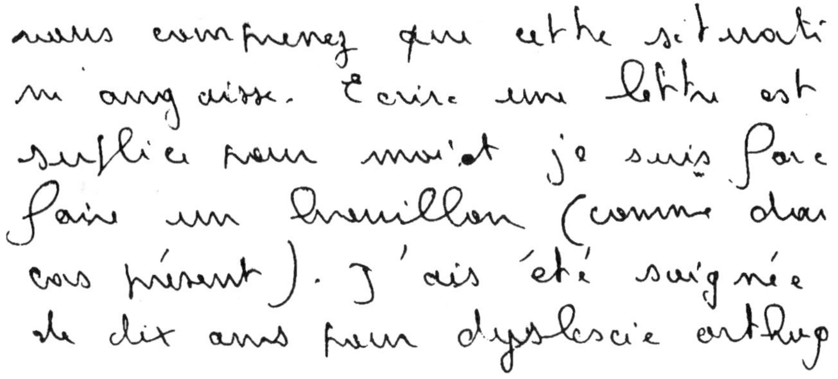

[handwritten text in French]

238 **Girl, 21 years**
Used to suffer from dyslexia. No need to comment.

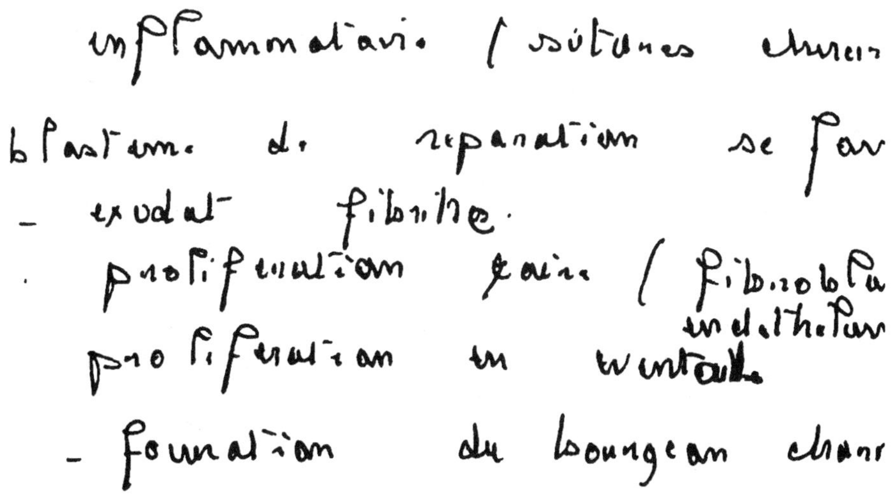

[handwritten text]

239 **Man, 22 years, medical student**
Stiffness, tenseness, slowness, chopped cursive progression, jerky, with lots of breaks, creating a static disconnected writing, with lapses of continuity and

enormous spaces with no rhythm. The forms are badly proportioned, inharmonious and too structured.

239 *Big problems of adaptation and integration into the outside world, but the will to succeed and the good intellectual level have enabled the writer to be successful at school, although on the late side. He will manage, after the age of 22, to improve his writing considerably, helped by a therapy which he will take very seriously.*

Girl, 21 years

Dysgraphic and ambidextrous since the earliest age, she keeps on changing hands when she writes, even in a single sentence, with considerable tenseness and clumsiness, stiffness of the arm, bad posture, which all exceed the severity of classic dysgraphia in children.

The writing shown here is that of her left hand, and is a little smaller, in spite of its dimension, and a little better than that of her right hand.

240 *The very strong pressure attempts to compensate for the difficulty in forming the letters. The cursive progression is made with strong jerks which appear mainly at the end of the movement.*

The writer, who has a good level, manages to retain a good layout and satisfactory spacing between words, owing to a desire for clarity[35].

An only child, with serious problems regarding affective relationships, the writer has never been able to make up her mind as to the choice of one hand rather than the other. When younger she wrote, for a certain time, holding her pen with both hands.

---

35 As far as interlinear spacing is concerned, one finds rather few writings with tangled lines among dysgraphics; they leave space probably in order to be more legible, unconsciously [61].

The above sample is similar to what is called writer's cramp, a very strong tenseness which appears as soon as the person suffering from it wants to write, with a stiffness which may affect not only the fingers, but also the whole arm and shoulder, and can sometimes even go as far as total incapacity to write : this cramp has the peculiarity of affecting only the handwriting, a coded act of communication. Drawing is still possible, and in some cases the signature, a freer movement, can be unaffected, or nearly so.

From the point of view of the script, the effects of cramp are shown by a light and trembling stroke or, on the contrary, by very strong and tense pressure from writers who, through an effort of the will, try to fight their handicap. Jerks are present in both cases, as are stops, irregularities, frequent smothered letters, etc.

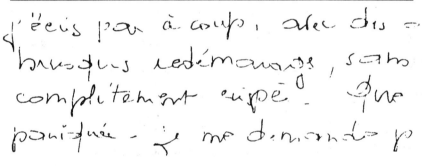

241   **Woman, 40 years**

"I need endless time to manage to write a sentence", a 40-year old woman remarks, who is affected with a writing disorder close to cramp. "I write in spurts, with breaks followed by sudden renewed starts, with no co-ordination, completely tensed-up. What am I to do? I am in a panic."

When this cramp occurs only in adulthood, which is fairly frequent, and therefore affects a writing which is already personalised, one can perceive the socio-cultural level and the level of the personality of the writer, just as one can in the case of writings damaged through ageing.

This cramp develops mainly among people with hyperemotive and phobic natures. In any case, it does not prevent those suffering from it from having a professional life and well-adapted behaviour. One does not know to what extent it is used as a protective outlet and a compensation for emotional difficulties.

Cramps are not easily curable by handwriting therapy.

The graphologist is normally warned in advance, when he has to analyse this kind of writing. His judgment must remain nuanced, but the main points of the personality can still be perceived, provided the writer's graphomotor ability is sufficient.

Woman, 44 years

242 *The evolved socio-cultural level, the feminine, but authoritative writing, the need to impose her ideas, to shine, to captivate, can be seen in the writing, in spite of the motor difficulty.*

[handwritten text]

Man, age unknown

243 *Light, trembling, jerky stokes in this writing which has retained all the signs of an independent character and of a high socio-cultural level.*

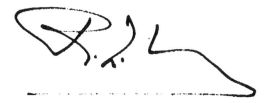

Man, 44 years

244 *This engineer, who has been affected by cramps for a year, has kept his cipher signature unimpaired, as well as his ability to draw and to make straight and firm strokes, whereas he can practically no longer write (a very slow, trembling writing, which chokes up after a few letters, not reproduced here).*

12

HARMONY, FORMLEVEL and RAPPORT between FORM and MOVEMENT

1. Harmony

"Harmony of handwriting is provided by its good proportions, its clarity and the balanced relationship between all its aspects. Simplicity, sobriety and freedom of movement reinforce its qualities. On the other hand, disproportions, discordances and exaggerations are enough to characterise a disharmonious writing especially if they are associated with confusion and complications" [84].

The choice of these criteria for harmony is based on the classical humanism so dear to Crépieux-Jamin. It is founded on qualities of self-mastery and respect for others, in the same way as it is related to ethics and social order.

A harmonious writing, for Crépieux-Jamin, was a writing which had attained a high level of balance and rigour in a personal way. It realised the highest degree of moral as well as intellectual superiority.

A priori, it would seem that these criteria for harmony were quite suited to a time when value judgments were made according to a very precise code of reference and when characterological theories had not been modified by depth psychology. In fact, the elements which warrant an individual's personal equilibrium, as well as his good integration, are still just as precious, and the importance of successful adaptation and good communication still seems valid.

Indeed, a harmonious writing is above all a balanced and nuanced writing. It indicates successful graphic gestures in an overall clear, orderly, homogeneous context with good proportions, sufficient suppleness and no superfluous effects.

By analogy, harmony in a writing shows a balanced personality, and the qualities of intelligence and emotion which it implies make for good adaptation and therefore adequate use of one's abilities, at whatever level that may be.

This is why we have no hesitation in using the Jaminian components of harmony, although we know that they are seldom found together in one handwriting, and that they will not necessarily represent a writing of a superior level in Crépieux-Jamin's sense. Nowadays, the spreading of education and contacts, and a standardisation of life-styles have brought the extremes closer, with the result that the handwritings have a medium degree of harmony in common. *This is also the reason why the concepts of harmony and disharmony are not used much to describe handwritings, whereas their components regularly are.*

The identification of signs concerning fundamental criteria which can be found in writings of very different socio-cultural levels is of prime importance, particularly in personnel selection.

Let us recall these signs : proportionate, clear, simple, orderly and homogeneous[1], sober and free.

We have already emphasised the importance of proportions in a writing, these proportions covering the vertical and horizontal dimensions of both the writing itself and the spaces. We know that a proportionate writing is not necessarily a perfectly regular writing, proportions being susceptible to variation within certain limits : those which are not detrimental to the

---

1   The term 'homogeneous' is not mentioned by name by Crépieux-Jamin among the factors of harmony, yet his own assertion that for a writing to be harmonious, there must be compatibility between all its parts, allows us to add the term "homogeneous", which in any case graphologists commonly use regarding harmony.

progression of the graphic gesture and which allow a rhythm to appear. This is a particularly important point regarding the quality of a writing, and one where both Crépieux-Jamin and Klages link up: for the one, all disproportion or exaggeration is symptomatic of inner conflict, and for the other, it prevents the formation of successful rhythmic continuity, a factor of life.

Clarity, both through the legibility of the forms, and the way these stand out in the space, is related to the structure of words; it implies a well structured personality and a clarity of mind, provided the writing is neither too slow nor slowed down.

Simplicity, as far as harmony[2] is concerned, indicates the naturalness of a writer who shows himself as he is; it belongs to the signs of common sense and objectivity.

An orderly writing is socially significant, showing acceptance of a type of order, and in terms of relationships, as it implies good mastery of spacing, a sign of balanced rapport with others. It is linked to good organisation of thought.

If sobriety is a sign of circumspection and moderation, it also shows the capacity to see the essentials and have a good sense of priorities.

Freedom (fluency), which implies well controlled graphomotor activity, shows, among other things, a spontaneous, skilful and supple progression indicating the writer's sound adaptation and efficiency.

Homogeneity is inherent in the very notion of harmony, inasmuch as compatibility between the different elements of the script is necessary for a writing to be harmonious. The homogeneity in question goes further than mere homogeneity of form, continuity and direction. It is goes together with the innermost quality of a unified personality.

Harmony, like rhythm, is a principle of cohesion. The level of inner security and therefore of resistance to frustration which it implies, considerably increases the strength of the writer. It is a source of dynamism because it makes it possible to accomplish stable projects, no matter at what level this may be.

---

2 Remember that a simple writing can also be a writing with poor forms.

Harmony does not exclude the originality of the writer, but it prevents this originality from intruding on other people's personalities.

Conversely, an inharmonious writing is disproportionate or excessive, heterogeneous through its discordances, confused, disorderly, complicated and clumsy. A graphic milieu containing all these elements would be decidedly negative; one of these elements on its own would not, however, be enough to make the writing negative, especially if it is found in the writing of someone from a modest socio-cultural background, who has not achieved good graphic mastery.

It is interesting to note, regarding harmony, that nowadays, one finds fewer exaggerations and less disharmony in handwritings; fewer writings looking like those of "crooks", to use Crépieux-Jamin's term [38]. The spread of culture may be responsible for this phenomenon, which makes dishonesty in writings even more difficult to spot. Apart from the fact that there can be, on the one hand, tendencies which remain only latent and, on the other, unexpected transgressions, dishonesty cannot always be perceived.

Nevertheless, Rhoda Wieser, through the study of many criminals' handwritings, managed to establish interesting relationships from the basic rhythm of the stroke [17].

Disharmony shows a weak ego, difficulty in reconciling a state of conflict which prevents the unification of a personality obliged to seek ways of defence, or compensation. It reveals a lack of inner security, difficulties in adaptation and sometimes, a refusal to accept the rules of life in society.

The significance of disharmony will be even more pejorative if the writing is well organised. Indeed, disharmony must not be confused with the clumsiness of the writing of those who have had little education and who do not write much.

The effect of the different components of harmony is to give, especially to the beginner, basic indications as to the tone of the graphic milieu.

2. Formlevel

Note on Klages. - Ludwig Klages, born in Hanover in 1872, died in Zürich in 1956. Doctor of chemistry, philosopher, characterologist and graphologist, he is the author of numerous works, three of which have been translated into French, among them, his fundamental work *Handwriting and Character* [23].

Klages, a great adept of the vitalist movement of that time - he had a profound admiration for Nietzsche - founded his graphological method on his philosophical conception of the predominance of richness and liberation, life forces and soul, over dryness, constraint and impoverishment due to the rationalising effect of the mind.

Thus he stressed the notions of rhythm, intensity and individuality. It is these notions making up his global perception of handwritings which he calls *Formniveau* (Formlevel), that is to say the level of life; *Form* here signifying quality of life force, inner richness, and not form in the psychological sense of *Gestalt* in German.

Klages also formulates a law of expression and puts the emphasis, in psychic life, on the polarity of a) the strength of drives and b) the weakness of resistance, insisting on the fact that the same action, seen from outside, can be carried out under the influence of one or other of these two tendencies.

This dualistic, antagonistic view led Klages to consider all the interpretations of graphic signs from the point of view of a positive-negative polarity. For instance, if we take the sign right-slanted writing, the meanings, in a positive context, will be social feelings, therefore warmth, self-sacrifice, passionate nature, etc, and, in a negative context, thoughtlessness, therefore licence, lack of moderation, of restraint, etc.

The graphologist Thea Stein-Lewinson based her system of graphometry on the subdivision of all the graphic variables, in terms of the Klagesian polarity contraction-release, into three grades of accentuation either way, going through 0, a central point of equilibrium [85].

Klages reckoned the Formlevel as having 5 degrees.

This numbered evaluation has now been abandoned by graphologists. On the other hand, all the notions of rhythm have been kept and deepened by means of studies on the relationship between form and movement, particularly by Prof. Robert Heiss and the graphologists Hans Müller and Alice Enskat, in works which have unfortunately not been translated into French.

In other ways, the excesses caused by a too rigorous polarity of the graphic context have been replaced, in France, by a more nuanced approach, enabling those who know how to handle them to use Klages's interpretations and to preserve something of great interest.

Use of the Formlevel. - In order to assist in the general grasp of a handwriting, French graphology has retained from the Formlevel whatever is thought to complement the components of harmony, which mainly emphasised moderation and balance.

This assimilation, free from any dogmatism, took place independently from the evolution of Klages' ideas and from the theoretical discussions which they may have provoked among German graphologists.

The most important thing has been to integrate into our view of handwriting, the concepts of intensity, plenitude and originality (meaning: that which is as it was originally, authentic). Indeed, Klages wrote: "degree of originality, individuality, intensity of rhythm and level of life, all these describe one and the same expressive phenomenon, and with it, the personal indication of Plenitude of life" [86].

In order to grasp the idea of the Formlevel, French graphologists have followed what Klages recommended in his writings, namely that "richness and poverty" of life are qualities ... whose contrasts can be described in many ways, as, for instance, with expressions such as "full or empty, profound or superficial, heavy or light, thick or thin, warm or cold, colourful or pale, strong or weak" [86].

This way of grasping a writing has fallen into disuse, but the idea of life in handwriting, synonymous with rhythm, has remained an important element of handwriting analysis, which we undeniably owe to Klages.

Rhythm is mainly perceived through movement, form and space distribution, which Klages used to call proportion, and in which he was, in fact, getting close to Crépieux-Jamin.

Formlevel emphasises the opposition between authentic, intense and evolved writings which are personalised (yet remaining sober and free from excesses), and devitalised, monotonous writings with poor, complicated, banal or "trivial"[3] forms.

Klages also specified that signs of culture must not be confused with the level of life. A writer with little culture will be all the more positively assessed if his Formlevel is good. Thus Klages links up with the notion of the writer's socio-cultural level, an immediate piece of information to use in analyses, as has been seen in the chapter on Organisation.

The elements of Formlevel, which clearly indicate the subject's presence, his capacity to radiate and his strength of conviction, perhaps do not appear sufficiently in harmony, though freedom of the graphic movement necessarily implies life in the writing. They are definitely of interest whenever qualities of competitiveness, communication and ability to stimulate are essential. In the same way as the elements of harmony, they generate cohesion and integration.

Klages always insisted on the limits of individualisation, which should remain compatible with respect for social order. Thus he links up with the fundamental notion of homogeneity in handwriting. The sometimes not very harmonious transgressions of certain movements are permissible only to the extent that they are not detrimental to the homogeneity of the script.

As Pulver says, all these elements, those of harmony and those coming from Formlevel, constitute an indication of all that which will be discovered by analysis, using the numerous established facts. Pulver replaced the term 'Formlevel' with what he called 'the existential quality of the writing'.

These elements are largely responsible for the general aspects which Crépieux-Jamin used to talk about. Their presence or absence is decisive for the evaluation of the graphic context, in relation both to the elements as a whole and to the distinctive peculiarities of each element.

---

3   Klages's term.

3. *Relationship betweem Form and Movement*

This concerns a guiding synthesis used in Germany, mainly following Prof. Heiss [87] and the graphologists Müller and Enskat [88]. From Klages's fundamental idea, namely that, essentially, life is rhythm, and that rhythm is found everywhere in nature, in biology, in the flapping of birds' wings ... and in handwriting, Prof. Heiss, after Carl Gross, founded a whole graphological system on the observation of handwriting under the three aspects of rhythm of movement, rhythm of form and rhythm of distribution[4], as well as the relationship between form and movement.

We do not intend in this book to give a didactic presentation of a system of graphology which would need a whole manual, but only to show what French graphology has integrated from these very rich concepts. A reciprocal relationship has indeed been created in the last decades between various graphological trends from which graphology has profited greatly. (Let us recall that in Germany at present , Klages's Formlevel, which we have just talked about, is mostly grasped through this approach of the relationship between form and movement).

Jaminian graphology does not have the same starting point as Klagesian graphology. It seems to be less philosophical, more experimental, but also particularly close to the graphic gesture which is a synthesis of both movement and form[5].

---

4   Each aspect is itself divided into three degrees, from the unevolved to the perturbed, going through a central degree: "marked" for movement, "accentuated" for space and "evolved" for form. In this way Crépieux-Jamin's most important signs are all practically covered. Let us note in particular that, regarding the aspect of movement, unevolved, marked, or perturbed, one finds, apart from signs describing the flow of movement, all the signs which concern the stroke according to Hegar, the type and degree of connection, and the speed. The stroke is inseparable from the movement in German graphology and the three aspects of movement, space and form regroup Crépieux-Jamin's seven categories.

5   In handwriting, movement exists only to produce a form. Movement is a means; it is directly expressive in so far as it is a psychomotor action and form is the aim; it brings into play an element of representation, which is more intellecutal.

In observing a handwriting, it is not true to say that Crépieux-Jamin's signs are envisaged analytically; this is an unfair reproach; the signs are envisaged within the main aspects of a writing and this ensures the correct interpretation of their meanings. So in Crépieux-Jamin, this notion of form-movement will not be found as in the case of the Germans.

What can be said of this approach from a developmental and French graphological point of view ?

The graphic movement, the impulse to scribble on a sheet of paper, is found in children before the age of two, if they are given writing instruments. As we have seen in the foreword on scribbles, it is expressive and probably accompanied with an inner image preceding verbalization [90].

Between two and three, children can produce some ideograms in a "tadpole-man" style, since they can draw sticks and circles [3].

Handwriting itself will become possible only through the maturation of the antagonistic muscles and the capacity to draw curves in both directions alternately with precision.

Therefore a child usually cannot learn to write before the age of 4. After a spontaneous period of pretend-writing, he sometimes continues by copying the model imposed at nursery school, or by using other methods which may vary according to schools and periods.

Handwriting necessitates an apprenticeship. Human beings have the developmental capacity to go through this apprenticeship if they have a sufficient I.Q. (intelligence quotient), but will not be able to write if they are not taught to.

Handwriting requires the reproduction of a visual model, of a form, which is difficult for a child when he is very young.

Children have *to make a mental picture* of what they are about to write, by means of an anticipatory image, when writing is under visual control at the start of the learning process. This anticipatory image will become semi-conscious as they learn to write and when their writing, in so far as it is a composite movement creating a form, has become a semi-automatic, well-coordinated physical action.

The integration of the graphic trajectory (from left to right in our models), when writing the letters down, also requires a long maturation;

this is why children's writings retain for a long time, that lack of suppleness and firmness which distinguishes them from adults' writings. A child, quite naturally, gives predominance to Form which is the aim of handwriting and needs all his attention, and there is no reason why this form should be transgressed. Children who do so too early have considerable graphomotor difficulties, the causes of which must be looked into (specific difficulties, disorders of personality or adaptation ...).

Adolescents who are well adapted to schoolwork, also retain this respect for form, which enables them to communicate both with others and with themselves, even if they change models, by adapting typographic forms, for instance, as they may temporarily do. On the other hand, if movement is too pronounced and disturbs the form, the writing may reflect refusal to face up to the classic process of adaptation, or communication.

In an adult's writing, one can arbitrarily separate the elements of form from those of movement, and one can make the hypothesis that movement, being more natural, since it corresponds to initial impulses, is closer to basic drives and reserves of life-force, and is more directly *expressive* of psychic contents, whereas *representative* form which is more related to a need to structure and fulfil one's personality, reflects attitudes towards others, social values, conformism, conservatism and ethics to a greater extent. It also lends itself more to a need to present oneself, to give an image of the self through the communicative role of handwriting[6].

It can be accepted as a general rule that good movement carrying well defined[7] forms which Heiss calls "form of movement", indicates satisfac-

---

6 We recall that Klages, in his vitalist philosophy, distinguishes between expression and representation. For him, movements connected with transcribing language are affected by an individual guiding image (*Leitbild*), very personal and unconscious, related to the personality, and which causes one person to write with curves and another with angles, etc. The graphologist interprets it symbolically, unlike movement which is expressive as it represents the flow of life and feelings.
   It is very regrettable that the translator of Klages's book into French has, mistakenly, translated "*Leitbild*" by "anticipating image" instead of "guiding image". One must clearly distinguish, in terminology, between this *guiding* image, Klages's theoretical hypothesis, and the *anticipating* image, which, having become gradually unconscious, can be taken for granted in our gestures when we write; this applies to all common physical activities (e.g. driving a car).

7 In the terminology of Heiss [87].

tory balance between drives and their realisation, control, acceptance of others, a stable personality, authenticity, adaptability and intelligence, when the movement creates evolved forms.

A predominance of movement, without the form being destroyed, indicates drives which are sometimes difficult to control, but also spontaneity, independence from conventions, or intense activity, if the writing has a good stroke and is firm. Predominant, but clear forms, carried by definite movement, indicates efficient acceptance of rules, solidity, patience, the capacity not to act on impulses, the interpretation being all the more positive, the more the form is evolved. With even more emphasised forms, we find acquired writings expressing the writer's desire to construct a certain personality for himself, to give others a deliberate, "impressive" image.

We are dealing with what Prof. Heiss calls "forms of structure" as against "forms of movement". These forms of structure, not always acquired, rigidify the movement when they become excessive. Then they express the writer's rigidity in conventional attitudes, keeping to the rules, and can, in some cases, mask deep conflicts, with possible flare-ups of these conflicts. If form is excessively dominant it is also worth mentioning certain forms that are very polished in a mannered way, stylised but lifeless, used by a small percentage of schizophrenic patients, plus all the complicated forms which should not be confused with the original forms one finds in the writings of creative artists, with a dominance of form, but where movement is not absent[8].

There are also inadequate movements, which produce monotonous forms, or perturbed movements which spoil the form, and movements which, being too strong or too weak, dissolve it. The interpretation calls the writer's balance into question, and here the quality of the stroke is very important, and is a positive compensatory factor when it is good. Indeed, the stroke is an integral part of movement and can guide the interpretations, whether negative or not, which can be given to the dominance of movement.

---

8 We shall not deal here with handwriting as a graphic art, which belongs to another field altogether.

It is noteworthy that women, more often than men, have a writing with a dominance of form, thus expressing their greater respect for traditions, their conservatism, their need for security, their potential for practical and steady efficiency, their emotional needs, and sometimes a narcissism still close to childhood. (In children's drawings, Ada Abraham has noticed that girls make more forms which are round, and that boys have a firmer stroke) [90].

Men's writings, which more frequently have a dominance of movement, are more spontaneous and less conformist, more directly express drives, the need for action, and for imprinting a personal mark on the outside world. Statistically, handwritings are sexualised [11, 91].

Another question arises : form being representative, or "impressive", should one support Klages's idea of the guiding image (Leitbild) of the unconscious expectation of what we write, under its various aspects, an image which is stronger where form dominates? It seems that that this hypothesis can be retained, and has been in fact, especially in Germany : for Müller-Enskat, the relationship between movement and form represents the factors of life and drives, and the way they are used through the control of the guiding images.

In French graphology, the breaking-up of handwriting into form and movement has made an undeniable contribution regarding the in-depth significance of both elements, and this is quite independent of a real knowledge of German graphology and its rhythms[9] : the predominance a writer gives to form or to movement is a matter of personality.

A remark is nevertheless necessary as to the influence of the educational level; a dominance of form is frequent among well-adapted writers with a modest socio-cultural level, since a positive dominance of movement necessitates an evolution and a graphic control rarely reached at that level. These notions are explained in the chapter on Organisation.

Remark: by comparing the notes, the curriculum vitae and a writer's letter of application, the graphologist can see that the same writer can

---

9   Here we shall not deal with another viewpoint of some German graphologists, who in an analysis, see movement mainly in relation to temperament, and form, in relation to intellect and intelligence.

switch from a writing with a dominance of movement, to one where he stresses form and structure, in order to be legible, in a conscious effort to adapt and communicate [92].

Below, for the interested reader, we reproduce a writing in which the relationship between form and movement has been studied according to the method of Müller and Enskat, authors who have not been translated into French [93].

245

"The form-movement relationship is very well balanced. Some slightly imprecise forms, a few letters with a filiform tendency, and sticks, show a slight dominance of movement. But the form remains firm and clearly shaped. The writing does not allow itself to be pulled along by an excessive forward movement. The movement carries the forms and makes them lively.

The element of structure is definitely present. It utilises good basic life forces, which, however, show no excessive intensity or violence. The guiding images are strong enough to control and channel the instinctual movements without having to exercise constraint. Also, the writing is too stripped of inessentials for the need to be "impressive" to play a major rôle. So the demands to structure the self seem aimed at satisfying an inner ethical need, rather than a desire to make an impression. In any case, this interpretation is confirmed by the general context of authenticity (not wishing to appear anything other or more, than what one is), which Müller-Enskat attributed to a good relationship between form and movement".

13

METHODOLOGY
Practical Application

METHODOLOGY
definition, interpretation

All through this book, we have endeavoured to define what constitutes the raw material of graphology, i.e. the signs classified into their categories, for didactic purposes. We have given their interpretations, showing their interrelationships, the importance of the graphic context and of the developmental and socio-cultural aspect of handwriting. We now have to know how to utilise that knowledge in order to do a clear graphological analysis which is true to the writing. Crépieux-Jamin used to say that signs are to graphology what the alphabet is to reading, thus showing their character, indispensable but also insufficient, as well as the whole complexity of their utilisation.

The document which the graphologist submits to analysis includes a text as well as a signature, the two being significant together and separately. We shall not talk of the signature again, since a chapter has been devoted to it, but the reader must of course take it into account, right from the moment he looks at a writing.

This initial perception concerns what first strikes one when looking at a writing[1], and the novice graphologist should not be tempted to focus his attention on precise points systematically applied to every writing, nor to aim at some interpretation or other, which at this stage would be very imprudent. The general impression maintains that initial contact and receptivity when faced with a writing for the first time. This remarks applies

---

1   This first perception was for a long time called the 'general impression'.

to students in particular, as a professional graphologist can immediately perceive a handwriting through a method which he has internalised. A global perception is important, for handwriting as "Form" (Gestalt) cannot be reduced to the sum of its components.

This method consists of three observations which are as follows:

1. First observation: this concerns the graphic context under the fourfold aspect of Organisation, Harmony, Formlevel and the relationship between Form and Movement, the notion of rhythm underlying the last two elements.

As we have seen, the signs which justify them are essentially qualitative, that is to say decisive regarding the tendencies and the innermost choices of the personality, also taking the socio-cultural milieu into account. They will make it possible to understand the writer's intelligence, emotions and activity.

Indeed these important signs help to pinpoint the interpretations of those which have a range of meanings varying from the most negative to the most positive. Remember that each one can cover different gestures arising from different attitudes and that it is the general tone of the graphic context which helps us decide.

If this initial observation applies more particularly to the four above-mentioned syntheses, the graphologist should not forget that the graphic context is also part of the overall regrouping of the signs in the definition.

2. Second observation : this is made up of the actual definition, that is to say the detection of the features which are very specific and essential to the writing under study. It is therefore no longer a matter of systematically using criteria applicable to all writings, but, on the contrary, to use the signs which differentiate one writing from another as much as possible.

These are the species called "dominants", whose number must be restricted, but can also vary according to the richness or complexity of the writing being studied.

The graphologist has to go through two processes:

a) *choosing the signs :* this choice is strictly dictated by the writing. This alone imposes the dominant signs in so far as they are factually indisputable and can be stated objectively.

This is an exercise which requires a lot of practice, application, a critical mind, precision and perseverance. "One must learn to see, to see well, and to see everything". The simplicity of the exercise is entirely theoretical "as the same quality is shown in different aspects and intensities; it is influenced by other qualities which restrict or enhance its functions in such a way that one sometimes has great difficulty in recognising it in the very complex and baffling context concerned (38). Incidentally, we do not conceal that "behind what a character looks like, there are infinitely more complex possibilities. But the visible qualities are at the same time the most operative, the others often being destined never to emerge". These first qualities are certainly those shown by the dominant signs.

This could be any sign such as, for instance, a strong right slant, when it pervades the whole writing, or a global sign with far-reaching significance per se[2].

Among these dominants, a small number of signs occur more often which can be called "standard" and which roughly correspond to the variables in foreign graphologies (which use fewer of them).

Crépieux-Jamin used few signs in his definitions, for he retained only those related to "the main aspects" of a writing, which at the same time explain and synthesize the minor ones. We make more detailed definitions at present in order to regroup the observations afterwards, according to their different interactions and bring out the syndromes (also called syntheses of signs) [3], as we shall make it clear in our third observation.

It is the essential that must be selected and correspond to the document, but it often happens that writings are characterised by a small sign, usually minor, or by the peculiarity of the signature, for instance.

Signs which already appeared in the first observation can be used again in the definition if they are characteristic.

---

2   Conventional, inhibited or animated, for instance.
3   We are using the term as Gobineau saw it, slightly differently from Crépieux-Jamin's notion of resultants.

Along with the building up of the definition, the graphologist thinks of the various, possibly suitable meanings.

b) *Hierarchisation of the signs* : the procedure leading to the interpretation is greatly clarified by the hierarchisation of the signs. This is probably what is most difficult. It is the result of long practice and a process in which the graphologist's intelligence and finesse are involved, as are his common sense and his aptitude to choose.

The beginner, more often than not, tends to pick too many signs which he thinks are dominant and does so in a disorderly fashion. So he will have first to cut down and afterwards organise the signs in a hierarchy.

The hierarchisation of the signs is done according to how specific they are, that is to say, the signs most suitable for qualifying the writing are put first[4]. The rigorousness of this hierarchisation is fundamental and any mistake compromises the next step in the analysis, particularly the choice of syndromes.

If rigorousness forces one to restrict the number of signs, it is none the less true that a thorough definition must be completed with lesser signs which it would be wrong to place first.

The more one progresses in the study of a writing, the more everything corresponds and becomes complete, including the first perception, which must then find its justification, if the graphologist was correct in the first place.

The signature, an integral part of the document, appears at all levels and sometimes more markedly at one of them.

3. Third observation : the one which builds up the graphic syndromes, that is to say the various associations of signs seen before. These groupings enable one to widen the interpretations considerably, as well as to particularise them at the same time. They will also indicate interpretations which would not have been established directly at first.

---

4   The hierarchisation in 3 successive levels, as practised in the past, has now been abandoned.

These syndromes can be of very different sorts:

a) Syndromes of signs *pointing in the same direction* : for instance, strong pressure, connected, regular, dynamic. This synthesis of signs enables one to intensify the conclusion already drawn from one of the dominant signs taken up again and placed first in the syndrome. It is the one which pinpoints the most significant conclusions by enhancing the more intense character features which will most likely remain dominant, whatever happens.

Moreover this type of syndrome has the advantage of reinforcing the graphologist's judgment by bringing in elements which confirm one another.

b) Syndromes of signs *affecting one another* : for instance, strong pressure, connected, dynamic, diminishing and filiform.

c) Syndromes of signs *bringing out contradictions* which can operate :

- either positively (compensation), for instance : small, irregular, wide, strong pressure and dynamic,

- or negatively, for instance : small, connected, descending, with heavy and low diacritics.

d) Syndromes *bringing out original associations* belonging to a particular writing and which immediately stand out and yet do not belong to the syndromes quoted above. They sometimes bring new psychological meanings to light[5].

The construction of the syndromes aims at going beyond noticing the presence of the dominant signs objectively; it aims at deducing interpretations which have greater depth than those derived from mere observation of the signs. The syndromes must be based on concrete cases and it would be dangerous and illusory to conceive and apply them with preconceived reasoning, when they must be dictated by the writing.

This is neither the most difficult nor the least interesting discipline in graphology, and it does seem that the beginner graphologist quickly learns

---

5   In the same way as psychological knowledge is indispensable for understanding the writer's personality, conversely, one could envisage that the study of the graphic syndromes helps discover a new psychology through the expressiveness of gestures [94].

to handle it, but a maximum of information should be drawn from it. It is perhaps at this stage that intuition, maturity and experience are most precious as they enable us to give more depth to the already listed signs with sometimes forward-looking insight.

These syndromes are all the more important as they constitute the framework of the analysis, and the solidity of the line of reasoning will depend on how soundly they have been assembled.

All the observations must form a coherent whole which will enable the analysis to be drawn up.

When it comes to wording the analysis, the understanding of the conclusions is linked to both the simplicity and the clarity of presentation, in keeping with the client's request, as also to the prudence and tact required by respect for the person.

Besides, the graphologist is bound by professional secrecy (article 378 of the Penal Code), but a letter belongs to its addressee.

This classic method of French graphology may have appeared a little complex in its explanation. To a certain extent, it is simpler to use once its rules have been assimilated. It seems to us to preserve both the necessary rigour in assessing a writing, plus a certain amount of freedom in the graphologist's personal judgement.

PRACTICAL APPLICATIONS

Below we give two practical applications : a study of capacity for professional adaptation, designed for the employer (writings 246a and 246b), and a brief study in depth, designed for the writer (writings 247a and 247b). The samples are presented in two ways : an excerpt from the writing, and the whole document, reduced to one third, to show the layout and the signature.

durée de 3 à 4 semaines, sur la base opp
tire d'un mi-temps, sans engagement d
de part ou d'autre. Un habillage précise
du type "Chargé de mission" pourrait peut
convenir.

— de rédiger à l'issue de cette période
court document analysant la situation
proposant un plan détaillé des actions
mener à court terme ainsi qu'une list
actions à plus long terme.

rect "challenge" du poste que vous prez

246a see also 246b overleaf

Man, 35 years - Married, 2 children
*The writer entered professional life with no diplomas (bank, then a management
consultancy), where he very quickly gained ground, while preparing for
l' Institut Supérieur des Affaires [6], where he was accepted. At the time of the
document, he applied to a PME [7] which was looking for a financial director.
He is now its deputy general director.*

---

6 A higher business institute (T.N.).
7 PME (Petite et Moyenne Entreprise): a small to average size firm with up to some
   200 employees (T.N.).

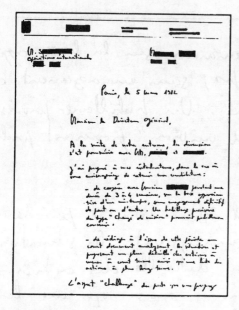

246b

First perception : a very mobile and lively writing with an important signature which is much larger than the text and placed in the centre.

1. *Organisation* : the graphic level is superior to that usually met with among those writers who, early on, have had no higher education.

In spite of insufficient spacing between lines, a layout slightly shifted to the right, uneven control of black and white, and of movement and form, the general arrangement of the small, rapid and rhythmic writing is personal, appropriate and efficient. The elements making up the layout are well placed and the paragraphs clear.

The candidate shows a good level of personal evolution and intelligence at the same time as certain signs of his career development, and the mark of his character; he chose to enter the world of work at an early stage.

2. *Harmony* : the writing is simple in its forms, but is not sober, due to the

signature and the moderate control of movement. Quite orderly, although in a personal manner, and it is relatively clear. It cannot be called free, but it remains quite homogeneous in its mobility, in spite of the disproportion of the signature.

3. *Formlevel* : without having intensity, the writing has a lot of life given by the irregularity and the mobility : there is a rhythm. The proportions of the different elements are not sufficient to give a rhythm of distribution.

4. *Relationship between form and movement* : Predominance of a vibrant movement slightly reared (causing an animated writing) over a form which is unequally individualised but simple, open, with simplifications and right-tending.

Hierarchised definition. - Rapid and and animated writing, small, irregular in dimension and above all, slant, with strong pressure, some relief and sharp points, a very large, superelevated, underlined signature, semi cipher-shaped and placed in the centre. Hopping writing, with semi-angular wide garlands with a few jerks, a well-kept baseline, no starting strokes, irregular finals and t-bars, some of which are at an angle, or restrained, or descending, precise and slightly thrown, bird-shaped diacritics, held back third letter in the signature, and some held back lower extensions pulling a little towards the left, rather prolonged upper extensions , and a few large 'M's.

● Syndromes (or : syntheses of signs) :

1.a. The strong pressure with the vibrant and reared movement (animated writing), the rhythm, the hopping writing, the irregular dimension and slant, the rapid, small and dense overall context, the variety of forms, with simplifications and right tendedness, the left margin - large - which adapts and the right margin - small -, and the absence of starting strokes, can all be grouped to indicate dynamism with mobility, diversity and rapidity of approaches and reactions.

1.b. The slightly irregular spacing, the lines close together, the small wide angles, sometimes jerky, associated with the restraint of some letters, the hopping writing, with a dominance of movement, the reared aspect, the irregular finals, the varied t-bar and the sharp-points, all confirm the slightly impulsive, impatient and critical reactivity.

2. The very large and superelevated signature, much larger than the text, constructed and dynamic, underlined and placed in the centre, the 'M's, the relief and the strong pressure, the reared aspect of the movement, indicate considerable ambition, a desire to succeed and to be at the centre of activities and attention, which motivate projects and guide behaviour.

3.a. The well kept line, the clear paragraphs, the personal and efficient general organisation, the lines further apart at the beginning than at the end under the effect of control, the relief, the signs of restraint, the very precise diacritics, all indicate the control of which the candidate is capable when it is related to syndrome 1.b. (reactivity), and his realism.

3.b. The signature placed in the centre with its held back letter (the position in the centre cannot be a sign of hesitation in this context and this dimension), associated with syndrome 1.a. (need for mobility) and syndrome 2 (ambition), enable one to conclude that the candidate wants to preserve his independence and to keep open other routes to personal success.

Analysis. - Intuitive, open and mobile (syndrome 1.a), the candidate is very much all there (density of the whole, the relief) and very quickly at the heart of situations. He wants things to move, has lots of ideas, but considers them carefully and organises them, in order to make them as efficient and profitable as possible (syndrome 3.a.).

His active mind, his varied and very critical thought (sharp points) quickly make him spot flaws at the same time as causing him to envisage all possibilities in order to provide for all contingencies immediately (speed, and lines close together).

His rhythm is fast, easily impatient (syndrome 1.b.). Only the desire to succeed (syndrome 2) by taking a realistic view, serves to moderate his impatience to reach the expected results rather fast, results which he criticises and questions if necessary (openness, restraint, straightenings-up), and which seldom satisfy him (an overall vibrant context, a little tense, a little prolonged up (syndrome 1.b. and 2). He looks for improvements and new opportunities.

He is keen on his independence (syndrome 3b), not liking to be either influenced or manipulated.

He stimulates, he persuades, has the knack of saying the right thing, enjoys discussion and tactics. By nature he finds his best equilibrium in action and ever renewed interests and contacts (vibrant movement with pressure and syndrome 1.a.). He is not always easy to live with, because he is impatient, quickly reactive, a little abrupt at times, or clumsy (dominance of movement, jerks, lines close together). He tries to distance himself from his easily affected sensitivity (attempts at spacing, clear paragraphs, restraints), he forgets his reactions and tries to make others forget them. He is open, direct (vibrant movement and open, simple forms), yet wishes to assert his place over a wide field (syndrome 2 and margins).

He is highly ambitious and directs his activity in accordance with his desire for success. He is motivated by a need to be competitive, a need to take on challenges (relationship of the small middle zone and the signature with the left margin, in this overall reactive context with strong pressure).

On the other hand, his destabilising factors are to be found in his fear of being limited, or too closely guided, and therefore of seeing his freedom of action curtailed (syndrome 3.b.). While respecting social and professional rules (layout), he wishes to leave himself a supple margin for manoeuvring and for ample opportunities to get involved in things. He needs, for his personal comfort, to be able to keep his eye on possible avenues of escape, should certain unforeseen events or restrictions occur. He fears routine and stagnation, becomes anxious and annoyed with himself if he cannot prove himself (vibrant movement, strong pressure, relationship between the dimension of the text and that of the signature, bird-shaped diacritics, descending t-bars).

His dynamism and his ambition are well suited to what this PME is looking for, which needs to be stimulated with regard to its new goals. He will provide it with that independence of thought, that mobility and that new critical outlook which he bestows on whatever is around him. He will know how to adapt to objectives coming his way (mobility and lines close together) but will also be capable of making longer-term plans intelligently (the general level, the paragraphs), in order to ensure the success of his actions.

Moreover, even if he does not wish to stake everything on his professional life because he wants to have a wide field of action (signature in the centre with its restrained letter, in this active and mobile context), he involves himself in it with ardour (density, pressure, relief, fairly homogeneous context), always taking a real interest in it, and sees in this promotion new opportunities, and the stimulus to surpass himself and to investigate new possibilities (open, wide and right-tending).

His application for the job is positive. Even with his demand for independence and success, he should be a strong asset to the firm.

Note : the graphological justifications of our interpretation have been inserted in brackets in the text of the analysis, for teaching purposes.

The very detailed syndromes have the same purpose.

247a

Woman, 40 years - Single[8]

The writer is in a Professional Trade Union Office.
Self-taught.

---

8   This writing was given for the written exam of the Société Française de Graphologie in 1984.

247b

Ma chère Janine —

Je m'excuse de ne pas t'avoir au plus tôt le compte rendu de la du ▮▮▮▮▮▮, mais les journées tellement vite que je n'arrive à Je le joins également ma cotisat aussi que ma carte à pointer et remercié de bien vouloir faire le qui qu'elle ne soit retournée. —

First perception : Cohesion, intensity and restraint of this writing.

1. *Organisation:* it is successful and personal in view of the writer's educational level.

2. *Harmony :* the components which are most evident are homogeneity, clarity and order. The writing is fairly simple, sober (in spite of a large middle zone). The proportions are personal (not much upper extension). The freedom is medium (association of skilful and restrained gestures).

3. *Formlevel* : The life of the writing is revealed more by the quality of the stroke and the intensity contained in this dense writing, than by a rhythm of movement. The form is relatively personalised on a conventional, albeit genuine basis. In spite of the tendency to compactness between the lines, the distribution of the graphic groups is good, within a very circumscribed frame.

4. *Relationship between form and movement* : The dominant form of "structure" is carried by a slightly constrained movement.

Hierarchised definition.- Homogeneous writing with a large and dominant middle zone, firm, connected, restrained, a little reared and left-slanted, narrow letters, deep, looped garlands with a few overhanging arcades and a few secondary widths with a little deviated pressure, well nourished and pasty writing, straight left margin, very well-kept baseline, short upper extensions, double-joins and small lassos at the base of letters, reverse letters, open-curved finals both diminishing and enlarging, legible signature similar to the text, rising underlined and placed slightly right of centre.

● **Syndromes :**

1. the large writing, the deep and looped garlands, the open-curved finals; the well-nourished and pasty writing, the small lassos at he base of letters, the double-joins, the tendency to compactness between lines, can be grouped here to indicate an important affective dominance, receptivity, femininity, presence, and a desire to assert herself.

The dominant middle zone in this context, the homogeneity and the intensity, increase the strength of the affectivity and give emotional intensity.

The clear and legible signature, similar to the text, in this authentic graphic context, give genuineness and a desire to be understood.

The dominance of form in this generally large and narrow context, makes it clear that the emotions and the desire to be understood go together with a need for security.

2. The slightly reared and left-slanted writing, narrow, looped, double-joined, reverse, with covering strokes, '*o*'s connected with arcades at the top, the either enlarging or slightly diminishing finals and the dominance of form, all constitute a graphic syndrome expressing restraint and control, against a defensive background.

The dominance of form giving the control of reactions in this syndrome, is to be related to the wide, straight left margin, which itself contrasts with the density of the text with its rather conventional forms; it can explain this restraint which is found at two levels in the writer, deep within herself, as well as ethically and socially.

Syndromes 1 and 2 are in opposition and show the ambivalence of the character (strong affective demands and fear of deep relationships), apparent self-assurance and apprehension.

3. The homogeneous, large, firm and connected writing, orderly with well-kept lines, well-nourished, a little reared, some secondary widths with deviated pressure, and enlarging finals, show that the contradictions have been integrated with seriousness, courage and discipline.

The dominance of form with the large, dense middle zone, and the orderly writing - yet with lassos and loopings - pinpoints the practical efficiency.

The large, reared writing with the signature similar to the text, also shows a search for lucidity and the ability to live according to her own choices.

Analysis.- This handwriting indicates a personality which asserts itself by its intensity and cohesion, just as much as it limits itself by its restraint.

It is immediately apparent that the writer is efficient, tenacious and controlled, and indeed, she is so. Then contradictions become clear and bring to light the inner complexity, in spite of the apparent control.

Feelings play a preponderant rôle, in that they are potentially intense and that the writer has difficulty in living with them in a natural manner. One can perceive the writer's aspirations; capacity for affection is clearly shown, distinct assertiveness and a representative self-image. But one can also see what in fact happens: a receptivity which suffers because it cannot express itself spontaneously, the search for deep affective relationships and the fear that this might disturb a hard-won autonomy, an acute sense of her personal dignity which is linked to a demanding moral sense and to activities free from any slackness.

The closed field of the writer's emotions and feelings is tightly and firmly circumscribed. She is keen on keeping control in this respect, and accepts, although this is painful to her, the frustrations due to her inability to let go.

However, her character remains fairly supple and her taste for life strong enough to enable her to adapt to reality and to other people, positively. Whilst being on her guard, she disregards her regrets, and faces the world with an attitude which is at once determined, skilful and cautious. She manages not to isolate herself.

Her work gives her the opportunity to maintain these contacts, the value of which she understands. She commits herself to them totally. Hard-working, organised, persevering, applied, precise and patient, she is an efficient and devoted secretary. She knows how to make herself indispensable through the quality of her work as much as through her moral rigour and her stability.

Involving her feelings in all circumstances, she is categorical and subjective, but pulls herself together, thanks to her qualities of intelligence and her discipline.

The certainty of having found, in her profession, her right level, in keeping with her aspirations, and of being appreciated at work, enables her to feel independent and to remain unaffected. There is a certain elegance in her behaviour.

14

HANDWRITING of LEFT-HANDERS using the left hand

The object of this chapter is not to study the occasional use of the left hand, necessary sometimes after an accident or an illness, or used for the purpose of forgeries, in anonymous letters for instance. The great clumsiness and changes which appear in such cases, by comparison with normal right-handed writing, has been the object of studies by Doctor Locard in particular. They are of greater interest to experts than to graphologists.

On the other hand, the usual handwriting of left-handers requires a certain number of comments which seem to us interesting to put forward, this question having been studied more often from the point of view of the particular rather than that of general reflection.

Laterality is the term used to define the dominance of one side of the body in relation to the other. It is called harmonic when the whole side of the body has the same dominance, i.e. the foot, the hand and the eye, and dysharmonic when this is not the case, which is rarer. It seems a proven fact that only laterality of the hand matters as far as handwriting is concerned, although the eye is the guide.

The question of laterality of human beings, right-sided in the great majority of cases, has given rise to many a hypothesis regarding its historical, sociological and cultural origins [95]. Among them one might mention the carrying of a shield with the left hand to protect the heart situated on the left side, thus developing laterality of the right side of the body with the hand that carries the sword, the instrument of attack.... .

The phenomenon of laterality is further complicated by the fact that a small percentage of human beings, about 7%, are different and have a dominance of left laterality, particularly regarding the hand.

This left-handedness has given rise to many hypotheses concerning its origins, and they are far from being unanimous.

First, the relationship between cerebral dominance and manual prevalence gives rise to further questions as to which of these factors is the first to emerge. Then, whereas it was thought for a long time that left-handers had reversed cerebral lobes, with the centre of written language in the left part of the brain, it is more generally thought now that this hypothesis has been exaggerated and that in left-handers, it is rather a matter of a more diffuse specialisation of the cerebral hemispheres. The fact is that , for scientists [96], left-handedness is still a bit of a mystery, as is also the overall functioning of the brain, although a gradually deepening knowledge of the very differentiated specialisation of the zones of the brain has been acquired.

Besides, one cannot easily deny a hereditary factor in the phenomenon of left-handedness, the proportions of left-handers in families where the parents (or one of them) are left-handed being considerably higher than in families where the parents are right-handed.

Finally let us mention and bear in mind that in some definite cases, a psychoanalytical origin of left-handedness can be found [97].

The question of the manual skill of left-handers gives rise to various reflections; in everyday activities, left-handers can have some difficulties with a whole range of instruments designed for right-handers, such as gear-levers in cars[1] and various tools. In apprenticeships, the difficulty can be increased by the necessity of imitating right-handed teachers or instructors, which forces left-handers to transpose the movements they imitate.

But against this, the considerable and significant proportion of left-handers with a high level of skill [98] in sporting activities in which the hand is used, as in fencing and tennis in particular, shows that perhaps left-handers might have an advantage over right-handers, because of a faster transmission from brain to hand.

---

1   Remember that in France, as in most other countries, people drive on the right, and
      gear-levers are mostly placed on the right of the driver's seat. (T.N.)

Coming now to the actual phenomenon of the left-handed writing of left-handers, several questions arise:

- Is the left-to-right direction of copybook models a handicap?

- Regarding manual skill itself, particularly in the case of very fine psychomotor activities such as handwriting, do left-handers encounter more difficulties than right-handers?

- Being left-handed, do left-handers have a different handwriting, identifiable as such and hiding the expression of their character?

- Can a graphologist analyse a left-hander's handwriting in the same way as that of a right-hander, or does he not run the risk of an incorrect analysis if he does not know that the writing he is analysing comes from a left-hander?

The two last questions are related to the possible graphomotor difficulties of left-handers, the application of the symbolism of space and, perhaps in the background, the idea, not consciously formulated, that by his unusualness, a left-hander might be someone apart; a sportsman, for instance, is often singled out as left-hander, thus acquiring an identity arising from the fact that his laterality makes him different.

1. Left-handed writing and cursive movement (continuity)

It can no longer be denied that the left-to-right movement across the page poses a problem for a left-handed child as compared to one who is right-handed, regarding our connected school model which progresses from left to right; instead of pulling, he pushes.

Indeed, the hand placed below the line quite naturally has a tendency to travel from the writer's body in an outward direction (abduction) to produce the writing, with a maximum of motor freedom.

The normal direction corresponding to this movement would therefore be, for a left-hander, right to left, and not left to right, which suits the right-hander perfectly.

This statement is substantiated by two observed facts:

- *When they learn to write, it is noticed that a large number of left-handed children quite naturally try to write from right to left, starting on the right-side edge of the paper* and producing mirror letters [4] or, more accurately, getting close to mirror writing[2], the wrong way round. Indeed, real mirror writing is quite rare and can also be produced by right-handed children.

In some schools, a red dot is put on the table of a left-handed child for him to know on which side of the paper he must start.

- In our writing models, left-handers mostly make their free signs, t-bars, underlinings and spontaneous strokes, from right to left, i.e. in the direction which suits their gestures naturally[3].

- *Similarly,* right-handed writing produced in writing models in which the cursive movement goes in the opposite direction to ours, as soon as the writer is freed, shows spontaneously thrown graphic gestures from left to right [99], appearing also in the accentuation of letters such as *d* in Hebrew writing, which goes from right to left.

So if the direction across the page which is easier for the left hand is from right to left, a graphologist can envisage a few difficulties for left-handers regarding continuity in our connected handwriting models, such as breaks in the rhythm of movement in the progression, co-ordination difficulties[4], a less rapid writing than that of a right-hander (this latter peculiarity is very clear in children, specially from the age of 9 onwards).

A little less rigour in the rules of learning how to write gives left-handers the possibility of choosing positions, both for the paper and for the hand,

---

2   Real mirror writing is that which is read in a mirror. It rarely has a neurological origin. Liliane Lurçat, in her experiments with writings done with both hands simultaneously starting from a central point, with children, has noticed also that loops made with the left hand were produced more easily in an anti-clockwise direction, and that the shapes of the letters came close to mirror writing.

3   88% of children and adolescents writing with their left hand, produce their free signs from right to left [44]. These already old statistics are confirmed by daily observations. The statistical study has not been done for adults. It would seem that the percentage is smaller.

4   In the left to right direction, the loops made by a child's left hand tend to become narrow. A percentage of children compensate for this difficulty afterwards with spread-out secondary connections, or juxtapositions.

which may sometimes be surprising, but which in fact make it possible to get closer to the movement of abduction. We should also note that modern graphic instruments, unlike former pen-nibs, make these positionings possible, as contact with the paper can be produced from various directions.

2. Left-handed writing and the fine motor skill of the hand

Given the fact that right-handers, in Hebrew and Arabic[5], do adapt to a cursive direction which is not the best for the movement of progression and that no higher percentage of graphomotor difficulties among right-handers has been reported than among left-handers, one wonders in what way writing difficulties are related to left-handedness itself.

The answer, in fact, needs qualifying, due to the fact that a left-hander rarely is the symmetrical counterpart of a right-hander, and that there are many different sorts of left-handers. Right-handedness is more forceful than left-handedness in the sense that, faced with tasks requiring very differentiated movements, with no social aspect involved, such as threading a needle, rubbing out, etc., most right-handers prefer to use only their right hand ,whereas left-handers use their left hand for a lesser number of tasks, and this varies from subject to subject [100].

Apart from left-handers called "true" left-handers, i.e. who preferentially use their left hand for a considerable number of actions and who may amount to between 6 and 7% of writers, there are practically as many less definite left-handers, or left-handers whose laterality occurred later in childhood, and, incorrectly called ambitextrous, who very often have graphomotor difficulties, and more frequently so than true left-handers. To this fact one can also add the reluctance to interfere with left-handers, which results in a larger percentage of left-handed writers, a phenomenon

5   The writing models are, it is true, different from ours: they are not connected and have a preponderantly top-to-bottom movements.

particularly apparent in the U.S.A.

So, in the case of a percentage of left-handers in a broad sense, one can actually acknowledge difficulties in learning to write[6], arising from a delicate motricity which is less adapted to handwriting. But one can also state, as experience has shown, that in adulthood, *owing to practice in writing, these difficulties have been compensated for, in the majority of cases, even if, statistically the hand used by left-handers is less efficient, i.e., less rapid than that of right-handers* [101].

3. Is there a handwriting of left-handers identifiable as such?

All sorts of characteristics can be put forward, those coming from difficulties of co-ordination (jerks, disconnections, trailing or skipped finals, *a*, *d*, *g*, *q* starting on the left....), of direction (left slant, irregularities, diving signatures), of pressure (reversed pressure on the ovals, Meyer's sign, i.e. roughness on the left side of the stroke, which is not very visible with modern graphic instruments). But it is sufficient to observe enough writings from both hands in order to notice :
- first, that all left-handers do not have these signs,
- second, that all these signs, the list of which it is unnecessary to lengthen, can be found in the writings of right-handers [102].

There is therefore no left-hander's writing as such.

One characteristic alone makes it possible to identify the writing of a left-hander; that is the free signs and underlinings drawn from right to left, but the difficulty of spotting them with certainty diminishes their interest, quite apart from the fact that this is not true of all the writings of adult left-handers.

As far as the inversion of the slant axes is concerned, which is relatively frequent in left-handers, we ask the reader to refer to the following pages.

---

6   In a population of 144 dysgraphic children, Ajuriaguerra found 16% of left-handers and 22% of children with poor laterality.

4. Can a left-hander's writing be analysed as reliably as a right-hander's?

This question, very often asked, is justifiably surprising.

It is a well-known fact that handwriting is a *purposeful function directed by the brain*[7], expressive, as are all our movements, and that the hand is only the chosen tool for that purposeful function (with specialised training, handicapped people can write with their mouth or feet) and *whether the left or the right hand is used cannot therefore make any difference to that expressiveness.*

In its general aspect, a right-handed writing would have been the same if the left-hander had been right-handed or if he had been forced to write with his right hand ("a frustrated left-hander")[8], which is particularly evident if one refers to Klages's guiding image (Leitbild).

But is the analysis not going to be distorted because of a clumsiness which has not disappeared, or by the symbolism of space which should be applied differently?

a) For the sake of prudence, a graphologist can minimise what could be negative in the interpretation of the clumsiness of right-handers' writings, but *in adulthood, graphomotor clumsy elements of childhood, if they once did exist, are usually compensated for.* If they persist, nothing proves that they are not an integral part of the features of the writing, thus expressive of difficulties which are not due to the tool used and which the left-hander would have had, just as much, with his right hand, had he been right-handed.

Also, the very type of clumsiness, different in each individual, can be interpreted (is expressive) : for instance, the way of counteracting the

---

7 And even if it was the case that there was not only an anatomo-physiological differentiation between left and right-handers, but also some pathology connected with left-handedness [8], the extreme diversity of left-handers' handwritings is, to a graphologist, the best proof of their expressiveness.

8 Gobineau, in her studies of ambidextrous people, reported that she had met only four cases (three of which were mirror writings), in which left-handed writing was more expressive of the character, less socialised [19].

possible difficulties of moving across the paper, with jerks in a connected writing, or on the contrary with breaks of continuity in a slack writing, shows a different way of solving the graphomotor difficulties, a more tenacious character in the first than in the second case.

However, we draw the graphologist's attention to a specific point: when he knows that a writing is from a left-hander, and when that writing has a left slant, he must interpret the left slant only if the graphic context and the other signs reinforce the meaning of that left slant. By the same token, faced with a writing whose left slant is at odds with the meaning of the writing as a whole, the graphologist has the right to wonder if the writing is not that of a left-hander, and must try to obtain the information.

Indeed, the position of the hand placed underneath the script, similar to that of right-handers, tends to make the writing slant to the left [103][9] and this left slant, having a "mechanical" reason, is not very expressive in itself.

It should be noted that the percentage of this formerly very frequent left slant has been very much reduced, probably owing to the different sorts of penholds and to modern graphic instruments.

A few left-handers can also produce plunging signatures, in a dynamic context, and this is caused by a movement freeing itself rapidly. The graphologist should be cautious with his interpretative hypotheses, but these cases are relatively rare.

---

9   This assertion has been checked with many observations, as much among children as among adults, although it cannot apply totally. The hypothesis of a correlation between the right-slanted writings of right-handers and the left side of the brain, and the left-slanted writings of left-handers with its right side, cannot be retained, in view of the increasingly smaller percentage of right-slanted writings in our copybook model* together with the very doubtful neurological aspect of the hypothesis. This idea, put forward in Israel [99], where a majority of right- to very right-slanted writings (80%) is found, would rather incline one to think that right-handers mostly have a normal hand position, or write from beneath; that they thereby may compensate for the right-to-left direction of their writing model, or that this corresponds to a social phenomenon. On the other hand, and correspondingly, the left-hand slant, very often seen in left-handed writings in that right-to-left writing style, corresponds to a normal movement of abduction.

*   Only 25% of French adolescents according to the SFDG's European survey [11] (Société Française de Graphologie).

b) *Can one apply to left-handed writing the same symbolism of space applied to right-handed writing? i.e. the symbolism of left and right,* the symbolism at the top and lower zones obviously not being involved.

The answer seems simple to us.

The possibility of a symbolism in reverse, claimed by some people with regard to spontaneous drawings, but very controversial anyway, cannot really form a hypothesis in the case of handwriting, since a left-hander, adapting to our copybook model, also adopts both the graphic space and the movement across the page, of right-handers; in this very differentiated acquisition, the left-hander has taken on the mould of right-handers.

Therefore the layout generally and the margins[10] have the same symbolic significance.

The same is true for the right- or left-tending direction of a writing in its form and continuity; some left-handers have very right-tending writings and one cannot put down to left-handedness the exaggerated left tendencies of a few writings...

The only exception to this is found in free strokes, underlinings or paraphs, which are no longer conditioned by the writing model, which regain their autonomy in the right-to-left direction, and whose interpretation must follow the normal interpretation of centrifugal gestures, towards the outside (a left-hander's underlining from right to left, clubbed or sharp-pointed, means that the club or the sharp-point is directed towards others and not towards himself, as we shall see in the samples further on.

As a result, in any analysis concerning a writer whose laterality is not known, a graphologist, seeing t-bars, underlinings with sharp-points or clubs pointing leftwards, must envisage the possibility of a writing which is perhaps written with the left hand, with these signs drawn from right to left, but he must not overstress the importance of what is only a detail in the study of a writing.

Below we show a few writings which illustrate this chapter, but do not result from any choice in particular. The reader can see for himself that they

---

10 In some cases, the position of the hand writing from below the script, linked with a certain position of the paper, favours a wide left margin. But why would a left-hander accept this wide margin if he did not conform to a space distribution which he endorses more or less consciously? The same applies to the right-hand margin.

do not have much in common, that there is no such thing as a left-hander personality, and that all of them are expressive and can be analysed on an individual basis, regardless of the left-handedness and the possible persistence of clumsiness.

matin, ami

midi ennemi, monde, quille, r

soir

Boy, 8 years 3 months, left-handed for writing, ambidextrous tendencies in his other activities

248

At the top, the child spontaneously reproduces from right to left[11] a model of strokes given to him by the person conducting the experiment, without any commentary. The stroke is firm and rapid.

Below this, the child's writing, is clumsy, stiff and slow. Putting down the letters and the left-to-right direction cause him trouble. T-bars go from right to left.

Boy, 14 years, left-handed

249

Position of the hand from above the script.
Very right-slanted writing, small, connected and thrown.
A very intelligent and reactive pre-adolescent. A passionately curious mind.

11 For this experiment, the statistical results, regularly confirmed, are of the order of over 90%.

249

250

Boy, 14 years, left-handed

Left-slanted writing, 'a' and 'g' drawn the wrong way around, light pressure, weak movement. The hand position from below facilitates the left slant. But one can see that the signature, in the middle, is more left-slanted than the text, larger, more angular, firmer and illegible (it is the Christian name, the initials representing the family name are hemmed in, on the right, by the underlining paraph which crosses itself in a back and forth movement). The left slant, which goes much beyond mere left-handedness, is very expressive of the child's character, the other signs confirming troubles with communication, an underlying aggressiveness, a need to have enhanced standing outside the family environment, against a background of weakness and of refusal when faced with the demands of reality.

Nous ne nous sommes pas vues depuis très longtemps maintenant, mais je pense souvent à toi, en pa culier aujourd'hui pour te souhai ainsi qu'à Bertrand, une très heu

Woman, 25 years - Single, true left-hander

The writer has always done everything with her left hand, and never had any difficulty in learning to write.

Her present writing is a little conventional, well-nourished, connected with a few breaks, restrained, slightly angular, both left- and right-tending, slightly right-slanted. One should notice the very narrow lower extensions, with covering strokes, and at the same time the important, round and double-joined ovals. The fairly large middle zone is irregular in dimension. Accents are very precise, the spaces create a sufficiently aerated writing. The line is very well kept.

251

Affective, but not opened out, this young and intelligent woman, conscientious in her work, has not been able to free herself from a constraining upbringing, or find an identity and an autonomy as a woman, in spite of her wishes. The graphologist does not need to know her laterality to analyse her writing; nevertheless, the t-bars, when detached, are written from right to left. The t-bar in "Bertrand" is not a t-bar rising to the right, but quite the opposite, descending and in keeping with this writing which is sad as a whole.

In order to see it, all that is needed is to notice that the inking, in this writing, is increased by extra ink in the finals (letter-endings not connected to the next ones), and to see where the inking is placed in the flying t-bars.

Woman, 30 years - True left-hander

252

This small, very rapid writing1, connected, right-tending with a tendency to filiformity, supple and aerated, is very different from the previous one.

The graphologist immediately perceives the writer's efficiency, her qualities of adaptation, but also her need to assert herself and her capacity to make decisions. One can see that the free strokes go from right to left. The lines over the 'j's would show very little compatibility with a movement which would start right back from the left: for the writer, this is a centrifugal movement with strong pressure.

Man, 35 years, describes himself as left-handed in his letter

253
A small, simplified and irregular writing, a little descending, keen on speed, but slowed down by spasmodic pressure, breaks in the continuity and slightly smothered letters. A well aerated writing with large spaces between the lines, but the layout makes the absence of a left margin and the presence of a wider right -hand margin noticeable; a signature on the left, and complicated. In this writing with a very good intellectual level, some features seem to be related more to personal problems and the fear of committing himself than to the "pretext" of left-handedness.

Vous en souhaitant bonne ucc/ tric d'agrécs monsieur l'assuran trafaite considération .

Man 35 years, left-hander

How different from the previous one this writing is, in blue felt-pen, left-slanted, disconnected, close to typographic letters, with superelevated 'p's and curved lower extensions. A good layout between the words, and between the lines, a considerable left margin, social margins, very small right-hand margin, signature to the right.

The socio-cultural milieu is less evolved, but the sensuous writing, in search of contacts, suggests to us the hypothesis of a left slant caused by "mechanical" reasons probably due to the position of the hand, which we will not interpret.

254

---

right hand

Woman, 34 years - Ambidextrous Israeli

The right-handed writing, at the top, is slightly right-slanted.
In this right-to-left, disconnected Hebrew model writing, one can observe flying strokes with strong pressure towards the right. The left-handed writing

255

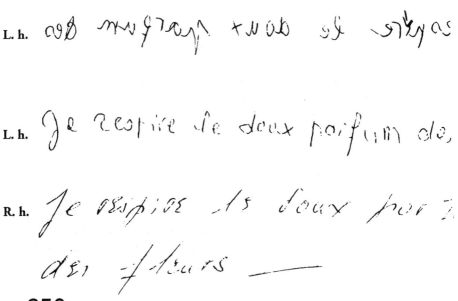

left hand

underneath, is vertical to very slightly left-slanted, with more strokes with strong pressure towards the left, looking similar, likely to be slower because more constructed (ambidexterity rarely corresponds to totally equivalent possibilities).

L. h.

L. h.

R. h.

256 Woman, 45 years
True left-hander, forced to use her right hand for writing

This rather caricature-like sample will enable us succintly to mention the case of frustrated left-handers, which in fact is less and less frequent, the principle of letting children write with their left hand having been more or less accepted universally for some twenty years.

This woman, left-handed in all her movements, had the peculiarity of using only mirror writing up to the age of 8 1/2. As she was incapable of following a direction and a normal style with her left hand, she was at that time made to use her other hand; she was re-educated and after the initial difficulties, the girl was able to acquire normal writing.

Let us note that this child had no difficulty at all in learning to read and only a relatively slight spelling disorder (double letters, common words) which she was able to make up for afterwards.

She would now be incapable of writing with her left hand skilfully, as she does with her right hand. She can still do mirror writing with her left hand if asked to do so.

In sample 256 we show :
- her present mirror-writing with her left hand (which she no longer ever uses),
- an attempt to write the normal copybook model with her left hand: light, dented and very clumsy,
- her present writing with her right hand. Large, with irregularities, right-slanted, disconnected (original typographic forms mixed with flying strokes and superelevations). Good pressure.

The three examples look alike, in spite of the clumsiness of her left hand.

What is of special interest to us is that this left-hander who is very clever with her left hand, has been totally reconditioned in her nervous circuits regarding her right-handed writing, which does not bother her in the least (the disconnectedness, the "taking-flight" are related to her reactive character).

It is the same for most frustrated left-handers, about whom graphologists do not have to ask themselves as many questions as for left-handers[12] who have not been interferred with, the movement across the page causing no problem to the writer, nor the application of the symbolism of space to the observer.

(The very coercive attitudes used in the past to interfere with left-handers, sometimes caused blockages, inhibitions and stuttering, which were visibly expressed in a clumsy, stiff, disturbed and amended writing. It was often difficult, in these cases, to assess exactly what was due to frustrated left-handedness, and nowadays, although those methods have disappeared, one is often faced with the same difficulty of judgement as to the origin of the dysgraphy, or the stuttering of a left-hander, as the etiology of these disorders can seldom be put down to just one reason [8]).

---

12 In statistics which are already old, the authors have shown that frustrated left-handers write better than left-handers who have been left alone [101].

APPENDIX 1

SYMBOLISM OF THE GRAPHIC SPACE

The diagram reproduced, founded on the archetypes, necessarily outlines only the barest essentials.

No value judgement is to be attributed to one direction rather than another.

Each direction has its own importance. All must be interpreted in accordance with the graphic context.

The symbolism of space applies to all aspects of handwriting: emphasis of one zone (by means of dimension or pressure), direction of the letters, of the free strokes, of the cursive movement, etc.

To the classical division into four parts, we have added the Greeks' division into three parts, which puts the emphasis on the middle zone (θυμος, heart, courage), which is particulary reliable, being related to the centre, that is the very kernal of gestural activity.

Handwriting is indeed a living dynamic whole, and its subdivision into zones, once written down, is a field for the application of the symbolism of space. This requires much prudence, particularly regarding the upper and lower zones, as the reader will have been able to see from the chapter on dimension.

This symbolism rests on a representation of space on the sheet of paper[1], a natural representation, in keeeping with the terms "upper extensions" and "lower extensions", as well as with all the other rules of learning. It cannot, in particular, be replaced by a projection which would make the poles swing by 90 degrees.

The "depth" dimension, relative to pressure, the differentiation of which can give rise to writing more or less in relief, to arcs in space, makes no difference to the general distribution of the graphic space.

The symbolism of space which has always been used to interpret drawings and handwriting has been validated by several researchers, especially for drawings, and by Renée Stora in particular, through the tree test [104].

The Swiss graphologist, Max Pulver, [24] founded his entire graphological system on the application of this symbolism, with a psychoanalytical background. His viewpoint is very interesting, in spite of a few exaggerations.

---

1 The representation of space cannot be discussed, whereas a symbol "which represents something else by virtue of an analogical correspondence" (Petit Robert) can always be.

CHART 6

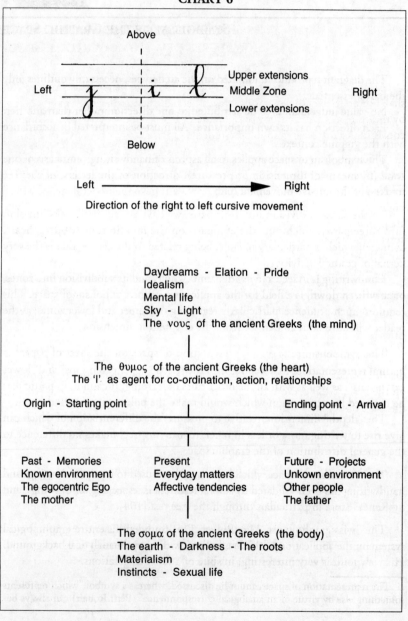

Above

Left ——— Upper extensions / Middle Zone / Lower extensions ——— Right

Below

Left ——————————————→ Right

Direction of the right to left cursive movement

Daydreams - Elation - Pride
Idealism
Mental life
Sky - Light
The νους of the ancient Greeks (the mind)

The θυμος of the ancient Greeks (the heart)
The 'I' as agent for co-ordination, action, relationships

Origin - Starting point   Ending point - Arrival

Past - Memories   Present   Future - Projects
Known environment   Everyday matters   Unkown environment
The egocentric Ego   Affective tendencies   Other people
The mother   The father

The σομα of the ancient Greeks (the body)
The earth - Darkness - The roots
Materialism
Instincts - Sexual life

APPENDIX 2

REFLECTIONS BASED ON THE OBSERVATION OF THE SIGNATURES OF A HOMOGENEOUS GROUP

An account of statistical methods would go beyond the scope of a manual. We shall limit ourselves to illustrating a few aspects of their applications in graphology by means of a statistical study of signatures, carried out on a very particular group consisting of first-year graphology students in Paris.

It consists of a group, of which the vast majority are women, which in many respects is very homogeneous. The students are young: 46% are under 30, 78% under 40. Their training is of a high level. All have their baccalauréat, 71% a higher education diploma, 28% of which are in psychology. Most of them (78%) are involved in professional activities. The proportion of unmarried women is very considerable: nearly three times that which can be observed in a group of Frenchwomen in the same age structure.

The study was done on a sample of 125 women students (here we do not count men students, whose number was insufficient).

Each signature was studied from the point of view of the different characteristics brought forward in Chapter 10 of this book.

To simplify, we reproduce, in Tables 1 and 2 below and next page, only the distribution of the signatures according to the following characteristics: position on the page, distance from the text, signature "similar to the text" (and whether these are underlined or not), or "in cipher".

TABLE 1

Numbers

	Position on the page			
	to the right	in the middle	to the left	together
- similar to the text	76	17	8	101
of which : underlined	57	13	6	76
not underlined	19	4	2	25
- in cipher	20	3	1	24
Total	96	20	9	125
	Distance from the text			
	far	normal	near	together
All forms	49	70	7	125

TABLE 2

%

	Position on the page			
	to the right	in the middle	to the left	together
- similar to the text	75	17	8	100
of which : underlined	75	17	8	100
not underlined	76	16	8	100
- in cipher	83	13	4	100
Total	77	16	7	100
	Distance from the text			
	far	normal	near	together
All forms	39	56	5	100

The analysis of the act of signing, different from the act of writing, suggests the possibilities of interpreting the presence, in a signature, of each characteristic in particular, and of interpreting the combinations of these characteristics which give each signature its identity.

The search for the identity of the signature, and through it, that of the personality of the person who signed, brings into play a large number of data and of combinations of data. Each has its meaning. All are not equally significant in the statistical sense of the term, and do not bring the same amount of information.

Considered in isolation, a characteristic which appears very often in the signatures is a piece of information of lesser "added value" than a characteristic which one meets with only rarely.

It is known that it is frequent for the signature to be underlined. This observation, common enough, is useful only if the notion of frequency is specified. The absence of underlining would bring little information if it were not decidedly rarer than its presence, but even more information if it were more the exception, at least in the category of people where its presence enables one to connect the author with the signature.

In the sample of 125 signatures of students, only 25% are not underlined. This lack of underlining certainly brings some information. However one would need similar observations on other categories of population in order to determine whether this result is general, or whether the lack of underlining contains more information in one particular category of population than in another.

In the absence of statistical data giving points of reference regarding frequency, a graphologist has only his personal empirical knowledge to go by. He may, consciously or less consciously, have acquired his own points of reference, and can if necessary, make use of a characteristic such as the absence of underlining, because he knows it is rare. Equally, he may have no point of reference of frequency at all to go by, either because he has paid no attention to it, or possibly, because underlining is not significantly more common than the lack of it, in those categories of population with which he is more familiar.

The above Table shows that in the sample studied, the proportion of signatures on the left is only 7%. This figure is not surprising: the position on the page is very largely dictated by usage. In France it is usual, if not the absolute rule, to sign on the right. The fact that one departs from current usage by signing on the left, is in itself an important piece of information (apart from what may be deduced from the left side of the page being occupied).

A signature which would be both on the left and not underlined would contain two pieces of information, each of a certain value. However, one would add nothing to the other if the two facts were linked, not invariably, (as it is clearly incorrect that someone signing on the left never underlines), but by a statistical correlation, i.e. if the statistic showed that people signing on the left underline their signature much less often than those signing on the right.

Table 2 shows that for the 101 signatures "similar to the text", the proportions of signatures placed on the right, in the middle, or on the left (horizontal percentages) are practically identical, whether the signature is underlined or not. So, there exists no correlation, at least in the case of the group studied and the signatures "similar to the text", between the underlining and the position of the signature on the page.

The proportions of signatures on the right, in the middle, or on the left are not identical for the 101 signatures similar to the text and the 24 cipher-shaped signatures. This is probably due to the chance "extraction" of a sample reduced to 125 signatures, of which only 24 are cipher-shaped. It could however be significant and the cipher-shaped signatures could be placed less often on the left than those similar to the text.

It is up to statistical analysis to validate the intuition, which is not sufficient here, by providing rigorous methods making it possible to decide whether it is legitimate or not to come to a conclusion one way or another.

A statistical test like the X^2 test is likely to show that the statistics of Table 1 are insufficient, in view of the observed differences of frequency and in view of the numbers involved in the sub-samples, to conclude to a significant difference of the position on the page according to whether the signature is similar to the text or in the shape of a cipher.

Statistics is a mathematical discipline. Itsconcepts are not without pitfalls, so statistics must be handled with respect. Yet they are only a matter of common sense reduced to arithmetic. With present-day calculators, which have the usual statistical functions in their memories, a calculation such as that of X^2, or of a coefficient of correlation, when it is necessary, is no longer off-putting.

The distance of the signature from the text shows a use of the space, the meaning of which is well known. A signature far from the text shows uncertainty and fear of commiting oneself.

However, only 56% of the students' signatures are set at a distance which the graphologist who made the study considered normal, 5% are closer than normal and 35% further away than normal.

This is a remarkable result, likely to show that these students are probably trying to establish themselves as a genuine group, (which, quite apart from the underlining and the similarity with the text which we have observed, other characteristics would confirm) often uncertain of itself, its choices and its prospects of success. This does not contradict what is known in other ways of the socio-logical structure of this group.

Let us note, however, that that particular feature "far from the text" is as yet defined in this study only with reference to a "normal" distance which is not made explicit.

The distance in relation to the text is a continuous dimension (and not a "discrete" characteristic like underlining). It is an objectively measurable dimension, provided the "appropriate "yardstick" has been devised. It is distributed in a given group, in accordance with a certain law (not inevitably Gaussian).

Knowledge of this distribution in a control group would make it possible to define the distance from the text considered as normal, according to conventions : the central part of the distribution, comprising, for instance, 80% of the group, excluding the two tenths on either side, in which the distances defined as far from, or as near to the text, would be situated.

It is likely that the graphologist who classified 35% of the signatures of his sample as being far from the text, based his judgement on a similar but implicit point of reference. If this is the case, the 35% observed are highly significant. We would be certain of this if a statistic had existed enabling us to establish the standard point of reference for certain.

In the state of graphology at the moment, such points of reference remain to be established, by means of systematic statistical observations.

It is not surprising that, at present, graphology lacks figures[1]. It is an activity which is carried out individually. It is difficult to imagine bringing together statistical material, which is bound to be collected in a haphazard way, in accordance with precise criteria, which have not been defined, because they could not be exploited (such as the objective measurement of the distance from the text)....

It is not impossible to think that this state of affairs may change with the spreading of personal data processing - perhaps by simply using minitel[2] - which would enable the community of graphologists to collect statistical data and to process information which at present is not within reach of the individual.

Arranging bases of statistical data, thus progressively broadened and polished, would perhaps also make it possible to add another opening , a kind of social graphology. It would aim at describing not the personality of an individual but that of a group, such as that formed, specifically, by graphology students.

---

1   Graphometry, based on precise measurements on the graphic variables (T. Lewinson, J. Salce, M.T. Prenat), already uses application programmes for some factorial analyses. Signatures have not yet been the object of systematic studies.
2   Home terminal of the French telecommunications system.

BIBLIOGRAPHY

[1] COHEN M. - *La grande invention de l'écriture et son évolution.* Imprimerie Nationale, Paris, 1958.

[2] HÉCAN H. ANGELERGUES R. et DOUZENIS J.A. - "Les agraphies", *Neuropsychologia,* pp. 179-208, 3, 1963.

[3] LURÇAT L. - *Étude de l'acte graphique.* Mouton, Paris, 1974.

[4] LURÇAT L. - *L'activité graphique à l'école maternelle,* 3ᵉ éd. Éditions sociales françaises, Paris, 1984.

[5] BERNSON M. - *Du Gribouillis au Dessin.* Delachaux et Niestlé, Neuchâtel et Paris, 1957.

[6] LOMBARD A. - *Le Gribouillis.* Monograp for the G.G.C.F., 1968.

[7] HEGAR W. - *Graphologie par le trait.* Vigot, Paris, 1962. Out of print.

[8] AJURIAGUERRA J. de, AUZIAS M. et DENNER A. - *L'écriture de l'enfant.* Tome I : *L'évolution de l'écriture et ses difficultés,* 3ᵉ éd. Delachaux et Niestlé, Neuchâtel et Paris, 1979.

[9] WALLON H. - *L'évolution du caractère de l'enfant.* Presses Universitaires de France, Paris, 1957.

[10] Lectures of the January 1984 international Congress in Paris. *La Graphologie,* no. 176, 1984.

[11] "Recherche européenne chez l'adolescent en classe Terminale". *La Graphologie,* nos. 158 & 159, 1980.

[12] FAIDEAU P. - "L'écriture en sillon", *La Graphologie,* no. 1218, pp .29-38, 1970.

[13] BOURREILLE C. - "Application graphologique de la théorie Jungienne de l'introversion et de l'extraversion", *La Graphologie,* no. 162, pp. 29-36, 1980.

[14] CRÉPIEUX-JAMIN J. - *A B C de la Graphologie,* 8ᵉ éd. Presses Universitaires de France, Paris, 1983.

[15] POPHAL R. - *Zur Psychophysiologie der Spannungserscheinungen in der Handschrift.* Greienverlag Rüdelstadt, 1949. Not translated into French.

[16] BOSE DE C. - "La physiologie du mouvement et son interprétation graphologiques d'après l'oeuvre de Pophal", *La Graphologie,* no. 124, pp. 3-22, 1971.

[17] WIESER R. - *Rhythmus und Polarität in der Handschrift. Ein Beitrag zur Rhythmus Forschung.* Ernst Reinach Verlag, Munich, 1973. Not translated into French.

[18] BOSE DE C. - *La Graphologie,* no. 101, pp. 6-16, 102, 8-15, 1966.

[19] GOBINEAU DE H. et PERRON R. - *Génétique de l'écriture et étude de la personnalité. Essais de graphométrie.* Delachaux et Niestlé, Neuchâtel et Paris, 1953. Out of print.

[20] DELAMAIN M. - "La tenue de la plume". *La Graphologie*, no .87, pp. 24-30, 1962.

[21] Figures extracted from *La Graphologie*, no.142, pp. 10-12, 1976.

[22] MICHON J.H. - *Méthode pratique de graphologie. L'art de connaître les hommes d'après leur écriture, pour fair suite au système de graphologie.* Pp. 116-120, 6ᵉ éd. Marpon et Flammarion, Paris, 1893.

[23] KLAGES L. - "L'expression du caractère dans l'écriture". *Technique de la graphologie*, 23ᵉ édition(translated into French from the German by E. Reymond-Nicolet). Delachaux et Niestlé, Neuchâtel et Paris, 1953. Republished by Privat, Toulouse, 1976. Original title : *Handschrift und Charakter* (1917).

[24] PULVER M. - *Le symbolism de l'écriture*, p. 103 (translated into French from German by M. Schmid and M. Delamain). Stock, Paris, 1953. Republished by Stock-Plus, Paris, 1982. Original title: *Symbolik der Handschrift.* Orell Verlag, Zurich, 1931.

[25] TORBIDONI L. et ZANIN S. - *Graphologia, testo teorico pratico*, 2ᵉ éd. La scuola, Brescia, 1978. Not translated into French.

[26] DELAMAIN M. - *Découvrir la Graphologie.* La Signe, Paris, 1980.

[27] KLAGES L. - *L'expression du caractère dand l'écriture, op. cit.* pp. 192-214.

[28] GILLE-MAISANI J.C. - "La graphologie à rebours", *La Graphologie*, no. 178, pp. 9-32, 1985.

[29] DELAMAIN M. - "L'affaire du script", *La Graphologie*, no. 54, pp. 7-15, 1954.

[30] PEUGEOT J. - *La connaissance de l'enfant par l'écriture.* p. 46. L'approche graphologique de l'enfance et ses difficultés. Collection "Époques", Privat, Toulouse, 1979.

[31] KERGALL N. et PINON J. - *L'effet filiforme.* Monographfor the G.G.C.F., 1980.

[32] DUBOUCHET J. - *L'écriture des adolescentes.* Le François, Paris, 1967.

[33] TAJAN A. - *La Graphomotricité.* Que sais-je? Presses Universitaires de France, Paris, 1982.

[34] MATHIEU H. - "L'accentuation des finales". *La Graphologie*, no. 136, pp. 7-11, 1974.

[35] LAMBERTO T. et ZANIN L. - "Les trois largeurs de l'écriture selon Moretti", translated by J.C. Gille-Maisani. *La Graphologie*, no. 172, pp. 9-22, 1983 and no. 173, pp. 37-47, 1984.

[36] PULVER M. - *Le symbolism de l'écriture, op. sit.* p. 59.

[37] PULVER M. - *Le symbolism de l'écriture, op. sit.* p. 60.

[38] CRÉPIEUX-JAMIN J. - *Les éléments des l'écriture des canailles.* Flammarion, Paris, 1976.

[39] CRÉPIEUX-JAMIN J. - *L'écriture et le caractère*, 17ᵉ éd. Presses Universitaires de France, Paris. 1975.

[40] BRESARD S. - *La graphologie, méthode d'exploration psychologique.* Scarabée et Cie. Paris, 1984.

[41] PULVER M. - *Le symbolism de l'écriture, op.cit.* chapter IV.

[42] CRÉPIEUX-JAMIN J. - *A B C de la graphologie, op.cit.* première partie, 15 premiers principes.

[43] KESTEMBERG E. - "Notule sur la crise de l'adolescence", *Revue Française de Psychanalyse,* 3-4, pp. 524-530, 1980.

[44] PEUGEOT J. - *La connaissance de l'enfant par l'écriture, op.cit.*

[45] KESTEMBERG E. - "L'identité de l'identification chez les adolescents", *La psychiatrie de l'enfant,* 5, no .2, pp .441-522, 1962.

[46] FAIDEAU P. - "La juxtaposition". *La Graphologie,* no. 108, pp. 3-14, 1967.

[47] MAUBLANC H. DE et BÉRIOT C. - "Construction et juxtaposition statique". *La Graphologie,* no. 169, pp .19-28, 1983.

[48] SÉBILLEAU L. - "Les écritures anglaises". *La Graphologie,* no. 134, pp. 12-18, 1974.

[49] FONTAINE F. - "Les écritures Anglo-saxonnes". *La Graphologie,* no. 181, pp .6-38, 1986.

[50] CRÉPIEUX-JAMIN J. - *A B C de la graphologie, op. cit.* 1ᵉʳᵉ partie, p. 57.

[51] BRABANT C.P. - "Les modes d'accentuation". *La Graphologie,* no. 58, pp. 13-17, 1955.

[52] SAINT-MORAND - *Les bases de l'analyse de l'écriture.* Vigot, Paris, 1950. Out of print. And "Le geste-type de Saint-Morand", *La Graphologie,* no. 162, pp. 9-22, 1981.

[53] DELAMAIN M. d'après STEIN-LEWINSON T. - "L'inclinaison et ses variations", *La Graphologie,* no. 103, pp. 40-43, 1966.

[54] GILLE-MAISANI J.C. - *Psychologie de l'écriture.* Payot, 1984. 2ᵉ éd. revised.

[55] CRÉPIEUX-JAMIN J. - *A B C de la graphologie, op. cit. 1ᵉʳᵉ partie, les quinze premiers principes,* pp. 21 et 22.

[56] SARTIN P. et BORIE N. - "L'adaptation de la femme à la vie
      professionnelle", *La Graphologie*, no. 141, p. 50, 1976.
[57] SAUDEK R. - *Experiments with handwriting*. Allen and Unwin, London,
      1928.
[58] DUBOUCHET J. - "Méthode de mesure de la vitesse d'un tracé". *La
      Graphologie*, no. 123, pp. 58-66, 1974.
[59] MICHEL F. - "Méthode de recueil dt d'exploration quantitative de
      paramètres temporo-spatiaux du geste graphique". *La Graphologie*,
      no. 148, pp. 32-45, 1977.
[60] HECHT D. - "Le scriptchronographe de David Katz". *La Graphologie*,
      no. 36, pp. 17-18, 1949.
[61] TROITSKY - *Approche de la dysgraphie chez l'enfant. Evaluation métrique et
      projective d'un niveau graphique*. Sciences de psychologie et d'éducation de
      l'Université, Liège, 1982-1983. Mémoire.
[62] VINH BANG - *Évolution de l'écriture de l'enfant à l'adulte*. Delaux et
      Niestlé, Neuchâtel et Paris, 1959.
[63] DELAMAIN M. - "Perspective et relativité de la vitesse". *La Graphologie*,
      no. 94, pp. 3-12, 1964.
[64] DELAMAIN M. - "Essai d'une orientation psychologique par l'écriture aérée
      et l'écriture compacte". *La Graphologie*, no. 1, pp. 15-22, 1935.
[65] PRENAT M.T. - "Sur l'étude Graphométrique de la sinuosité en tant
      qu'expression du rapport émotivité contrôle". *La Graphologie*, no. 114,
      pp. 30-35, 1969.
[66] MUEL A. - "La méthode statistique d'analyse graphique appliquée à un
      groupe de garçons inadaptés de 5 à 14 ans. Autour de l'élement M27,
      lignes descendantes", *La Graphologie*, no. 126, pp .21-40, 1972.
[67] MONNOT J. -"Considération générales sur l'ordonnance. La marge de
      gauche". *La Graphologie*, no. 147, pp. 26-28, 1977. "La marge de droite".
      La Graphologie, no. 155, pp. 11-28, 1979.
[68] COSSEL VON B. - "Signatures françaises et allemandes". *La Graphologie*,
      no. 120, pp. 37-46, 1970.
[69] TAVERNIER M. - "Importance de la signature en sélection professionnelle".
      La Graphologie, no. 150, pp. 22-32, 1978.
[70] STEIN-LEWINSON T. - "Les signatures de Hitler". *La Graphologie*,
      no. 162, pp. 44-48, 1981.
[71] MONNOT J. - "A propos des signatures; reflexion socio-psychologique". *La
      Graphologie*, no. 166, pp. 28-43, 1982.

[72] LIÈVRE F. - "Signature et mise en oeuvre du potentiel". *La Graphologie*, no. 177, pp. 71-77, 1985.

[73] BOBLET J. et HOUEL S. - *Les femmes dans les professions libérales.* Monographie pour le G.G. C.F., 1985.

[74] OLIVAUX R. - *De l'observation de l'écriture à la personnalité.* Éditions sociales Françaises, Paris, 1969.

[75] SARDA A., TRIPPIER G. et LOMBARD A. - "Article sur l'alcoolisme". *La Graphologie*, no. 161, pp. 6-31, 1981.

[76] KLAGES L. - *L'expression du caractère dans l'écriture, op. cit.* p. 16.

[77] *La graphologie,* collection of articles by different authors under the direction of P. FAIDEAU. M.A. Éditions, Paris, 1983.

[78] DESURVIRE M. - "Nouveaux métiers, nouveaux hommes, nouvelles écritures". *La Graphologie*, no. 177, pp. 98-109, 1985.

[79] PEUGEOT J. - "Recherhes : Étude de l'écriture de candidats à un poste de conducteur receveur". *La Graphologie*, no. 183, 1986.

[80] PEUGEOT J. - "Recherhes : Adresse manuelle, intelligence et maladresse de l'écriture". *La Graphologie*, no. 129, pp. 16-23, 1973.

[81] BELIN C. - "L'écriture des suicidaires". *La Graphologie*, no. 147, pp. 42-54, 1977.

[82] *Revue belge de graphométrie et de graphologie scientifique.* Liège, 1984.

[83] AJURIAGUERRA J. DE - *Manuel de psychiatrie de l'enfant*, 2ᵉ éd. Masson, Paris, 1977.

[84] CRÉPIEUX-JAMIN J. - *A B C de la Graphologie, op. cit.* p. 79.

[85] SALCE J. - "Graphologie psychomotrice, méthode de Théa Stein Lewinson". *La Graphologie*, no. 84, pp. 3-25, 1961.

[86] KLAGES L. - *Graphologie*, translated from German into French by E. Reymond-Nicolet, Stock, Paris, 1943, 3ʳᵈ ed. 1975.

[87] HEISS R. -*Die Deutung der Handschrift*, 3ʳᵈ ed. Claasen, Hamburg, 1966. Not translated into French.

[88] MÜLLER ENSKAT - *Graphologische Diagnostik. Ihre Grundlagen, Möglichkeiten und Grenzen*, 2ⁿᵈ ed. Huber, Berne, 1973. Not translated into French.

[89] BOSE DE C. - "Le rhytme dans la méthode du Pr Heiss". *La Graphologie*, no. 107, pp. 15-23, 1967.

[90] ABRAHAM A. - *Les identifications de l'enfant à travers son dessin.* Privat, Toulouse, 1985.

[91] LISTENOW W. - Congrès de Cologne 1983. Classification of sexes through handwriting (double-blind experiment).

[92] GIRARDEAU A. - Monographie pour le G.G.C.F., 1984.

[93] BOSE DE C. - "Méthode graphologique de Müller-Enskat : application concrète". Extraits. *La Graphologie*, no. 154, pp. 8-12, 1979.

[94] BRÉSARD S. & WILLI M. - "Recherche pour un lexique de graphologie illustrée", *La Graphologie*, nos. 167 and 168, 1982; nos. 170 and 171, 1983; nos. 178 and 179, 1985.

[95] DAILLY R ET EFFENTERRE VAN H. -"La droite et la gauche dans l'évolution des formes d'expression symboliques". *La médecine infantile*, pp. 243-378, Maloine, Paris, 1983.

[96] HÉCAEN H. - *Les gauchers.* Presses Universitaires des France, Paris, 1984.

[97] CADDY S. - *La latéralité : étude psychanalytique.* Thèse de Doctorat de 3ᵉ cycle, 1980.

[98] "La latéralisation chez l'enfant". *La médecine infantile.* Maloine, Paris, 1980.

[99] RATZON H. - "Sur la graphologie de l'écriture hébraïque moderne". *La Graphologie*, no. 176, pp. 11-25, October 1984.

[100] AUZIAS M. - *Enfants gauchers, enfants droitiers. Une épreuve de latéralité usuelle.* Delachaux et Niestlé, Neuchâtel et Paris, 1975.

[101] AJURIAGUERRA J. de et HÉCAEN H. - *Les gauchers. Prévalence manuelle et dominante cérébrale.* Presses Universitaires de France, Paris.

[102] VILLARD C. - "Le problème de l'écriture des gauchers". *La Graphologie*, no. 131, pp. 5-16, 1973

[103] AUZIAS M. - *Les troubles de l'écriture chez l'enfant..* Delachaux et Niestlé, Neuchâtel et Paris, 1975.

[104] STORA R. - *Le test du dessin d'arbres.* Éditions Universitaires, J.P. Delarge, Paris, 1975. Out of print.

INDEX OF SIGNS
AND GRAPHIC CHARACTERISTICS

Accelerated 281
Accents 229
Acquired 85
Aerated 298
Amended 226
Angular 104
Animated (Movement) 195
Arcades 91
  - over-curved 93
  - looped 93
Arc in space 24
Artificial 85
Ascending tiles 307

Bizarre 84
Blurred 44

Carried away (Movement) 190
Chimneys 301
Clear 113
Clubbed 30
Combined 213
Comfortable (see Effortless)
Compact 292
Complicated 81
Concave Lines 305
Confused 114
Congested 40
Connected 201
Constrained (Movement) 177
Controlled (Movement) .. 173
Conventional 87
Convex Lines 305
Copybook 75

Covering strokes 225
Cylindrical 156, 357

Descending - lines 305
            - tiles 307
Deviated 24
Diminishing 137
Disconnected (Juxtaposed) 204
Dissociated Letters 218
Diving 307
Double Curves 100
Double-joined 118
Dry 45
Dynamic (Movement) 185
Dynamogenic (Movement) 186

Effervescent (Movement) 193
Effortless (Movement) 182
Envelopes 309

Embellished (see Ornate)
Enlarging 134
Expanded 161
Extensive Movements 160

False connections (Soldering) ... 219
Filiform (Thready) 108
Finals 241
Fine 42
Firm (Stroke) 50
Flat 23
Floating (Movement) 180
Flowing (Movement) 182
Flying Strokes (see Thrown)

Fragmented 217
Furrowed 31

Garlands 94
        - cupped 99
        - looped 98
        - square 96
Grouped 208
Harmonious 379
Homogeneity/eous 123, 380, 385
Hopping 216
Horizontal Lines 302

Inflated 103
Inharmonious 382
Inhibited (Movement) 177
Initial Strokes 238
Inter-word gaps, with 295
Irregular - continuity 216
          - dimension 163
          - direction 255
          - pressure 55
          - spacing 300

Jerky 220
Juxtaposed (see Disconnected)

Lapses of continuity 224
Large 127
Lassos 118
Left-slanted 249
Left-tending 263
Light.....................................19
Looped - see Arcades
         - see Garlands
Low 154

Margin   - absence of 311
         - bottom 309
         - left....................310
         - right 310
         - top 309
           - typographic 311
Mirror writing 423
Moirée 46
Muddy (see Smeary)

Narrow 144
Nuanced 216

Obstructed (Movement) 195
Open 120
Ornate 82
Over-connected 210
Over-curved (see Arcades)

Paragraphs 312
Pasty 36
Personalised 78
Plump....................................101
Poised 280
Porous 37
Precipitated 283
Precise 33
Progressive 121
Prolonged down 153
Prolonged up 151
Prolonged up and down 149
Proportionate 380
Propulsive (Movement) 188
Pulled-about (Vacillating) 256
Punctuation...........................229

Rapid 281
Reared (Movement) 197

Regularity (Dimension) 162
Relief, in 22
Resolute (Movement) 174
Restrained (Movement) 177
Reverse 264
Rhythmic 168
Right-slanted 252
Right-slanted, very 253
Right-tending 259
Rigid (Lines) 302
Ringed (see Looped arcades
     and garlands)
Rising Lines 305
Rounded 101

Secondary Connections 212
Shark's tooth 226
Sharp-pointed 28
Signature 317
Simple 111
Simplified 79
Slack (Movement) 181
Slow 275
Slowed down 276
Small 130
Smeary (Muddy) 41
Soaring 263
Sober 148
Soldering (see False Connections)
Spaced-out 294
Spaced-out, very 295
Spacing between - lines 308
                    - words 290
Spasmodic 27
Spindle- shaped 30
Static (see Still)
Starting strokes 238
Still (Movement) 169

Straightened-up 251
Strong pressure 16
Stylised 90
Superelevated 158
Supple (Stroke) 49
Supported 227
Suspended 223

T-bars 235
Tangled lines 308
Taut (Stroke) 53
Telescoped 221
Thin 43
Thready (see Filiform)
Thrown (Movement) 190
Tiles - ascending 307
       - descending 307
Trembling 370, 372, 375, 377
Twisted 264
Typographic - form 89
              - layout (see Margins)

Unfinished 224
Unevenness (Dimension) 163

Vacillating (see Pulled about)
Variably-slanted 256
Variegated (see Moirée)
Velvety 40
Vertical 247
Vibrant (Movement) 192

Washed out 46
Wavy Lines 303
Weak (Stroke) 52
Well-nourished 39
Wide 139

ALSO PUBLISHED BY SCRIPTOR BOOKS :

GRAPHOLOGY. VOL. I. The Interpretation of Handwriting, by Renna Nezos, 1992, 1st reprint, 315 pages, 70 handwriting samples.

ADVANCED GRAPHOLOGY, VOL. II. Twenty Lectures on Selected Subjects, by Renna Nezos, 1993, 388 pages, 115 handwriting samples.

JUDICIAL GRAPHOLOGY, VOL. III, by Renna Nezos, 1994, 178 pages, 13 illustrations.

LEARN GRAPHOLOGY. A practical course in fifteen lessons, by Gabrielle Beauchataud, 1996, 1st reprint, 320 pages, 217 handwriting samples.

CHARACTERS AND HANDWRITINGS, by Emile Caille, 1991, 307 pages, 103 handwriting samples.

PSYCHOLOGY OF HANDWRITING, by Dr. J.Ch. Gille-Maisani, 1992, 462 pages, 205 handwriting samples.

THE SOUL AND HANDWRITING, by Ania Teillard, 1993, 288 pages, 210 handwriting samples.

THE SYMBOLISM OF HANDWRITING, by Max Pulver, 1994, 371 pages, 186 handwriting samples.

GRAPHOLOGY AND THE ENNEAGRAM. Personality in Light and Shadow, by Usha Mullan, 1994, 381 pages, 17 diagrams and 152 handwriting samples.

POETS' HANDWRITINGS, by Dr. J.Ch. Gille-Maisani, 1995, 265 pages, 87 illustrations and handwriting samples.

SCRIPTOR BOOKS
123 Bickenall Mansions
London W1H 3LB, UK

Tel. +44 (0)171-935 9884
Fax +44 (0)171 935 6098
Email: j.simopoulos@ic.ac.uk